SONGS WITHOUT RHYME

SONGS WITHOUT RHYME

Prose by Celebrated Songwriters

EDITED BY ROSANNE CASH

New York

Library of Congress Cataloging-in-Publication Data

Songs without rhyme : prose by celebrated songwriters / edited
    by Rosanne Cash.—1st ed.
        p. cm.
      ISBN 0-7868-6277-7
      1. American prose literature—20th century. 2. Songs,
    American—Adaptations. I. Cash, Rosanne.

    PS659 .S65 2001
    818'.540808—dc21   00-049896

Book designed by Jennifer Daddio

FIRST EDITION

10   9   8   7   6   5   4   3   2   1

CONTENTS

ACKNOWLEDGEMENTS

Thank you to Peternelle van Arsdale, executive editor at Hyperion, and her assistant editor, Alison Lowenstein, and to my agent, Merrilee Heifetz, and her assistant, Ginger Clark.

INTRODUCTION

I published a book of short stories, *Bodies of Water,* in 1995. It was my first (published) attempt at prose, having been a dedicated and fairly successful songwriter for more than twenty years. I got a lot of comments, some from close friends, along the lines of, "Well, now you're a *real* writer." This was meant to be a compliment. I was appalled and frustrated to discover that songwriting was still perceived as not-quite-legitimate writing, a poor cousin of poetry, without the reverence. In truth, the demands of serious songwriting are rigorous, solitary, and require the same degree of commitment as any other writing. I often lament that true songwriting will end up as an arcane folk art, like Appalachian basket weaving or divining water with a stick. In dark moments, I suspect that no one really appreciates the beauty of a precisely rhymed couplet, sewn perfectly into a heartrending melody, delivered by an honest voice. I have devoted my entire adult life to the pursuit of that beauty, to discovering the internal rules of each individual song, to revealing the truth, and not the facts, of its subject matter, and to understanding the subtleties of tempo, feeling, and tone. And these thirteen writers, whom I invited to make the leap with me, a leap of writing medium and faith, have devoted their lives to the same principles.

When I began writing prose, I worried that I would have far too much rope and too many opportunities to hang myself. I missed the structure imposed by songwriting, the rhyme schemes and the welding of lyric to melody. Then I began to enjoy the liberation, almost to the point of giddiness. As Shawn Colvin said when she turned in her story for this book, "What a *relief* to write something and not have to rhyme it!" I asked these writers to choose one of their own songs as a departure point and to take a theme, or a character, a line, or even a word from that song and turn it into a prose piece. They rose to the task magnificently—not to say that there wasn't a rustle of anxiety, particularly among those attempting prose for the first time. It's a leap, but not a leap like ballet to brain surgery. More like oils to watercolor. Different pool, same water.

As the stories started to roll in, I was awestruck. The voices were so original. I could hear the sound of the singer's voice in the unrhymed phrases. Reading each story made me realize again what drew me to that person's songwriting, and why I had invited each of them to be in this book. Thirteen of the fourteen of us used one of our songs as a jumping-off place for a story. My dad, ever the iconoclast, chose to submit a story he had written in 1953, a highly original, and unexpected, futuristic story written partially in phonetic language. (I recalled him showing me this story more than fifteen years ago, and it had always stuck with me, so I was delighted to include it, even though it referenced no song. However, he is represented lyrically in Rodney Crowell's autobiographical song and story "I Walk the Line Revisited."

I made new friendships and deepened old ones during the development of this book. I was humbled by the gifts of these people. I thoroughly enjoyed nudging the more anxious and reticent types and then reading the breathtaking results. I hated delivering deadlines, and then stretching the deadlines to accommodate a touring schedule or a record, and then delivering an even more adamant deadline, only to move it again, but I got over it. I am immensely proud to introduce these well-known voices in new roles, as talkers instead of singers, freed from the structure of time and rhyme and obvious melody, but intensely poetic and musical in their narrative forms. It is an honor to be included among them.

Rosanne Cash
New York City
August 2, 2000

SONGS WITHOUT RHYME

A SELF-MADE MAN

David Byrne

LOSE YOUR BOSS'S HEAD? NOT WHILE
CRAY GENTECH HELPERS ARE ONLINE.
CRAY HORMONALS—THE DIFFERENCE
THAT MAKES THE DIFFERENCE

THE ZETA CHALLENGE—GO UP AGAINST
YOUR FORMER SELF.
THE RESPONSE—SIMPLE AS Z-5000

IF LIFE HAS ALL IT HAS TO GIVE THEN
GIVE IT ONE MORE TIME!
NOTHING COMES AROUND LIKE IT GOES
AROUND.
USED BY LADIES . . . AND MEN!

NO MORE DAYS SPENT WONDERING—WILL
I BE THE ONE TONIGHT?
BE ON FIRE WITH TURNER TIME
TRIALS . . . PROVEN IN THE JUAREZ
OLYMPICS.

HOPE HAS NEVER SOUNDED SO DEAFENING
BEFORE.
KEEP YOUR DEFENSE AN OFFENSE.
LOSE IT *AND* PROVE IT!

JESUS LOVES ME, YES I KNOW
FOR HE ALWAYS TELLS ME SO.
FOR MORAL GUIDANCE AND SPIRITUAL
STAMINA
ASK FOR JESUS BY NAME.

15 FEET AND RISING
A NEW GENERATION
A NEW EXPECTATION
EL PODEROSO—FOR THAT TOWERING
FEELING.

NOT FOR USE BY MINORS
PLEASE CONSULT YOUR TECHNICIAN.

New York Times ONLINE EDITION
February 23, 2020

ATLANTA. TIMES NEWS SER-
VICE. Last week's categoriza-
tion of G6 hormones, which
increase the brain's ability to
maintain a sense of pleasure,
well-being, and amiability, as
controlled substances has been
contested by a number of states
and also by many other
nations, including U.S. eco-
nomic partners Honduras and
Nigeria, who have taken exception to this ruling. The eco-
nomic health of these nations
depends on their development
of hormonal stocks, essences,
and operating system hybrids,
so their interest in the ruling is
more than casual.

A spokeswoman for the
powerful Honduran board of
genetic industries made a statement shortly after news of the
ruling was announced, saying
her government sees Dramatic
Software as the wave of the future, and they view this emerg-
ing technology as safe and
beneficial to all mankind. She
also stated that tighter regula-
tion of their industry, represented by the new G6 rulings
in the United States, could sti-
fle growth and development
of new technologies, which
would only hurt the consumer.
Her government's Washing-
ton lobby and National Advertising Ministry will make
every effort to have the ruling
reversed, "for the benefit of
all," she said, in closing.

The Nigerian consulate,
another nation with a powerful
lobbying organization, had no
statement as of this afternoon.
See later Online Updates for
further developments.

So, I go into the bar and my guy is sitting there. I recognize
him by the flower growing out of his head. Tucked in
amongst his blond dreadlocks, as if it is just a casual deco-
ration and he's really not trying to be noticed too much. A

fucking flower! Growing out his head! A geranium, I think. I'll bet he waters it! The fashions in genetic software are truly nutty these days. I wonder to myself what a pain in the ass it must be watching out for that thing . . . I mean, it's not exactly sturdy . . . it's a goddamn plant! Growing out of his head! And it's part of him.

Pays off, I guess . . . the girls seem to go for that kind of thing. He's got his arm around one that seems to have everything money could buy—she strokes his pansy and he rubs her tummy . . . and except for the ferocious mane of hair on her head . . . she's completely hairless. Shiny skin, like a new car. She's all glossy, like a bug. That's a new thing this year too. The hairless thing. That, and the flowers. Slightly unhealthy, this particular look, difficult to maintain and keep up, and very expensive. She actually looks like she's made of plastic, like a doll. Which I guess is the point. I must say it's arresting and hits some sexy buttons that I sure didn't know I, for one, possessed. Although God knows what buttons I possess now.

I introduce myself to the pair. She kisses me on the cheek and I notice that, like those Mexican hairless dogs, her body temperature seems slightly jacked up, a degree or two above normal, like she's in a permanent fever, I guess to compensate for the lack of insulating body hair . . . but maybe that heat was something else I felt . . . maybe it was me. Watch out, Dave.

"Join us in a drink?" Flower boy asks.

"Ummm . . ."

They look at each other like idiots. But I must remind myself they're probably as smart as a couple of Mensa hackers.

"We're celebrating."

Pause, how can one tell? They're almost always high.

"Jama's pregnant."

"Really? . . . Congratulations . . . lucky you. What are you gonna have?"

They look at each other again . . . a look that says they've got something in mind. Something brilliant and stupid.

"We've been talking about it. . . . which is how we heard about you."

"Hmm . . ." I glance at the Moon girl sitting over in the corner, in the dark. "Just curious, how exactly did you hear about me?"

"Through Fern, remember her?"

Poor Fern. Little Fern decided she didn't want to sleep . . . life was too short, she thought to herself, so why miss any of it? So she went ahead and did it . . . no drugs, no pills . . . pure genetic software. Brilliant. Or at least for a while it was. An incredible thing to watch. She'd be everywhere, all night . . . all the time. Nonstop. Dancing. Talking. Singing. No one could keep up with her. She seemed to be living about three normal lives at once. Four guys in four separate apartments, or so I was told, she was so active and constantly on the go they never even noticed, each one thought he was getting her full undivided attention.

After a while she began to see things. And eventually

she couldn't make them go away. Just like with drugs and plain old boring shit like that, but this wasn't a "thing" doing it to her, affecting her consciousness, this was actually part of her. Genetically, who she was. Her being, her identity, her existence, became that of someone having waking dreams. And to not know the difference between what was a dream and what was what we like to laughingly call reality. It seemed like some sort of moralistic or Karmic comeuppance when all that started happening to Fern, so we all thought, and we looked the other way. We looked the other way a little too long.

But boy, talk about burning the candle.

"Yeah . . . I miss her . . . what a shame," I said.

"Well, we didn't actually know Fern, not personally . . . but we knew her friend Jason."

Jason, I think, was the idiot who ran the code for Fern's batch . . . figures these two would know him. I wonder what nutty combo-creature these two have in mind. I haven't bothered to keep up with the fashions. What they do with the stuff is their own business. A program doesn't tell you what to write, be, or do with it. I did see a goat-boy driving a scooter the other day, though. He looked awfully cute, too. Wonder how he drove with those hooves.

"Jason . . . yes, I know who he is . . ."

"Do you know that actor on Web TV with the . . . ?"

She scrunches up her nose, or what there is of it.

"He's kind of cute . . . got a kind of sly look."

"I don't really watch that much . . ."

"Wasp, that's his name."

I figured maybe she wants a kid to look like some cute guy she's seen on the Web. Or maybe she wants me to clone this actor guy for her . . . and she'll be the mom. OK, this is fine. But that seems almost too normal for these two . . . even if this actor guy is real and not one of those Web thingies.

"OK," she says. "Try and guess . . . if you can't guess, do we get a discount?"

Now I know for sure they've got something peculiar in mind. I should have known from the start. Otherwise, why call me? My contacts are at various labs, "bootleg" basements, and thermo bubbles scattered around the world, mostly in out-of-the-way places. Chiapas, Burma, Kazakhstan, Honduras, Nigeria . . . the field people always let me know when something radically new is available. And the latest one that I've heard about is a beta G6. An outgrowth of the outlawed G6 hybrids. It's reported to be both a facilitator, a catalyst, and a metabolizing agent, so it allows connections to happen that otherwise would be impossible. As if a plant growing out of your head wasn't impossible enough.

I myself won't touch the stuff, but if they want to do the unimaginable, well, why not?

Flower boy whispers to me, his pansy flopping against my ear. "I heard that Prime connections aren't limited . . ."

"Uh-huh . . ." I nod. "Not limited in what kinda way?"

I wonder that flowers and goats are maybe too limited for the imagination of this crowd.

"Well . . . well . . . ," he hesitates, "I've heard that pleasure can be a done deal."

"Uh-huh." I nod again, wondering if he is talking about irreversible changes, still a hypothetical development, not proven to be possible . . . yet. But with these new Hyper molecules, who knows?

"And Jason says maybe it's possible to metabolize thingies."

"You mean, inanimate objects?"

"Yeah, any fucking thing."

"Well, I dunno about that . . . it hasn't gone that far . . ." Although it's true I've heard rumors. Shiny girl leans in.

"We heard that there's a guy that maybe you know."

"There is?" Actually I do know a fool who decided he wants to be able to remake himself over and over . . . and has decided to internalize some sort of soft machine to willfully change his own genetic structure. Mind over matter, his own matter. Over and over he can change himself, like a batch of jelly or a morphing torus, he becomes a 3-D hypothetical form that turns itself inside out continuously, almost imperceptibly, reinventing himself each time.

They look at me, just staring for a second, waiting for a response, so why deny it?

"I do know of one case, but I haven't had contact with him in some time."

"What did he do?"

"Strange guy . . . I don't think what he's doing is for everyone." As if these two are not strange?

The guy says, "OK, if it's what we think it is, maybe we want to try just a little bit."

"It's expensive . . . ten billion a pop."

Flower boy shows me his marker . . . and quickly punches up his stock balance and shows me.

"OK, what this guy seems to have developed is a beta version, and as far as I know he's the only one who's tried it. So, no guarantees. It is, as you seem to have heard, a kind of continuously evolving molecule. Nothing else like it. Like evolution in hyperdrive. You sure about this?"

They look at each other, heads swiveling like two sur- veillance cameras in love.

"You should try it," he says to me.

"You both want this?"

They nod.

"Yes? Why not one at a time?"

Flower boy hands me his marker.

"OK, gimme a few days." I touch his marker to mine and transfer the stock. "OK. See you here next Monday?"

We shake hands and the heat of hers reminds me that my own must seem awfully cold.

When I get into a taxi I check to see if I have any mes- sages, and, as usual, I have to throw out a whole stack of ads before I even see who called . . . ads from who knows where, that have somehow found my address.

YOUR MOTHER HAS A NEW HEAD.

**YOUR FEELINGS ARE TWICE AS BIG
AS EVER.**

**YOUR CHEEKBONES ARE AS BIG AS
CHARLIE SKADIA'S.**

YOUR SISTER HAS GIVEN YOU HER ASS.

Every one of these pops up as a little film. And every line
of ad copy speaks to me in a familiar voice: it's my mother
telling me she has a new head, my sister reminding me of
my feelings, and my high school girlfriend audibly smiles as
she mentions the cheekbones. If I didn't know better I'd
think my family had something against me, but they're all
synthesized.

My accountant:

**"YOUR TEETH ARE INSURED FOR THREE
BILLION, OR FUTURE SHARES IN
AQUABELLA STOCK."**

My sister's girlfriend (I had a crush on her and she knew it):

**"YOUR LIPS ARE LIKE TWO BALLOONS
WHEN YOU WANT TO ATTRACT THE**

OPPOSITE SEX, AND LIKE GEORGE BUSH IV'S, WHEN YOU WANT TO BE FORCEFUL."

A TV sex provider:

"YOU ARE MORE MAN THAN ANY WOMAN YOU KNOW."

My doctor from when I was a kid:

"YOU HAVE NU-SKIN IN YOUR FREEZER FOR A RAINY DAY."

My mom, again, in a new dress:

"YOU NEVER NEED CLEAN CLOTHES, NEVER WIPE YOUR ASS, AND NEVER BLEED, EXCEPT WHEN CALLED FOR."

A few days later I'm sitting in my place, well, my place this week. If these putzes have the stock they seem to I'll be moving to a place with a window soon enough. A real window this time. I look at the stuff, it's in a cheesy Korean medical wrapper, but I know it's from Honduras by the way the package is sealed. They're the only ones who use that metallic strip. And I wonder to myself how it works. Not how the G6 stuff works, I sussed that some time ago, but this morphing development has me puzzled. It just doesn't seem possible. I wonder how it feels. I wonder if each person, or whatever they are, has distinct personalities, do they have memories of the previous ones, or is it like past life memories? Old data, dead format, unretrievable.

I watched them as they did this stuff. Over the course of several weeks. And they seemed to be having a wonderful time. Just fantastic. Looking different every couple of days, then every day, then almost every few hours, then every fifteen minutes. What must it feel like inside, I wondered to myself.

Every time I saw them they were all smiles, loving to show off their new exteriors. And happy to show off on demand.

"I know what you like," she says to me.

And the next minute I'm looking at my high school sweetheart, not as she was, but as I dreamed her.

"Jama, stop that. It's not funny."

She laughs, and the next minute she's the model of an intelligent sophisticated woman, a cartoon almost. But it works, appearances matter, and she's got my trust back. I can't believe I'm so easily fooled.

I thought to myself, "How bad can this be?" They seem to be having such a great time. And look at the advantages . . . they're like living ads, one could play to everyone's weak spots, their prejudices and desires. So, after watching them over the course of a little time and noticing they didn't seem the worse for wear, I decided, hell with it, I'll try some myself.

Of course, I reasoned, it would be different for me. I'd do only enough to see what it's like. I'd be doing it for different reasons, not purely for amusement, for kicks, or to gain some material or strategic advantage over my competition. I'd be doing it in order to will myself into a more evolved form, to truly become the self-made man our ancestors imagined.

New York Times ONLINE EDITION
April 5, 2020

ATLANTA. TIMES NEWS SERVICE. A man and woman were arrested today for violating code 6 of the genetic laws, instituted just last year. In a case that is sure to be viewed with much interest, they were arraigned on bail totaling almost 2 billion dollars for allegedly selling modified types of G6 hormones without a license.

The couple, a Mr. Stein-Davis and Miss Jama-Scott, he of Atlantan and she of Mexican and Iraqi descent, were arrested at a bar in the Brookthorne neighborhood here.

The arrested couple were allegedly carrying four vials of a new type of Dramatic Software. A box of forty skin patches and lumbar clocks were also found behind a nearby barstool. Investigators are considering whether or not to include the bartender and staff in the investigation.

Federal agents had been keeping a watch on a number of establishments in the Brookthorne neighborhood, known locally as G-Cell Gulch. It is a part of town notable for its many large houses—most of which are rentals, due to the transient nature of the businesses here. Most work takes place in basements, which are easily converted into biosealed concrete bunkers. The area has boomed in recent years, attracting investors and the inevitable operators and dealers in biosoftware of dubious reliability.

Lawyers for Mr. Stein-Davis and Miss Jama-Scott maintain that their clients were not selling these substances but were approached by strangers at the bar who turned out to be federal agents. The lawyer also maintains that the samples being held by authorities were their personal property and were for research purposes only. No further details of the exact nature of the Dramatic Software they were carrying has been announced, but a man present at the bar when the arrest took place claims that there was talk of substances that the suspects claimed had irreversible properties, a valuable attribute in the booming world of hormone software, where time is seen as more valuable than money.

Well, the news was not exactly a surprise. Those two weren't exactly discreet. With me it would be different. Already I was holding down positions on the boards of three Judicial Corporations, *and* I had a position as a part-time fed as well. Not bad. For each job my physical appearance was completely different. So who knew?

My sex life was pretty much whatever I wanted it to be, and the main problem seemed to be maintaining a consistent look for the duration of a session. I still was holding a pretty sizable chunk of Jama and co.'s stock, but I guess they won't be needing it now.

New York Times ONLINE EDITION
May 19, 2020

THE HAGUE. TIMES NEWS SER-VICE. The World Court today found that the G6 variety of genetic software violates the so-called identity statutes, the recently instituted series of laws governing the nature and kind of biological identity. According to the ruling, G6-type software, and its accompanying technology, creates a situation in which identity, that by which an entity can by identified and even localized, becomes so much in flux and evasively intransigent that there often is no way to identify or regulate the entity and its offspring. This, the court claims, is counter to the basic tenets of biolaw, instituted in the early teens.

The ruling was instantly challenged by a number of representatives, both national and corporate. Among them was American Life, the global insurance company run by the alleged son of Bill Gates, Billy Gates 2.0, and Nigerian Spirit,

the entertainment and sports conglomerate, based in Havana.

In a related development three bodies were found recently in a wooded area near Atlanta. The bodies were thought to be the result of failed G6 beta versions. One body reportedly was part young man, part tree, and part child. An autopsy performed at Atlanta Medical revealed high levels of Prime pharmaceutical and hormonal relaxers, believed to be bundled with the G6 software package. These levels were reportedly seventeen times permissible limits. Although, as a manufacturer of Prime, American Life has access to G6 research, they have claimed no interest in any beta testing being done in the Atlanta Metroplex.

Representatives of American Life, and six other organizations, did make a statement urging caution and requesting that any beta testers allow their grafts to be examined by AmLife technicians, without ID or registration formalities.

An expected backlash reaction is expected, as tens of thousands of legal beta testers are now considered illegal and dangerous under the new ruling. Water and electronic supplies to the court headquarters have been sealed as of 10 A.M. today, as the ruling was announced this morning. Bio Hackers had apparently used the water supply as an entry point in a previous disruption of the court, in 2009, at one point leaving the court biologically sealed for a year and a half.

Dare I say that this is our destiny as humans? Never again to be imprisoned by our biology, history, or lack of imagination. Sounds pretty grand, although maybe a side effect. But really, this is a whole new world, a new kind of existence. Being is no longer a process of becoming someone, or somebody, it is almost a reflection of the mind.

A funny thing happened yesterday. I seem to have misplaced the stock from that couple. It seems to have vanished from my marker. Nothing to worry about, a few minutes' search and it'll probably reveal itself misfiled somewhere.

I wonder at what point the effects become permanent, or if that was just hype. Soon, I hope, or that damn World Court ruling is going to put a real damper on things.

A friend has forwarded a mail apparently sent to Stein-Davis.

Sender: CrazyWorld@ceeda.net
To: RealDeal@ChemicalNet.com
May 36, 2020
10:45 A.M. WST

Dear Stein-Davis,

She laughs, and the next minute she's the model of an intelligent sophisticated woman, a cartoon almost. But it works, and I kept my promise and only used it once, but apparently that was enough. My time has never been more exciting and more enjoyably useful, but I have a strange feeling that as this gets more popular, I'll be one of the early birds, left holding only the worm. Already 3 kids in the same residence are way ahead of me, and they're only 12 and 13 years old. I wonder how an old geezer like Jason can even keep up, what with post this and Zeta that. But maybe this is where I belong, losing sleep over material things.

I'll be around this Saturday, leave me space if you can. A yard will do- ;-).

Have you seen the recent genital genius? There's a cable version on VSL, but apparently there are cheaper ones out there too. Let me know if you find a brown one.

Dramatic Pause

How could he be getting mail if he's in jail? And who's Dramatic Pause?

New York Times
Op-Ed Page, May 37, 2020

How Many Does It Take?
By "Dramatic Pause"

Jim Venebal's response to the court ruling is, in this democrat's opinion, a looser portrayal of justice than we've seen in quite some time. Both parties know the consequences are negligible and that AmLife will stand by their research, as they have in the past. Truly, unless I am not the man I was before, Jim doesn't really believe that a loose beta version can infect the majority of the Atlantan people, at least I for one don't believe he does. I have a secret suspicion that Jim wants to think that freedom is only for the Real People and not for the rest of us . . . and that this is what is really behind his decision to back the World Court's decision.

I know how many lives I have, and I suspect Jim has been counting his once too often, at least that's the way it looks to this observer. My hands, while known as fine playing instruments, were never a problem until the People introduced the scrub-testing virus. As long as there are lives in me, and I'm on number seven this season, I'll never request that any version of G6, or any other lifting or irreversible software, be restricted. Not only is it against all of our interests, but it is against what life on this planet is about—namely, evolution and procreation.

Let Jim and the other Real People show us all a valid alternative, and we'll all be more than happy to donate a few years to the cause. At least I, for one, will . . . and I suspect that most of the rest of the 50 percenters would as well.

So I ask, how many of us

18

does it take to make a difference? Is 50 percent too little?
Have I lost what little say I
have, just because we're not
People? Double standards
have never been part of the
AmLife structure, and maybe,

if we are wise, we won't let
them creep in now.

*Mr. Pause is a six percenter
who recently won the Nobel
prizes for both physics and
kickboxing.*

I'm in Venezuela. Last night I joined some folks I've met here
for dinner and was introduced to an interesting woman who
seemed strangely familiar. Her skin is completely hairless, and
her body temperature seems elevated, like a kid with a high
fever. She acts like we've met, but how could she recognize
me? I haven't looked like I used to for months now.

This morning I check my marker and there's the stock from
that couple! As if it was there all the time. It's quadrupled
in value, there's a message attached.

Dear Mr. "Pause,"

*Long time no see. I'll bet you wondered how long it would
take me to get free of that position tag the feds implanted. Longer
than I thought, it still kind of hurts, but it sure is good to be
back. So don't be a stranger, no one will ever recognize you now.
Don't you miss me?*

Jama

A SELF-MADE MAN

We're living in a dump
Trying to figure out what sex we are

Exchanging chromosomes
Trying to bargain for a better future

Well I'll trade you my potential mental
illness for your bad teeth
How 'bout trading your sexy body for a
full head 'a' hair?

Well, we can't predict the future
But we're trying to do the best that we can

My cards are on the table
I'm gambling everything I am

And some of us are hoping
To end up with a perfect life
I'll trade you everything that I got
For the chance to be someone else

And what you see is what you get
And what you get is what you choose
And what I am
What you see
Is exactly what I chose to be

And now we got a black market
A black market in designer genes

The most beautiful, most intelligent
Criminals you've ever seen

And now you're paying top dollar
For what you used to get for free

They'll stun you with their looks
And charm you with effortless ease

They've taken everything from you
The way that you walk
The way that you smile
The sound of your voice

Don't even know
Who you are
Who are you now?
Who are you now?

I'm a self-made man
(I've got nothing left to give)
I'm a self-made man
(I've got nothing left to lose)
On down the hallway
The freaks are waiting for you
Somebody calls me
The freaks are waiting for you
The clown will laugh in your face
Ho ho ho ho ho ho ho ho ho ho
The clown will laugh in your face
Ho ho ho ho ho ho ho ho ho ho

Colin Bell

DAVID BYRNE, primarily known as the musician who co-founded the group Talking Heads, has also been involved in many other projects, including work with Brian Eno, Twyla Tharp, Robert Wilson, Jonathan Demme, and Bernardo Bertolucci. In 1989 he began solo recordings, including *Rei Momo*, the self-titled *David Byrne* (1994), and *Feelings* (1997). Byrne has his own record label, Luaka

Bop. Since 1991, he has had a number of photo and art exhibitions. Born in 1952 in Dumbarton, Scotland, he currently lives in New York.

THE HOLOGRAFIK DANSER

John R. Cash, 1953

Fil Gravr sat at the bak ov the klasrum wher he always sat, payeing no partikular attenshun tu the techir, Professor Ivan Klewicki.

The "Investigashum of Thought transferuns, E.S.P, and Hipnosis" bord him to tears. The klas was kumpulsori, yet aftr awl thez yirz the skul had grown lax in its skolastik demans. The kovitid red star for acheevmint wasn't so kovitid inymor. A blu star or evn a whit star wud pas him so whi bothur wasteng hiz tim.

For almost twenty years now the Soviets had tried to "occupy" the United States. One of the first things they did was to desecrate the English language. Words had to be written the way they sounded to the USSA occupation forces.

The old English still, after all these years, was used by the general public in all personal correspondence. When Phil wrote his brother, who still lived on a farm in Manhattan, Kansas, he would take his chances. He could not address his dear brother as Der Bruthur.

But this problem with the language was minuscule compared to what his father and mother had gone through. They, along with hundreds of others, were executed. Executed for refusing to pledge allegiance to the USSA.

Phil was a small boy on that sad day in 1998, when he lost his parents. He had been taken from his home by the SS Habilitation Corps and given a "home" in a church that the Soviets used to house orphans, malcontents, bums, prostitutes, and migrant workers.

At the age of eight, he had worked on a road construction gang and studied the Russian language and the new English, as well as Russian history. Due to the lack of manpower following the holocaust and as was compulsory, he, at the age of twelve, had served four years in the B.A.C., the Boys Army Corps. At sixteen, he donned a Regular Army uniform. For the next four years, he was a member of the Youth Workers Police.

He had learned to live peaceably with the Soviet presence. He saw at an early age that the die-hard Americans who resisted the Red Star die hard.

Topeka, Kansas, had been somehow spared the bomb.

Wichita hadn't been so fortunate. As a matter of fact, there was no longer much of a place known as Wichita, Kansas. The city had melted in the first thrust of nuclear missiles. The Red Army, the Red Guard, and the KGB had practically stormed the quiet grain-belt city of Topeka. Within days, all resistance had been destroyed. Now, for all these years, Topeka had gone about its business, but in a much different way than before. Wheat, corn, and soybeans were brought into storage facilities as always, but the communal farmers received nothing for it. Food was plentiful in the State stores, but in return for a bountiful harvest, the farmers received only extra rations at the co-op supply store, if they didn't mind standing in line for hours.

Phil Graver donned the uniform now only once a month for three days' time during which he studied science, engineering, political science, accounting, and language.

The bell rang, marking the end of his hated class. Tomorrow was Sunday, and Sunday was off, thank God. He hurried out of the church and into the dark daylight. The weather was very cold for July. The temperature must be freezing, or near it. The nuclear cloud, which had covered the planet for years, showed no signs of dissipating. Winter was, for some, a time for hibernating in the underground shelter dug out in every hillside. A few minutes outside in the sixty- to eighty-degree-below-zero weather and a man could freeze to death in his tracks. Winters were fearful.

Even in the cold of July, fresh food was grown in large greenhouses by the communal farmers under the supervision of Soviet administrators. Meat, dairy, and poultry products were flown into all the surviving population centers from South America and New Zealand.

Phil's wife, Kitra, would be at the commissary when he returned home. She would be standing in line for hours, as usual, for the weekly allotment of bread, sugar, flour, meat, and other necessities.

Kitra had served her time and had been discharged from the Y.C.L.A., the Young Communist League of America. In her fourth year, she had proven herself a warrior. The four Soviet soldiers who attacked her to try to rape her one night on her way home from the Y.C.L.A. camp didn't know that she had a black belt in karate. One by one, but quick as a flash, she chopped and kicked them down. At least two of the four she stomped in the crotch before she ran.

Kitra was a gentle woman by nature. She never raised her voice regardless of her struggle to keep her home in some kind of reasonable order.

Phil had a quick temper but usually reserved it for venting his anger on the Soviets, and more especially on the puppet government in Topeka and the Americans who, for a few dollars more per year, forced upon their neighbors the ideals and demands of the enemy living among them.

On his walk home Phil passed the corner kiosk, which was nothing more than a newsstand and television tollbooth. He browsed for a moment, looking over the meager selection of reading material. *The Topeka Truth* carried a front-page picture of a local party official smiling under the caption "Grain Production above Expectations." Big deal! A few magazines such as *Independent Farmer* (a pictorial voyage) and *National Government Policy* also were available at the kiosk.

He looked at the programs listed on the board. There were two categories, television and holovision, and various prices depending on which program you wanted punched into your home receiver and at what time.

Kitra wouldn't be home for a couple of hours, maybe, so he looked at the list to try to decide what they might enjoy together. There were a few movies listed that he had seen, such as *Gone with the Wind, Moby Dick,* and *Oh, God. Oh, God,* he thought, will they ever stop protecting us from ourselves? There were cartoons, animated movies, and, of course, *Old Yeller.*

He moved around to the hologram board. Holographic viewing was more expensive, but the choice was more varied. Still, he was sensitive about who or what he would have projected in three dimensions into the middle of his living room. Cossack dancers, the Soviet army, the Soviet army chorus, chess players, a celebrity aerobics event, a boxing match, and so on were his choices.

To his surprise, a new category had been added, adult entertainment. He asked the vendor, an American woman, "What's on adult entertainment?"

"Flamenco dancing," she said, "or Egyptian belly dancing."

"Nothing with women and men?" he asked.

"Yes," she said, "a Ukrainian wedding ceremony, or thirty minutes of Ivan Bolsovol."

"Who's he?" Phil asked.

"A Russian poet," she said, "reading his poetry in new English, which being translated from Russian isn't very poetic if you ask me."

"How much is the flamenco dancer?" he asked, then added, "Is the dancer a man or a woman?"

"She dances for twelve dollars," the woman replied. "Don't ask me how long. I don't know. The program is supposed to be half an hour."

Phil paid his twelve dollars and gave her his tele number. "Punch it in about ten minutes from now," he said, turning toward his apartment building.

He picked up two liters of bock beer at the state store, got his liquor ration card punched, showed his identification, and paid his two dollars. Although beer was on the luxury item list, it was still relatively cheap, brewed by the State through collective production. The beer was warm, but there should be enough room in the boxlike refrigerator, which also sat on the kitchen cabinet.

As he climbed the six flights of stairs, he occupied his mind with nothing more than whether or not the beer would be any cooler or how much cooler before the hologram came on.

Kitra was not home, as he suspected. Only one liter of beer would fit into the refrigerator, so he opened the other, splattering himself with foam but putting his mouth over the bottle and catching and swallowing all the warm beer he could. He walked into the living room dripping beer and burping. He'd clean it up before Kitra returned, but for now he'd plop down on the living room easy chair and drink his beer.

He kept watching the wall, waiting for the flamenco dancer to be projected into his room. He finished the liter and still no dancer, so he took the empty bottle to the trasher in the kitchen, grabbed a towel, and wiped the counter, the floor, and then the window where the beer had squirted. He was opening his second liter when the sound of flamenco guitar began in the living room.

He walked in expecting to see a dancing girl, but the only hologram in the room was a man wearing a sombrero, an old man in an old sombrero, probably from Juárez.

Phil was fuming with anger, but he sat with his beer and watched dirty fingers playing "Malagueña." Half his beer was gone when the image disappeared and a beautiful Mexican girl whirled out of the glass wall and into his room. Four feet into his room she shook and wiggled to the music, which continued from the tele speakers. The guitarist wasn't visible.

Phil took a long draw from the bottle; as he stood up and walked over near her. She was beautiful; her lifelike image played with his mind. He walked around in front of her and watched her for a while from the other side, then from the front.

"You're beautiful," he said, inches away from her face.

She was in a studio somewhere in Mexico, but her image

in Phil Graver's living room couldn't be any more lifelike. Phil flopped back down in the chair, and finished the last half of his beer as he continued to watch her dance.

Two liters of strong bock beer hit him harder than he had planned. He hadn't eaten since breakfast and his head was spinning, even as his eyes stayed on the woman.

"Thought transference," he said aloud to himself, laughing. What about body transference?

A stupid idea, he knew, but how could he exist in this society if he couldn't dream, couldn't make believe? Make believe he was somewhere else, someone else, with someone else. Kitra was as bored with life as he was.

His eyes half closed, his body in a stupor, his mind dulled and blanked out except for some little part of it zeroed in on the dancer.

"Body transference," he mumbled. No, that isn't it, he thought. "Energy transference," that's it! His eyes closed on the woman and a smile crossed his face as he felt the release; the release of energy and consciousness from the body.

He looked down at his own lifeless form and turned to the holographic dancer. He grabbed her and she fought him screaming. The guitar playing abruptly stopped as she, fighting to pull away from Phil, pulled him through the tele and out of sight. Her screaming continued and a man was shouting in Spanish, then there was a sound of a guitar splintering.

Kitra climbed the last flight of stairs and sat her shopping bag on the kitchen counter. She smelled beer and so wasn't surprised to see Phil sprawled on the chair apparently asleep.

"Phil," she said, shaking him, "you must have really tied one on to keep sleeping through that noise."

"Phil," she called again, and getting no response from him she was losing patience with the screaming and Spanish curses coming from the tele.

Without looking at it, she picked up the remote control switch and turned the tele off. Angry now, she pushed him and shouted his name. He didn't respond, but slid to the floor and lay still.

She felt a chill as she felt his face. He was cold and he wasn't breathing.

I wrote "The Holografik Danser" one night in early 1953 at the base where I was stationed in the Air Force in Landsburg, Germany. I was a high-speed radio Intercept operator, and the Cold War with Russia was hot. It was my job to sit at a position with my typewriter and radio receiver and copy Morse code from Russian ground stations and aircraft.

We had no television at the base in Germany, but it was all the rage back home. Letters were full of mentions of favorite programs and unusual broadcasts. Someone had predicted live holographic broadcasts in the twenty-first century. From somewhere in the dim, dark corners of my mind came this idea for a story. If the images could come out of the television, what would happen if I went into the television, and it was turned off?

I don't remember exactly, I think there were a couple of German beers involved in this story.

JOHNNY CASH began his career in 1955 at Sun Records in Memphis. Since then, few if any artists have accomplished anything close to what he has achieved. The Songwriters' Hall of Fame, The Country Music Hall of Fame, and the Rock and Roll Hall of Fame have all inducted him, a feat that no other artist has yet to achieve. He has received countless other awards and honors, including the Grammy Living Legend Award and the prestigious Kennedy Center Honor for lifetime achievement.

He is truly an original. He is deeply compelling and instantly recognizable. Johnny Cash will most certainly be considered one of the most important musicians of the twentieth century, and he continues to make vital music into the twenty-first.

bells, ink, sand and roses

Rosanne Cash

Sera gave birth at 4:24 A.M. on Tuesday the nineteenth, and the DNA Profile and Predictive Testing was done by 9:30 that morning. The baby, a girl whose name had been chosen several months before, lay sleeping in the tiny water-bassinet next to Sera's bed. The microheaters glowed a soft red on the control plate at one end of the curved plastic cocoon. The baby wore a funny little silver skullcap on her miniature head, which was perfectly shaped, although a little red and wrinkled. Sera was lying on her side, staring at the baby, full of unexpected feelings of love and new impulses, when the nurse walked in and handed her the paper. Sera looked at the nurse, shocked, and took the paper with a trembling hand. She had handled paper only a few times in her life, with the exception of the botanical prints she had framed

for her studio apartment and the old newspapers she had
bought from the antique stores.

Certificate of Live Birth
Manhattan Center for Reproductive Sciences
Baby: Bellarosa Utone

Date of Birth: 2.19.2107   **Time of Birth: 0424**

Weight: 3800 grams   **Length: 55 cm**

Gestated by (check one):

    Mother __X__

    Extra-Utero Gestational Device (EUGD) _____

Weeks gestated: 39.2

If gestated by mother, labor was natural _X_ induced ____

Mother: Sera Utone

Mother's Global I.D.: 55-24-22-18.USA.F

Age of mother: 47

Father: n/a

Age of father: n/a   **Father's Global I.D.: n/a**

Assisted Reproductive Technology Utilized for This Pregnancy (levels 1–5): level 3

Genetic Manipulation Used During This Pregnancy: none

Fetal Repairs during Pregnancy: none

Distinguishing Benign Physical Abnormalities:

  brown/black eyes

  excessive foot length (slight to moderate)

---

inequitable lips (slight to moderate)

shortened torso (slight)

Predictive Genetic Analysis: normal to long lifespan, superior intelligence, normal fertility, reduced capacity for logic and mathematics (see accompanying document), enhanced capacity for art and music (see accompanying document), propensity to stress-related diseases (see accompanying document), possible cancer of reproductive or eliminatory systems in 7th to 8th decade, high likelihood of nerve damage in neck, head, and face (see accompanying document).

Sera looked up at the nurse. "What document?"

The nurse handed her another sheet of paper.

Documentation of GENETIC ABNORMALITY

This document is intended for educators, psychotherapists, physical therapists, and employers under the Genetic Anomaly Full Disclosure Act of 2089, article 7712b of the Global Genome Project. This information is fully encoded on subject's DNA I.D. chip.

Specific Genetic Abnormality: Multisensate, 11 degrees

Characteristics and Prognosis: Beyond the common six physical senses, subject has been found to have five additional senses. Complex prognosis, see following.

Statistical Probability of Genetic Abnormality: (average of all five superfluous senses): 1/7,524,045

Specific Additional Senses:

1. *The ability to hear color,* particularly vibrant colors. Red and indigo may be perceived by subject to shriek or wail. Pastel colors may produce only a low humming sensation. Colors may appear unexpectedly in subject's field of vision to the accompaniment of a loud bell sound. Bells may also presage the appearance of color in subject's vision field. Prognosis is unanalyzed at this time. *Suggest tutorial @ age three to activate filters. Advise soothing visual environment.*

2. *The ability to see sound.* Slightly more common than other superfluous senses. (S.P.:1/800,220). Subject has enhanced enjoyment of music. Sound/vision of traffic, construction, screaming, airships, white noise, etc., may have cumulative effect and produce nerve damage in area of eyes, ears, head, and neck. Music becomes linked to visual experience, and over time, particular pieces of music can evoke extreme anxiety in subject. Subject may be musically gifted but may find the pursuit of musical virtuosity to be fraught with psychological distress, due to visual/emotional triggers. Prognosis undetermined, although nerve damage is highly likely. *Prophylactic measures strongly advised.*

3. *The ability to smell memory.* A peculiar sensory abnormality with a statistical probability of 1/22,661,599. Not the same as recalling smells, or having a smell provoke a memory,

although these abilities are deeply enhanced. A phenomenon whereby a random memory produces a distinct and original fragrance. Pleasant memories tend to evoke flowery or citrus fragrances. Unpleasant, painful, or sad memories produce musty odors, to which the subject may develop a physiological allergy, with symptoms ranging from headaches and itching to muscle spasms. Guilt produces for the subject a pungent, acrid, and chemical-like smell, which provokes various physical complaints. Fear elicits a burning odor quite overwhelming in its intensity, which activates the first additional sense, in that the odor becomes both visual and auditory, with a high-pitched wail in the 4k range and a charcoal haze perceived by the subject to descend upon her. Both odors of fear and guilt, powerful as they are, are exceeded in intensity by the smell of roses, which is inextricably associated with feelings of regret, longing, and nostalgia, sometimes for a past that does not exist. (This particular phenomenon, a longing for something that has never been experienced, is also a separate aspect of the multisensate personality.) The fragrance of roses can be overpowering and deafening. It is the one aspect of multisensism that has been clinically proven to exist on an objective basis: it has been found that the slightly musty smell of healthy old people, which some find similar to dried roses, is actually the smell of decaying memories. *Advise tutorial in memory control and filtering, beginning @ age 7. Advise medication in alphablocker class of drugs. Prognosis undetermined.*

4.   *The ability to perceive emotional content by contact with objects and rooms associated with another person.*   An

enhanced version of the normal sixth sense (intuition and precognitive ability). Subject can walk into a room and internally graph the chronological order of suffering experienced by former occupants. (Subject may be aware of more positive emotional content, but in a very peripheral way). Graphing happens very quickly, sometimes in less than a minute. As well as rooms, subject can also internally graph the provenance of objects such as furniture, glass, clothing, and artwork. Subject is ideally suited to a career in the buying and selling of art and antiques, as the accurate tracing of the provenance of those items has a subjective and biological irrefutability that can be substantiated by objective sources. When this sense is combined with a sincere education, subject can be extremely successful if she learns to detach from the psychological residue that "sticks" to objects. If subject does not learn to detach from the experience of graphing, prognosis is very poor. Subject will magnetize perhaps hundreds of years of suffering and carry it in her body and psyche as her own. Physiological ramifications devastating. *Strongly advise ERR (Emotional Regeneration and Rehabilitation) on weekly basis for lifetime.*

5. *The ability to see inside one's own body.* A most peculiar sense that is activated in dream or meditative states, sometimes unwillingly, with unsettling consequences. Subject has ability to peer down her own vertebrae, into the recesses of her internal organs, which have an inky appearance, and even into the folds of her brain. Other multisensates have described a sensation of sand in the bloodstream, scratching and rubbing against the joints and muscles, whenever this extra

sense is activated. It is an unusual subject who can learn to employ this ability to her benefit, as a diagnostic tool to treat herself or seek medical care when necessary. Most subjects choose to completely deactivate this sense, which is possible with rigorous neuroprogramming and ERR. If sense is not deactivated, prognosis is unclear but may lead to mental illness, as subject may become "lost" in the recesses of her body and may never return to objective awareness.

Cumulative Prognosis: Although multisensates endure varying degrees of disability and difficulty, multisensism is not *necessarily* a fatal or devastating defect. However, subject must be indoctrinated from early childhood in the construction of internal filters. Subject must also avoid intense emotional experiences of all kinds. Some multisensates find that it is healthier for them to choose a solitary life, forgoing love and romantic relationships, as the normal physical and emotional components of love and sex will prove to be too overwhelming, in a very literal sense. The subject will be lost to herself in the flood of these sensations. As mentioned above, a career in art and antiques seems extremely well suited to this particular subject, as her fourth additional sense can be turned from a liability into an asset, with proper education. Specific tutorials in filter activation are available by request, by contacting the Genetic Resource Center at *Global I.D. 790779-224-afl.usa.0.*

Sera looked up at the nurse, the document shaking in her hand.

"Why do I need this piece of paper? Isn't all this information encoded on her I.D. chip?" Sera gestured to the baby's umbilicus, where the chip had just been inserted by the technician, moments before the nurse had come in.

The nurse shrugged. "Yes, it's all on the chip, and I don't know why, dear. It's just the law." The nurse patted Sera's foot. "I'm sorry. It's one of those things we can't predict or cure. Yet." The nurse glanced at the baby, sleeping contentedly. "With good care, she'll be fine. You just have to protect her, and then teach her how to protect herself." The nurse smiled at Sera. "I've heard about multisensates, but she's the first one I've come across."

Sera stared at her, still as stone. The nurse looked slightly embarrassed.

"Well, good luck anyway, dear. Just hit the button if you need me." She turned and left the room.

Sera put the paper on the nearby table and turned to look at her baby again. She gently slid her hands under the baby's body and lifted her to her shoulder. She stroked the back of her little head and kissed her ear, cheek, and chin delicately. "You're special, Bellarosa," she said quietly. "I'll help you figure it out, I promise."

2149

Bella unlocked the door to her shop and glided in silently. This was her favorite time of day to be here, in the early morning, before she was open for customers and while the streets were still relatively quiet. This morning was even better, as the flowers and candles left over from her birthday party last night were still here, giving the room and the antiques a festive and sumptuous air with the morning light pouring in through the high windows. She glanced around with pleasure. Each piece of furniture and work of art was perfectly arranged. The footstools and the benches, the china and the armoires, the paintings and mirrors—each was separate and in its own place. She had found that if she overstocked the store the sense of crowding was too much for her and tended to activate the fourth extra sense, which she had spent so many years getting under control. She glanced in one of the ornate mantel mirrors. She was not tall, but long-legged, and she wore skirts that showed her legs to their best advantage. Today she had on a simple black sheath dress, made of one of the new luxury synthetics, with short black boots and a lavender shawl. Her hair, which fell straight to her shoulders, was a deep burgundy. She could not remember when she last saw its natural color, but she believed it was a medium brown—probably salt and pepper by now. Her face was still unlined, clean and pale, set off by very dark eyes. She was forty-two, as of yesterday. She had never been married and had no children or siblings. Sera, her mother, had been dead for eight years. She was aware that her friends who didn't know about her abnormality felt sorry for her, but the only thing she felt missing in her life was Sera. She was acutely mindful that it was Sera's exacting and meticulous care of her that had prepared her for this simple, serene life she had established for herself. Sera was the patient overseer to the endless tutorials, the ever-changing drug regimens (which Bella had tailored down to one alpha-blocker weekly for the past seven years), the soundproofed and softly lighted rooms, the weekly walks in the state-protected woods, not far outside the city, to give her hearing a break, and the unwavering encouragement in total self-reliance. Sera had given her everything she needed. Bella knew of multisensates who had self-destructed at very early ages because of the lack of structure and understanding from their caretakers, but Bella had had the best of care and preparation from Sera. She had loved her mother, still loved her, totally and completely, and there was nothing in that love that was a trigger for her pathology. Bella was able to live with the grief of losing her only because Sera herself had taught her how to do it in advance.

Bella had a few friends who were married, and sometimes she did wonder about it. It must be a lovely thing, she would think, to have someone to talk with in bed late at night. Just to lie next to someone and whisper and laugh would be nice. I bet it would be very nice. She allowed herself a few moments of reverie about this, but only a few moments, and then she would become a little anxious and afraid of activating one of the senses. She had a breathing exercise she had been taught when she was eight years old that stopped the internal dominoes from falling and locked the filters in tight. Whenever the daydreaming started to trip her up, she stopped and did the breathing.

Bella looked around her shop once more with satisfaction. Her eyes came to rest on a lovely blue platter, newly acquired from a dealer in Munich. She had bought an entire lot from him when he had posted on the ArtWeb that he was going out of business. It was a rather small lot, but high quality: a pair of late-twentieth-century wall sconces, a couple of chairs and a lovely oak game table, a few decorative pieces, and this old platter. It was very old, actually; more than two hundred years. Bella had not had a chance since the shipment arrived to examine it thoroughly, and now she took the cup of tea she had brought in with her and sat in front of the aged Stickley sideboard where it rested on a shelf. She picked it up and turned it over in her hands. It was a type of design called "flow-blue," which was not a pattern at all but a mistake in the firing process. The deep blue curlicues and flowers were awash on the white field, which itself had a paler blue bleeding into it. The blue had run amok, had flowed through everything. It was gorgeous. Bella stroked the platter and turned it over again. No chips. It was in remarkable condition. Bella's hand started to tremble slightly as she lifted the platter off her lap and began to place it back on the sideboard. She stopped. Her hands felt warm and the warmth spread quickly up her arms and into her shoulders. A sure sign. Now was the moment to put it down, but she did not. Her body relaxed deeply and the room began to recede until all she could see was the blue, swirling and spreading, into her hands and around her body, a deep, deep blue. She still had another few seconds to react, to stop the activation, to draw her filters up with her breath, but instead, she drew the platter to her and bent her head over it, as if to inhale the story it was going to tell her.

The Dream of the Blue Dishes

My dress is a stiff material, a faux satin with a grosgrain pattern that gives it a slight shimmer. It is a pale peach color, fitted at the waist with a white sewn-in belt. It falls to just below my knees. It is cheap and out of fashion, but no one in Dresden has money to buy fashionable clothes since the war, so I don't feel ashamed when I go to the market or for a cup of tea. Everyone is too tired and sad to care about dresses anyway. The city itself, a hollow wreck, is a fitting backdrop for our collective frame of mind. Just after liberation, nearly fifteen months ago, there was relief, and jubilation even, but it was short-lived. Our city is gone. My dreams for my life are cut in half, and all the things I once held most dear for my future— my longing for children, my ambition to write a book, and even the simple, unspoken, implicit desire to grow old with my hus- band—all these things are ludicrously impossible now.

They took him not twelve weeks before the end of the war. I was in the garden, nearly a quarter mile away (an odd arrangement, but one that suited me as I loved the walk through the patch of trees both early and late in the day). I was walking back, around five in the afternoon, and from around the side of the house I saw them put him in a transport truck. I could see the top of his head bent over his chest, with his dark wavy hair sticking out behind his ears because of the funny way the heat made it curl. I watched them drive away. He never lifted his head. He did not see me. If it had been a year earlier, surely they would have come to find me as well, but the arrests in the last weeks of the war were both desperate and halfhearted. In some ways, it would have been easier if they had found me. I feel a lot of things about that day and guilt is the most intolerable. I felt an impulse then to run after the truck, but I did not. Whatever fate he has come to—and believe me, I still have a powerful hope that he will walk up the path to our front door one day—it haunts me that I do not share it. It is a bitter revocation of our marriage vows, four years old on that day last spring.

Now it is the fall of the following year. I go into town every day, to buy a little flour or sugar or oil, to look in the shop windows (still mostly bare), to observe the painstaking reconstruction of the city, and to have a cup of tea with Anna-Isaac. She is the only friend I have left, and one of the few Jews left in the city, among a spattering of children and old people who had been either hidden or overlooked. I am not a child, nor am I old, and although neither Anna-Isaac nor I understand why I am here among them, we don't mention it. The Gentiles in the shops and the tearoom treat us well, just as polite as always, but there is the Unspeakable between us. I don't think it will be breached or repaired in my lifetime.

The house had been ransacked.

I could not go in, alone, after seeing him being driven away, for the longest time. I sat against the back wall of the stone house as it grew darker. The moon was well in the sky when I got the courage to open the door to my own home. It looked as if a terrible wind had blown everything inside out and upside down. All the drawers were pulled out and turned over, the cabinets open and nearly empty, the bedsheets ripped from our double bed, and the *icebox left open. The block of ice inside had begun melting and the small pint of precious milk was standing in a few inches of water. Up to that point in the war, through the bombs and the detainments and the call-ups, I had been frightened, but never so much as that night alone in my ruined house, in my ruined life.*

A powerful, strange energy was there in my home, at the center of which was the enormous, gaping hole of my husband's absence. I could almost hear a hum, a tense vibration that was the sound of recent violence and forlorn separation. I slept in the bathtub that night, with a pillow and blanket, with the door locked. I was afraid to turn on the light, but also afraid of the dark and the hum. I lay in the footed tub and watched the moon arc its way across the little window near the sink, corner to corner, and then disappear. I fell asleep just before daylight. When I awoke, I left the house and walked the two miles to Anna-Isaac's. She came back with me and put my things in order. She was the one who noticed they had taken my dishes—a peculiar item for soldiers to take the time to steal. My dishes were special to me. They had belonged to my mother, a deeply refined woman who died early in the war. My mother had given the dishes to me as a wedding gift. They were what was called "flow-blue"—not the name of a brand or city, like Limoges or Wedgwood, but a description of something that had happened to the porcelain during the process of firing it. The pattern in the dish— the blue flowers—was not set properly, or didn't respond well to the firing, and the heat caused the blue dye to bleed over the white areas. The result was a deep, milky blue dish with the faint under-imprint of the original intended pattern. It could happen to any dish, from a fine bone china to a heavy faience. My dishes were a lovely French porcelain. They were a beautiful, magnificent mistake.

Anna-Isaac stayed with me for a few weeks, through the initial difficult period of my grief when I could not sleep or eat. She was a true friend, quiet and not overly demonstrative with her sympathy. She just made soup, swept the wooden floor, let me cry, and offered her wide bosom and strong, heavy arms for comfort. When she saw me begin to eat and to take an interest in my garden, she moved back to her own empty house. Her husband and grown son had been taken the year before.

It is no life for a young woman, Anna-Isaac says, and tells me I should leave Dresden. For America, or England, or even Israel. I have no desire to go. I would not know how to feel like myself in another country. The one thing that keeps me grounded to the earth, and rooted in my body, is the platter that belonged to my set of dishes. They had overlooked it. It was the one piece that was too big for the narrow kitchen cupboard, so I kept it carefully wrapped in newspaper at the back of the top shelf of the front room closet. I discovered it after Anna-Isaac went back home. I am not ashamed to say that I slept with it, under the blankets with me, for many nights. If Anna-Isaac knew this, she would chastise me. So I don't tell her about the platter, and I don't tell her about the hope.

fff

Bella lifted her head slowly. She struggled to focus her eyes, and when she did, the first thing she saw was the platter, still in her lap. She startled, and quickly set it on the sideboard. She stood and picked up her cup of tea. It was still warm, unbelievably. She felt as if she had been gone for hours, but she had lost only a few minutes. It wasn't even eleven o'clock, the hour she usually opened for business.

She wandered around the store, a little dazed, unsettled by the images of the girl with her vacant house and her cheap dress. Bella slid into the chair at her desk and touched the screen, which took up most of the space on the desktop. The ArtWeb materialized. She touched Germany on the map. The dealer's icons, with their photos, popped up. She touched the photo of the man she had bought the recent lot from, and his picture disintegrated. A message came up in its place: "Dealer disconnected from ArtWeb. No further information." The sun fell directly on her hands, from the high windows that ran in a line on the street side of the shop. There was an abundance of windows on three sides of the store, both the small upper ones and the huge ones at the front and side. It was why she had bought this particular store.

Bella ran her finger lightly across the screen and it went black. She got up and walked to the sideboard where the blue platter lay. She cocked her head, as if listening for a moment, then abruptly turned away and went to unlock the front door to begin her day of business.

She got to bed early. One late night a week was more than enough, and her birthday had gone on until the wee hours the night before. Her apartment was very spare, almost stark, and clean. It was perfectly silent, away from the street and thoroughly soundproofed. The walls were painted muted shades of ochre and vanilla. The bed was an old, dark-stained spindle bed, made up all in white. She climbed in and settled deeply in the pillows. This was a dangerous time of day for her. She had to be vigilant about her thoughts in that space of drifting just before sleep. So many things could happen then, when the filters were down and she had no activity to occupy her. Usually, she just read the ArtWeb newsletter on her bedside screen, which was attached to the wall like an old angled reading lamp, until she could turn it off with a light stroke, push it away, and nod off almost in the same instant. Tonight she just lay quietly, telling herself she was too tired to read but knowing it was the old platter, and the girl from Dresden, that compelled her and commanded her attention. With the milky blue design drifting in front of her, she closed her eyes. She fell asleep.

And then she was sitting up, leaning against the big white pillows. The girl was standing in front of her, the grosgrain dress shimmering a little in the moonlight that fell through the window. The girl smoothed her skirt and glanced down at her ankle-strap shoes.

"Silly shoes," she said firmly. "I much prefer yours." She gestured at Bella's short black boots, which Bella had kicked off at the foot of the bed.

Bella smiled. "You can have them, if you like."

The girl shook her head. "No. But thank you."

Bella waited. She looked carefully at the girl, who seemed agitated. She was squirming a little, shifting her weight from one foot to the other. She would not meet

Bella's gaze. The girl walked to the window and leaned against the frame. The moonlight fell fully on her face, making it appear pale and lusterless, like unpolished marble. Her hair, a soft russet wave that fell to her shoulders in a centuries-old style, seemed carved of wood under the opaque rays. She grew still, and cautiously turned her head to look at Bella.

"It is not a joy for me to tell you what I came to tell you. I'll say that first. But you wanted to hear it, so I'll tell you. The rest of my life was not happy. There is nothing redemptive about my story. My husband never returned, which was no surprise to anyone but me. Even from this distance, I'm still a little surprised. A person can hang on to a secret hope inside herself until it is as small as a saucer, until it is as small as a spool of thread, until it is the size of a matchhead, until it is the ghost of a speck of dust, and that is what I did. I hung on. Eventually, I remarried, too late for children, but I did not love him like the one I lost, and the lack of children did not concern me by then."

Bella was keenly interested in this girl. She wondered if there were rules operating here. Could she ask questions?

"What happened to the platter?" Bella blurted out suddenly. Immediately she wished she had asked a more important question first, and she felt a little annoyed with herself. It wasn't like her to speak so impulsively.

"I gave it away when I got married again." The girl shrugged. "It didn't seem fair to my new husband to hold on to it, even though he could never have known its significance. But I knew. I could have turned bitter, but I turned numb instead. Of course, I could not have told you then that this was the choice I would make. I didn't even know it was a choice. But once the life is over you see it all so clearly. You see how the most agonizing decisions are no different from the smallest, most careless actions that we make every day. Each one has consequences that are beyond measure, rippling down through the centuries, both backward and forward. And now I see everything, past and future. That's why I'm here. And that's why you need me."

Bella was alarmed. "But I *don't* need you, dear." Bella twisted uncomfortably in the bed. She didn't know what to think or say next, a completely foreign state of mind for her. A childlike feeling of helplessness swept over her.

The girl continued without answering. "I only had my senses to lead me through the world, but the world was nothing I took pleasure in, so they did not matter to me. The color of the sky, the sound of heels on pavement or laughter at the next table, the touch of real silk, the smell of morning tea and hyacinths in the early spring, all the hard and true content of days, these were no comfort to me, they held no information that I found useful and so I let it all become as nothing. Stiff, silent, empty, and gray. I became the ghost of the speck of dust and the only pleasure I knew was the pleasure of denying Life the opportunity to express itself through me. That's a hollow power, but like I said, I only know that from a distance."

The girl moved to the bed. She sat at the foot for a moment and then crawled up to lie next to Bella. She took Bella's hand. It was cold and Bella trembled a little. She felt a flash of anger that this girl had somehow managed to upset her, to get past the filters and make her doubt herself, and she couldn't even pinpoint how it had happened. But she let her hold her hand, and in fact, she gave a little squeeze. She felt oddly protective of this girl, and sorry for her. The anger passed.

"I'm not a ghost," the girl continued. "I go where I'm needed, and where I need to go. I go where I belong, where it feels like home to me. And you called, of course. Let's not forget that. You're the one who called."

The girl closed her eyes. Her breathing slowed, as if she had fallen asleep. Bella lay next to her, still holding her hand. She had more questions. They were surfacing one on top of the other, but she was afraid of disturbing the girl, who seemed to be sleeping. She was deeply interested in the era the girl came from, the Second War of the Twentieth Century, and relished the idea of getting a firsthand account from her. But what did she mean, that Bella had called *her?*

With her eyes still shut, the girl said, "When you look into the recesses of yourself, do you see me? Do you know my name? I am naked as the stars and silent as the grave, but I am as close as your bloodstream. And if your blood were like blue ink and your bones like white china, would you love them as you love a platter, or a teapot, or a saucer? Would you love them as you love me?"

Bella took a sharp breath in and held it. She felt dizzy. She did not want to exhale. If she exhaled, she might scream or cry or make unspeakable sounds that would lead to complete internal chaos. It would all be out of control, unless she held her breath. How could she possibly love this girl? And yet, she recognized the quiet surge in her middle as something akin to what she had felt for Sera; an experience of longing and satisfaction, all at once.

The girl leaned over Bella and stroked her cheek. A slow shudder began deep in Bella's body and she let her breath go. To her relief, there was no sound. The girl spoke again. "I am the part of you that has not been sacrificed on the altar of normality. I am the part of you that has not been tutored, drugged, filtered, and forgotten. I am the part of you you need the most.

"My name is the Sound of the Color of the Memory that is too much to bear.

"I am the sand in your shell, and that is my name.

"My name is the cross you can step down from, into the life you can change.

"My name is the bell that tolls for all departures and rings for your return."

The girl lay quiet for many minutes. She smiled. She squeezed Bella's hand in a handshake grip, as if she were meeting her for the first time. Bella met her eyes, questioning.

The girl whispered, "My name is Rose."

Bella laughed. She let the tears fall, rolling across her cheeks and into her ears. She suddenly recalled a tutorial she had taken when she was about ten years old. She had come out of the shiny white office into the outer room, where Sera was waiting for her. Sera asked how the session had gone. Up to that time, Bella had been called by her full name, Bellarosa. Bella told Sera that the therapist had decided in this session that she could no longer use the second half of her given name, because of the association with the scent of roses and the possible activation of the third additional sense—the ability to smell memory—that even the word "rosa" might provoke. So it had been eliminated on that day. Bella had not used that name in so long, she had nearly forgotten it.

She turned to the girl and smiled. "I'm also a Rose," she said. "And tomorrow I will take you to my shop, sweetheart. I have something that belongs to you."

bells and roses

everything was mine
but it's long slipped away
I stand here naked as the stars
and silent as the grave
if you see who I really am
will you still want to stay?
there's a danger in this love
and I want to be that brave

bells and roses
a sign of departure, but I love them just the same
bells and roses
a sign of survival on the door into this pain

I'll go in if you say I must
but I'd rather let it go
there are people I will never trust
things that I can't know
I'll kiss you 'til we turn to stone
I'll fight you 'til we're blind
but you love me when you're left alone
and it makes me want to die

bells and roses
wake up the senses to remind me who I am
bells and roses
the gifts of the spirit shall not be squandered on one
man

everything was mine
but it's long slipped away
will you love me if I'm naked
or I'm silent as the grave?
you don't have to answer now
but you might learn to pray
and I'll step down off this cross
into a life that I can change

bells and roses
fill up the silence
and the place where he once lay
bells and roses
a sign of survival
and the price I had to pay
bells and roses
bells and roses
bells and roses

Tom Tavee 1996

ROSANNE CASH is a Grammy-winning singer and songwriter who has released ten record albums over the last twenty years, which have charted eleven number one singles and earned numerous accolades for songwriting and performance. Her first book, *Bodies of Water* (Hyperion, 1995), received widespread critical acclaim, as did her recent children's book, *Penelope Jane: A Fairy's Tale* (HarperCollins, 2000). Her essays and fiction have appeared in *The New York Times, Rolling Stone, The Oxford-American, New York* magazine, and various other periodicals and collections. She also teaches a summer songwriting workshop. She is currently working as music supervisor for the film *Big Stone Gap* and will release a new record in 2001 entitled *The Rules of Travel* (Capitol, 2001). She lives in New York City with her husband, John Leventhal, and her children.

DEAR EMILY SARANE

Marc Cohn

Dear Emily Sarane,
   Tonight you were sitting on the edge of a hotel rollaway bed in California, playing my guitar. You were making up a song about a talking shoe named Bob:

> ONCE I HAD A SHOE NAMED BOB
> (your melody up half an octave on the word "Bob")

> THE SHOE SAID—"WHY DID YOU THROW ME AWAY?"
> (much movement of your fingers up and down the fretboard
>   while strumming downward—once for every 2–3 words)

> I SAID—"I DIDN'T KNOW YOU WERE A TALKING
> SHOE, IF I'D KNOWN YOU WERE A TALKING SHOE, BOB—
>   I NEVER WOULD HAVE THROWN YOU
>   AWAAAAAAAAAAAY . . ."

You went on with this for a while until you hit and held a perfectly hoarse high note, and then went on to your next song.

Give it up for . . . (said your name)
Singing . . . (said title of next song)

We were all laughing, applauding, cheering you on. Even your nine-year-old brother was doing the same. (A miracle of sorts, since at this point in your lives together, most if not all of your sweetness and charm is completely lost on him.) The next song was called "Dad's Punish-mint." At first, it was a song about paternal discipline that segued somewhere into an ode to peppermint patties, ending with extemporaneous wordplay between punish-MINT and pepper-MINT, sung over and over until dramatic crescendo with big flamenco-like flourish on the guitar.

You were particularly giddy tonight, having spent all day in the sun and sea and all night eating chocolate cake sent up by the hotel concierge for your old man's birthday. Maybe it's because it's my birthday that I feel like I need to write this down tonight—I don't know. But there are too many times at the end of the day that I try to remember something you said or did—a look, a gesture, a question you asked earlier in the morning or the afternoon—and it's gone. Tonight, I just wanted to write down a little bit about who you are, right now, in all your five-and-a-half-year-old glory. It's an attempt to preserve this tiny moment in time for you—to cordon it off and protect it from the daily onslaught of phone calls, faxes, and what to have for dinner.

Speaking of dinner, I'm having a little bit of a struggle with you in that regard. Here is a list of all the possible entrees in your current culinary repertoire:

1. Pizza (plain and thin-crusted from Domino's)
2. Noodles (with butter sauce or tomato sauce but not if the tomato sauce "looks gross" because it has visible chunks of tomato in it)
3. Chicken (only in McNugget form)
4. Hamburger (only if doused in ketchup to mask offensive meat taste)

To your credit, you have become an avid edamame fan, and you have never balked at a single serving of steamed broccoli, but it's been hard getting you to eat a reasonably well-balanced meal.

Part of the problem, of course, is that you live in two separate houses with two completely different sets of rules, dietary and otherwise. I know how hard it must be for you at times, trying to adjust to one or the other of your two worlds. I wonder if there is an emotional or psychic circuit breaker constructed somewhere deep inside you now that automatically flips over every time you move from one home to the other—something that switches your heart and mind into DAD-mode or MOM-mode each time a transition is made.

You've been asking me a little bit about the divorce lately, and I'm always careful never to tell you more than what you're actually asking. (There is such a thing as too much information.) Mostly, I listen to what you tell me and try to hold you in whatever it is you're feeling. (Christ—what a lucky girl you are!) I screw up a helluva lot, too. But for reasons I don't fully understand, I know that since the split I have become a better father.

You've been saying a lot lately about how whenever you're with Mom, part of you misses me, and how whenever you're with me, part of you misses your mom. I want to tell you now, little one (will you always be little one?), that I wish it could have been different. By the time you read this, we will have talked a lot more about it, I'm sure. But in case we haven't talked enough, call me up, or walk over to me if I'm there with you right now and let me know what's on your mind. I can still hold you—wherever you are.

I want to get back to this Bob-the-talking-shoe-singer-songwriter thing for a minute. Right now, you're telling everyone that you want to be a singer when you grow up, and everyone's telling you that you look and sound like your old man, especially when you sing. All of that's fine and everything, but I want you to know that I'm not pushing you one way or the other—really, I'm not. It is strange and wonderful, though, hearing that voice, deep and raspy, coming out of your little throat—like Janis Joplin dubbed over in a Shirley Temple movie.

Music already moves you. You listen to the melody and to the words. You repeat them, sometimes only phonetically, but you still seem to get the meaning behind them. Sometimes, you sit in front of the stereo speakers—eyes closed, body swaying, trancelike, singing inadvertent harmony to a song that has struck a chord in you somewhere. You play it over and over. You sing along, quietly at first, then louder and louder, until you are standing, performing for no one but yourself, hand choreography thrown in at the end. You are, in that moment, Motown's little undiscovered singing Jew.

Your favorite song right now goes like this:

VOCAL: I will lay down my troubles on the
ground
(Hands: *Palms down, pushing outward*)
VOCAL: In front of you
(Hands: *Index fingers pointing out*)
VOCAL: And play
(Hands: *Air guitar*)
VOCAL: Let me play just one more song
(Hands: *More air guitar*)
VOCAL: That's my res-cuuuuuue
(Last word sung LOUD while hands
touch heart)

In the hotel tonight, olive-skinned and hazel-eyed, you loosened your grip on my guitar. You faded quickly as the effects of your day out in the elements overtook your sugar rush. I caught the guitar (which is almost as big as you are) before it hit the ground. I sang a song or two, even though you and your brother were already fast asleep. I watched your chest moving up and down as you struggled to breathe through your ever present congestion. (The ear, nose, and throat doctor says your tonsils look fine, but I'm betting you will no longer have them by the time you read this.) The sound of the surf is coming through the open windows, and for now, in this moment, no divorce, no custody agreement, no alternating weekends, no every-other-Christmas hangs in the salty air between us.

THE THINGS WE'VE HANDED DOWN

Don't know much about you
Don't know who you are
We've been doing fine without you
But we could only go so far
Don't know why you chose us
Were you watching from above
Is there someone there that knows us
Said we'd give you all our love?

Will you laugh just like your mother
Will you sigh like your old man
Will some things skip a generation
Like I've heard they often can
Are you a poet or a dancer
A devil or a clown
Or a strange new combination of
The things we've handed down?

I wonder who you'll look like
Will your hair fall down and curl
Will you be a mama's boy

Or daddy's little girl
Will you be a sad reminder
Of what's been lost along the way
Maybe you can help me find her
In the things you do and say
And these things that we have given you
They are not so easily found
But you can thank us later
For the things we've handed down.

You may not always be so grateful
For the way that you were made
Some feature of your father's
That you'd gladly sell or trade
And one day you may look at us
And say that you were cursed
But over time that line has been
Extremely well-rehearsed
By our fathers and their fathers
In some old and distant town
From places no one here remembers
Come the things we've handed down.

Singer/songwriter MARC COHN re-
leased his self-titled debut in 1991. The RIAA
platinum album included the top-20 single
"Walking in Memphis," which propelled the
New York City–based artist to international ac-
claim during a period highlighted by four New
York Music Awards and the Best New Artist
Grammy. Cohn's second album, 1993's *The
Rainy Season,* included contributions from Da-
vid Crosby, Graham Nash, and Bonnie Raitt.

In 1998 he released his third album, *Burning the Daze*, to critical acclaim. He is currently at work composing material for his fourth Atlantic solo album, due in 2001.

BETHLEHEM

Paula Cole

Our secondhand spinet piano is painted garishly three times over: white, brown, then baby blue. It stands at the back of "the Cold Room," the entry room of our two-hundred-year-old New England Federal fixer-upper. This is where our snowy boots are shaken off and mackinaws and mittens huddle in damp piles. There's firewood, puddles, bicycles, the good old-fashioned Yankee thriftiness that pinches the pennies off the expensive electric heat . . . and the piano.

I play an annoying One-Five Melody from my beginner book. It's called "The Cricket." I'm six. How can this painful song look so complicated? I fume and my anger fogs in the unheated colonial air. I hear distant laughter coming from the warm kitchen and I promise to abandon these compulsory lessons from the woman with the smelly house and the blind dog. I will not play joyless music with brittle blue fingers.

Flash and fury, I grab my sharpened pencil spearlike and stab my book to pieces.

Murder. Self-deflated. Ashamed.

I repair myself eight years later: I'm fourteen with my feathers and bangs hair, cut in the Gloucester Mall (the closest thing to civilization for us unless you like the Christian Science Reading Room or the House of Pizza), and worse, a perm. I hide my Little Orphan Annie pom-pom under a hat, and then God really strikes . . . mysteriously I fracture my right metatarsal bone. Perhaps it happened during softball practice? . . . . Or maybe during my breakfast waitressing job at the aptly named "Peg Leg" restaurant. A podiatrist X-rays my foot and informs me slow healing is in order: I will not don a heroine's cast; I will wear a hideous wooden shoe. For a year. My mom has to drive me everywhere because I cannot walk any distance. And I swear at her. I am horrible. I feel hooflike, an orthopedic blockfoot who clomps in the silent school hallway. I ebb away from my friends who now seem mean. I am a monster, caffeinated on diet pills, depressed, and ugly, ugly, ugly. There is nothing for me in this world and my acid must spill.

I slouch at our new spinet. It's now inside by the antique wing chair and the maniacal ding of my mother's beloved grandfather clock. Obnoxiously bright in tone, the piano forces its sunshine into me; it wills me to sit up straight. I devour "Moonlight Sonata"; I flower unknowingly. Chopin's "Prelude in B," and three weeks later I'm singing. I have discovered a secret river of joy. I have found my Way. I have found Me.

BETHLEHEM

Pulling on the apron strings looking up
Standing on the chair to be grown up
I feel so little, I need my pillow,
I hate time, I hate the clock, I want to be a dog or I
want to be a rock.

Sunday's pancakes, Miss Mary Mack
Color Polaroids show my heart attack
In my secondhand pants and dusty shoes
The day that the playground laughed at my shoes
It's my birthday next week and what I want please
Is to turn on the heat so the fish won't freeze
The fish in the tank froze and died last week
Oh I want to be a dog or I want to be a leaf.

Quarry miners, fishermen, in my town of Bethlehem
Picket fences, church at ten, no star above my Bethlehem.

Now I'm only sixteen and I think I have an ulcer
I'm hiding my sex behind a dirty sweatshirt
I've lost five pounds the past few days
Trying to be class president and get straight A's

Well who gives a shit about that anyway?
I just want to be a dog or a lump of clay.

Quarry miners, fishermen, in my town of Bethlehem
Picket fences, church at ten, no star above my Bethlehem.

Still, I'm tired of standing still
Tired of living still
Every day I dream of leaving.

Everybody's talking 'bout Becky's bust
The boys on the basketball team just fuck
The same ten girls who don't know who they are
They're looking for some comfort in the back of a car
The six-packs of beer, the locker room jeers
I don't want to be me, I don't want to be here.

Quarry miners, fishermen, in my town of Bethlehem
Picket fences, church at ten, no star above my Bethlehem.
Red brick schoolhouse, dead-end dirt roads, daffodils
No star above my Bethlehem.

I want to be a dog or I want to be a rock
I don't want to be me, I don't want to be here
In Bethlehem.

Frank Ockenfels

PAULA COLE grew up in Rockport, a small Massachusetts town. In 1994 she had her debut album *Harbinger*. Her follow-up album *This Fire* was released by Warner Records. Fueled by two smash hit singles, "Where Have All the Cowboys Gone?" and "I Don't Want to Wait," *This Fire* blazed onto the pop charts, blanketing both MTV and VH-1 while garnering a remarkable seven Grammy nominations, including one for Producer of the Year. Paula is the first woman in Grammy history to receive that honor. *The New York Times* called her "a rising talent with tremendous artistic potential," while *Entertainment Weekly* praised Paula as "a feisty poet with a soaring voice and a funky groove."

BONEFIELDS

Shawn Colvin

we had to call the police again on the mexican bachelors
next door. it's kind of a thrill to call the police on somebody,
and my husband and i agreed that we weren't being reckless
because we had asked them twice already to turn the music
down and it was 2 a.m. and the last time this happened the
baby woke up. we live in an apartment complex and although each unit has a front door, most of the residents use
their garages to enter their apartments. we knew, therefore,
that the mexicans drove a mercedes and a lexus, a detail that
made an impression on my husband, who appreciates fine
automobiles. we could also see that the inside of their garage
was plastered with absolut vodka ads and pinups of naked
women. so we knew the mexican bachelors were young,
upscale, and liked to party, and that was fine, but enough
was enough.

i had the phone in my hand when i heard my husband coming back from next door, yelling over his shoulder, "my wife is calling the police and there's nothing i can do to stop her!" and indeed, i was just explaining to the 911 operator that i really didn't have an emergency, but that no one was answering at the police station. she said that was fine, she would take my information and pass it along. after what seemed like a long time my husband called 911 again. a man answered this time, and he asked, "has there been any violence?" my husband said menacingly, "no, but there might be," to which the 911 man replied, "it sounds like we need to check *you* out, sir, making threats on a recorded line." i thought, well shit, that's the end of that.

but the police did come, and it was all wonderful. the mexicans had the music going full tilt, just as we'd hoped, our case proven. we heard an officer say, "if you don't quit getting in my face i'm putting you in the car. you are drunk, sir, and most people in your shoes would say they were sorry and go back inside." my husband and i clung to each other in our dark garage, giggling nervously. the poor, young bachelors, who were only doing what came naturally after all, might be getting in trouble, and we didn't want that really, but it was exciting anyway. nothing happened, though. the police were nice and spent at least 45 minutes explaining how many better things they had to do on a saturday night besides coming over to break up their party. then the party broke up and it was quiet again.

by now we were wide awake, having called the law on our neighbors. my husband looked grave. he said, "i don't like this kind of trouble. they might try to fuck with me." this was not particularly reassuring. i told him i didn't understand and was he truly concerned that something might happen to one of us, or worse, to the baby? "no," he said, "they might hurt my car." the mexican bachelors moved out not too long afterwards, but not before trying to mend fences with us by giving our child a little stuffed bunny. my husband scowled at them as they knelt down to offer our baby the toy, defending his family even at peril to his automobile. our new neighbors have a child, too, and a range rover. we've never spoken.

BONEFIELDS

all in all i guess that
there's so many things that
we don't say but it's
what makes us sad I think
sometimes that makes us close
but I don't mind
I don't mind

in the alleys and the bonefields
of Arkansas past the piles of tires
and the smell of hot tar
you threw your papers in the rain
under your hat
you had a world
a world

there ain't no father
there ain't no mother
don't see my sister
ain't got a brother
running to no one
left to each other

in the valleys and the twilight
of illinois and under the new moon
i write my book and i walk the streets
where no one lives not even you
but you don't mind
you don't mind

and all in all i guess that
there's so many things that
we don't say and today
you think that i don't even
like you but don't you know
you are my world
you are my world

there ain't no father
there ain't no mother
don't see my sister
ain't got no brother
running to jesus
running to lovers
running to strangers
running for cover
running to no one
left to each other

Written by Shawn Colvin and John Leventhal
© 2000 WB Music Corp. / AGF Music Ltd. / Scred Songs / Lev-A-Tunes
(ASCAP). All rights reserved. Used by permission.

Katherine Wessel

SHAWN COLVIN is a native of Vermillion, South Dakota. One of Shawn's first breaks came singing backup on Suzanne Vega's 1987 hit, "Luka." By 1988, Shawn had found a musical collaborator in John Leventhal, who co-produced her first album, *Steady On*. Released in 1989, the album took home a Grammy for Best Contemporary Folk Recording. Her debut album's success led to appearances on benefit albums and as a guest vocalist on LPs by Suzanne Vega and Mary Chapin Carpenter. Then came *Fat City*, released in 1992, which garnered two Grammy nominations: Best Contemporary Folk Recording and Best Female Pop Vocal for "I Don't Know Why." In 1996, she released *A Few Small Repairs*, which won the Grammy Award for Record of the Year, as well as a second Grammy for Song of the Year for the hit single "Sunny Came Home." In 1998 she released a collection of all-new recordings of seasonal holiday classics and traditional children's lullabies. Shawn is currently working on her next album with producer/co-writer John Leventhal. It is slated for release in early 2001.

I WALK THE LINE
REVISITED

Rodney Crowell

Houston, Texas, 1956: Landscaped by whitewashed tree trunks, oyster-shell parking lots, roadside watermelon stands, sawdust dance floors, and Pentecostal tent revivals, it proudly proclaimed itself "The murder capital of the world." It remains unclear whether such dubious distinction was substantiated by statistical evidence, no doubt the Chamber of Commerce had facts to the contrary; but in the hometown of my childhood, statements made loud, stayed loud. A wise and simple man perhaps put it best when he said of the bayou city, "round these parts close is close enough." As a backdrop for my misspent youth there was no substitute for hot nights, fistfights, fat stock shows, rodeos, cherry bombs, Peeping Toms, and loudmouthed Texans.

Populated by lovable ne'er-do-wells and flatland hillbillies, the east side of our city was a post-Depression mecca for lost souls and poor people. Common labor was plentiful, honky-tonks were the cultural center of the universe, petty crime was an art form, and greasy hamburgers were considered a delicacy. The streets were full of high hopes and low I.Q.'s, and my family was among the proudest of its underachievers.

My grandfather, a hard-drinking ex–sharecrop farmer, lived very much in his element in the seedy area of Houston known as the East End. A connoisseur of decadence, he was a fixture in the neon nightspots lining Navigation Boulevard and a regular at Friday night crap games all over his side of town. On occasional Saturdays he would make ritualistic displays of grandfatherliness by announcing to my delight that he was "taking the boy to get a haircut." Coincidentally, a seaport bar of the finest ilk happened to be located two doors down from The Captain's Clippers Barber Shop.

Houston's fifty-mile, man-made ship channel reached its dead end at Navigation Boulevard and Wayside Drive, the exact location of The Old Navigation Ice House, and our true destination. Known locally as The Old Navigation, it drew its clientele from a deep pool of dockworkers, roughnecks, and hard-drinking merchant seamen living in the neighborhood or those just off the ship. With it being open all hours and walking distance from our house, my grandfather and I always seemed to wind up there and in trouble.

It's a mystery why my mother and grandmother agreed to let me go on these outings with the old man; the results were always the same. I would be propped up on the bar with some big-hearted barmaid oohing and aahing and carrying on about what a handsome little man I was while my grandfather in his gray fedora hat and scratchy old wool suit smoked hand-rolled Prince Albert cigarettes, drank his beloved Jax beer, and held court with one-eyed sailors and hard-core merchant marines.

Like clockwork, my mother and grandmother came charging through those swinging porthole doors wired on coffee and Salvation Army righteousness. Their battle plan called for a sadistic twisting of my ear as my mother marched me out into the blinding sunlight on Navigation Boulevard and my grandmother's equally harsh retrieval of my wobbly old crestfallen grandfather from the reverie of his mid-Saturday booziness. With the efficiency of a brick thrown through a living room window, our little boys' club was dismantled on the spot.

Quoting scriptures from the Bible like her words were crucifixes and those poor ice house patrons vampires, my grandmother rebuked everything in that beer joint from the liquor license to the pinball machine. Regular customers, though used to her sanctimonious tirades, cowered like whipped dogs when Sister Willoughby brought the wrath of God into that den of iniquity. As for me, I just wanted to be back inside where it was cool and dark with that red-headed woman and those salty old men.

My grandmother taught me about love and common decency, my grandfather, cussin', spittin', and cheatin' at cards. In a war of intangibles waged for my soul, my grand-parents settled old differences, like faith versus freedom and duty before fun, under the guise of "seeing to it I was raised up right."

Refuge came in the form of my father's guitar and his wealth of old songs. My father knew hundreds of songs, literally, and I learned most of them by osmosis, spending endless hours playing around his feet while he sang eyes closed to an audience of me and my toys. Though it would take years to surface and my father would never have the satisfaction of hearing me say these words, I learned who I was on that floor listening to his renditions of great songs like "May I Sleep in Your Barn Tonight Mister," "The Great Speckled Bird," "Put My Little Shoes Away," and "The Columbus Stockade Blues". . . . Along the way, my father also taught me how to fish, sharpen a knife, throw a curveball, shoot a shotgun, tie a knot in a necktie, and drive a used car.

My father drove an ice truck and city bus, but in 1956 he didn't own a car. The knack for making and keeping money would not introduce itself until much later in my father's life. Luck, however, was a timely ally; my uncle Porter had a friend with a strange fondness for lending my father his 1949 Ford two-door hardtop roadster with big whitewall tires and wire fender scrapers that stuck out like feelers to let you know when you were the perfect parking distance from the curb. It was jet black, loaded with thick chrome, and sported shiny full-moon hubcaps.

The proud owner of this palace on wheels was a man named Waymon Lowe, but we all knew him as Little Willie Smith. At Little Willie's insistence, with occasional engagements lasting two weeks, my father drove that Ford as if it were his own. He often gave Little Willie a ride to work in his own car. Little Willie, for reasons of his own, loved to see my father behind the wheel of that handsome automobile.

In the predawn hours one summer morning before I turned six years old, my life changed forever. It took less than three minutes. From the backseat vantage point of Little Willie's Ford, my chin resting on the front seat between my father, who was driving, and my grandfather, who rode shotgun, I watched as we headed deep into the heart of an East Texas morning on a two-rut wagon road. The high-beam headlights revealed a charcoal-sketched landscape of pine trees, salt grass, and armadillos. We were going fishing. My father smoked Old Gold cigarettes, my grandfather sipped Old Crow whiskey, and I entertained visions of white perch and gasper goo a foot long on our fish stringer.

Before this particular morning I don't recall having it brought to my attention that an automobile was capable of reproducing music. As far as I was concerned that function belonged solely to the icehouse jukeboxes of the world and my grandmother's old Victrola radio. That misconception was soon to be changed. Out of nowhere the slow rolling chugging rhythm of a freight train began to assemble itself. A hypnotic drone that I can describe only as the strumming of a sandpaper guitar made the first signs of an assault on my unsuspecting senses. Gradually I became aware that, like a genie, out of the dashboard a song was taking form directly in front of me.

A voice, sounding very much like Abraham Lincoln looked, started humming long, low, single-note passages with the gravity of an earthquake, making my front teeth more loose than they already were. Identifying itself with illogical directness, a melody wafted its way through the car, magic carpet style, carrying on it these exotic words:

I Keep A Close Watch On This Heart Of Mine
I Keep My Eyes Wide Open All The Time
I Keep The Ends Out For The Ties That Bind
Because You're Mine I Walk The Line

Spooky shades of blue and gray, like the light from a black-and-white television, saturated the interior of Little Willie's roadster; I couldn't tell if it was a haunting or a hallucination. My father and grandfather seemed far away and my words, if I could have spoken, would not have traveled the distance required to reach them. I had taken a direct hit from a sucker punch masquerading as a song, and reality as I knew it was long gone, like the air I had been breathing just a few minutes before.

We may well have been abducted by aliens that morning—strange were the events that took place. From the farther reaches of outer space it seems that song came, picked me up, took me away, and returned me sometime later to a world forever changed. Should the veracity of my recall be a cause for question, rest assured in the telling of this story no allowances have been made for a line of retreat. I can but press forward with rope enough to hang myself.

I don't know what my father or grandfather experienced that morning, if anything. I never asked. I don't know if we made it to our destination or if we caught any fish. But I do know this: until the day my grandfather died he had a strange and maniacal reverence for the music of the man he called the greatest singer in the world: Johnny Cash. I myself became obsessed by a deep longing to know where such an unusual song came from, how it got here, and if there were any more out there like it. The hours spent listening to my father sing about someone's son calling another man Daddy, holes in the bottom of the sea, and little Appalachian dead babies had not prepared me for the first time I heard Johnny Cash sing "I Walk the Line."

This experience/allergic reaction has disturbed me off and on for forty-plus years. Radio-activated blackouts don't just happen every day. Pondering the before-mentioned musical mirage's lack of traceable earthly origins I have drawn a conclusion concerning the nature of songs and how they come to be. Pretentious perhaps to the point of pedanticism, my conclusion is nonetheless this: somewhere, there exists a place where songs yet to be conceived wait fully written for bold messengers to reach this distant outpost of inspired originality where anything is possible and everything rhymes. Johnny Cash has been there . . . and back.

Galveston Island the summer of 1957 was the last seen and heard from Little Willie Smith and his '49 Ford. That year Little Willie's prized possession found itself at the bottom of the Gulf of Mexico.

By the carload family members and friends caravanned,

like dustbowl gypsies, down a fifty-mile stretch of two-lane highway leading to Galveston's sunshine and saltwater and the hard-packed sandy beaches we loved so well. There, cars were parked next to the waves and we slept out under the stars. My grandparents slept fully dressed sitting upright in the backseat of my uncle Kenneth's DeSoto; others found the beach, picnic tables, or an open car trunk suitable for their rest. My preference for the flat surface between the backseat and the rear window of Little Willie's Ford made the Big Dipper seem close enough to drink water from it with a straw.

Car radios were all tuned to the same station and blasting, grown-ups danced, kids played hide-and-go-seek, and the mosquitoes had a drunken feast thanks to my male relatives and their fondness for large quantities of liquid courage. On one of these Crowell/Willoughby seaside outings such as I describe, my uncles outdid themselves once and for all with a stunt that is now part of Texas Gulf Coast folklore.

Grandiosity and one-upmanship were the cornerstone of the Willoughby brothers' sibling rivalry long before their first taste of homemade liquor. The flat Texas coastland and blue expanse of open sky raised the ante on their scatter-brained escapades to the detriment of everyone involved, especially Little Willie Smith.

Under the influence of a case of Jax beer, my high-stakes double-dog daredevil uncles Raymond and Porter hit on an idea that, to them, was the absolute peak of their brotherly genius. The plan called for Uncle Porter to get a good head of speed going and drive Little Willie's roadster straight into the Gulf of Mexico just to see what would happen.

Here's what happened: with my uncle Porter at the wheel, and traveling somewhere between fifty and sixty miles per hour, that beautiful black Ford hit the water with a spectacular splash. The car sank, Uncle Porter swam, Grandma prayed, Grandpa cussed out loud and spit tobacco juice in the sand, and my father shook his head, mumbled something under his breath, then headed down the beach in search of a pay phone or a tow truck.

The day is gone when a good ol' boy on the periphery, like Waymon Lowe, got his goofball kicks watching some other guy parade around in his hot-rod Ford. They don't make people or radios like that anymore.

I WALK THE LINE REVISITED

I'm back on board that '49 Ford in 1956
Long before the sun came up way out in the sticks
The headlights showed a two-rut road
Way back up in the pines
The first time I heard Johnny Cash sing
I WALK THE LINE

I got my thrill behind the wheel upon my daddy's lap
Grandpaw rode co-pilot with a flashlight and a map
Cane pole out the window it was in the summer time
The first time I heard Johnny Cash sing
I WALK THE LINE

I keep a close watch on this heart of mine
I keep my eyes wide open all the time
I keep the ends out for the ties that bind
Because you're mine I walk the line

I never will forget that day I know the time and place
It sounded like the whole thing came right down from
outer space

I still can see those headlights and that dashboard in
my mind
The first time I heard Johnny Cash sing
I WALK THE LINE

I find it very very easy to be true
I find myself alone when each day is through
I'll admit that I'm a fool for you
Because you're mine I walk the line

All these long years later it's still music to my ears
I swear it sounds as good right now as anything I hear
I've seen the Mona Lisa I've heard Shakespeare read
real fine
It's just like hearing Johnny Cash sing
I WALK THE LINE

As sure as night is dark and day is light
I keep you on my mind both day and night
And happiness I've known proves that it's right
Because you're mine I walk the line

In the summer of 1972, RODNEY CROWELL moved to Nashville, and in 1974 he became the first member of Emmylou Harris's famous Hot Band and performed with her until he received his own recording contract three years later. Not only was Rodney recording his own music, but he also began producing records of other artists such as Johnny Cash, Jerry Lee Lewis, and Carl Perkins. Rodney's solo career produced such hits as "Leaving Louisiana in the Broad Daylight," "Viola an American Dream," "Till I Gain Control

Again," and "Stars on the Water." *Diamonds and Dirt* was the record that finally brought Rodney into the mainstream recognition he so well deserved. He became the first artist in history to perform, write, and produce an album with five number one singles. When "After All This Time" was named Song of the Year in 1990, Rodney won his first Grammy. Rodney's immediate projects include a soon-to-be-released album of autobiographical songs titled *The Houston Kid* and a book of memoirs of his youth titled *The House on Norvic Street*.

STUNTMAN

Joe Henry

It looks like he's gone back to sleep, yes. I guess he needs
it. They had him up and down the hall four times today,
and I think it sort of discouraged him, poor thing. I mean,
he's only been out of the cast since Tuesday, but I think he
was somehow expecting more, like maybe he was supposed
to drive us both home today. I'm not laughing, not *at* him.
Hey, I was there when they took it off, and that nurse had
to practically tear it apart with her bare hands; it went all
the way up to his hip, I'm saying. His leg was all thin and
puckered, like an old ear of white corn. It still smells sour,
and I've scrubbed it myself repeatedly. He's got steel pins
in his upper thighbone and knee, which gives him a leg to
stand on, but he's walking like a man on short stilts, if you'd
have seen him. Even with help. His upper body is another
story entirely, but that's going to take some time. No,

honey, leave it on; that light's not about to bother him, I don't guess. He's so looped on whatever that is they give him that you could all be making a break for it and I don't imagine he'd so much as roll over—alarms, lights, and all. No offense. He's a lucky man any way you look at it, and I make him say it every day of the world.

Was that your wife in here this morning? Pretty. Well, bless your heart. Thank you. I used to be, but not so's you could tell. I feel like my husband here has about doubled my age in the past two months. I mean it, I can see a difference. Not that *he* will, of course. I don't know what he's likely to remember. No, sugar, he couldn't have done this kind of damage in an automobile, even trying. Not unless you could get one up to ten thousand feet.

He started flying in the Navy, but he wasn't there very long. Wasn't ever involved in any ruckus to speak of. He got up with a colonel who just thought the world of him and spent most of his hitch flying his brass in and out of Virginia for briefings and whatnot. That's where I met him. And then we followed that same colonel out to San Diego where my Andy spent the next eighteen months logging maintenance, playing golf, and waiting for his orders to come through. Fine by me. All in all, though, the Navy didn't amount to much of an *experience*, like they talk about. The only exotic thing I saw was a cockfight behind an auto body shop in San Pedro, if that qualifies. But it did land him a job flying commercial for a couple of the major airlines, which he did for the next four years running. Nice work if you can get it, I always say. And I flew free, so there. Anyway, pretty soon he got some nicer work as a freelancer flying small planes in and out of Mexico for a fella he knew, an "independent importer." That's what he called himself. I was against it at first, not like I exactly *knew* at first; but once I did, boy, I had a thing or two to say about it. But the money was real good. So good that we didn't think much about it when Delta sent him packing. His supervisor got suspicious of all that sick time. But shit, they didn't even have a dental plan, not hardly, unless you call two cleanings a year a "plan." You want any more of these peanuts? Suit yourself.

No, things were going good for us, finally. We moved to Long Beach, I was in a little book club and whatnot. But then Tommy Reese, a flyboy that was trading runs with Andy, crashed and burned in the desert with full cargo, and I mean *full*. You probably read about it. And then everything stopped, like, overnight. We had put a little money away, but we'd both become a bit too "vested in the trade," is how we called it. Smoking, I mean. I should keep my voice down, but what *don't* they know at this point, am I right?

Smoking is what I was doing, anyway. I didn't know about any of the other with Andy for a while. Not until all our money was gone and I start finding Chuck Yeager here in a fetal curl on the couch, nodding in front of those family wrestling matches on television. Aren't those a stitch? Did you see the one with that stock analyst who liked to be put in diapers and called "Molly" or some such thing? *His* wife didn't know what was going on either. But the boy here doesn't remember anything he saw on TV. The smoke was just like soda pop to him and I couldn't do a thing with him. A few times he got work through a friend subbing for a charter service. Got to fly Kojak and his girlfriend up to Sun Valley for a weekend once. But we couldn't count on that. Andy started spending most of the time I could get him to work doing phone sales: auto insurance packages, juicers, home insulation, pagers. Anything people hadn't already decided they didn't need. And he was pretty good at it, too; padding around in his robe and corduroy slippers with the cordless phone, telling anyone else who might also happen to be home in the day that he's just been authorized to extend a special offer to select, prequalified customers. . . . Look at his foot going. Like a dog dreaming. I suppose that's a good sign of some kind, that he can move it like that by himself. I was saying about this job, and that. I really thought things were about to get better all the way around when he met the Fellers.

Carolyn and Ted Feller put on air shows all over the country, and Andy started flying for them last year. That was them here last night just about closing time. Brought the flowers and this nut dish. Like, the man is still eating through a straw and they bring fancy mixed nuts? But these shows were like county fairs, really; everything from livestock to corn dogs to classic car rallies. In Wisconsin and Minnesota there was even the added attraction of local artists who sculpted busts of celebrities like Bruce Willis and Roseanne Barr out of butter and cheese. But the real draw was the planes. Stunts, and whatnot. They started on Memorial Day weekend in Montclair, New Jersey, their headquarters, and they'd wind through Jersey, New York, Pennsylvania, and then the Midwest, making a loop that always ended on Labor Day in Cleveland. That's Ted's hometown. Then they'd stage special events on the West Coast that took them all the way through Thanksgiving. Then they'd disappear into Vermont where they spent the winter trading in antiques and folk art. For real: I'm thinking I might just get me some cardboard and house paint and become a Folk Artist. Have you seen it? I wouldn't *need* a dental plan; good teeth would be a liability.

Most of the flyers on the circuit were vets like Andy. No stories to tell. There would always be a few, of course, like Dave Patterson, who had nothing left *but* the story. He'd been an Air Force captain in N-a-m. Don't want to say that too loud in here, I bet. Somebody'll start flashing back. He flew fighter jets in a quad formation, but his specialty was a solo "peel-off," they called it, where he'd rage above the crowds like a bullet piercing a bullhorn. Loops, and whatnot. If you listened over the headsets he'd be screaming the vilest things known to man, but off the field he was the picture of civility. Clean, and always had something nice to say to me. It was Dave, I remember, who brought a Styrofoam cup of black coffee over to Andy that morning in the hotel lobby while we were waiting on the minivan to take us out to the field. Andy was sort of slumped over on a couch. "Buckle up," he said, and Andy laughed, but I swear I *freaked*. I mean, I had a feeling right then that we should've just gone back to bed. I still think we should've.

Well, they're going to throw me out of here in a minute, late as it is. I might just as well light up a cigarette and they can get it over with. Honestly, I don't know how they expect anyone to sit through those group sessions without smoking something. I don't know how Andy's going to. I sat in on one yesterday and I've already heard the spiel they've got on him. About how being a pilot's made him think he's supposed to be able to control everything; about him being angry and how what he really wanted to do was hurt me. Can you imagine? They should've been there. Yeah, he wanted to hurt me so bad that he nosed his plane into Lake Erie on as beautiful a day as God ever made. I think I'll be a damn psychologist after I get finished painting angels on cardboard. Shouldn't I though? I mean, can you imagine?

Well, I'll tell you what I *never* imagined was sitting in here with a magazine while some volunteer nurse's aid helped my husband vomit into a pan, and him half suspended from the ceiling. "Trouble comes to those who need it," I've heard it said, but I mean, there's a limit. I'm going to go home and take a hot bath for about a week, is what I'm thinking I need. And I'm leaving the rest of these damn peanuts, whether you eat them or not.

MEDICINE

Everybody knows the crash
Left me on my back,
Everybody knows that this is
Just my medicine;
I staked it like a claim
And it pushed me like a broom,
Now I'm straighter than a razor
Well anyway, I will be soon

Come sit down beside me
I'm your cripple little king,
The day once fell away and left
its rose on everything;
but now the sun, it keeps above my head
the meanest kind of blue,
I keep myself behind a cloud
almost safe from you

(La, la, la, la . . .)

I'm going to move myself into
That room above the bank,

And I think I'm going to buy myself
A brand-new pair of shoes;
I can feel it: everything's about to
Change and soon,
I won't even have to try
If I can just change you

(La, la, la, la . . .)

Words and Music by Joe Henry

Melanie Nissen

JOE HENRY is a critically acclaimed singer/songwriter. All of his albums occupy a different sonic landscape, the common thread being his voice and a unique lyric sensibility. His recordings have included forays into folk, jazz, atmospheric rock, and sound collages that verge on hip-hop. His recording bands have featured everyone from jazz legend Don Cherry to art-metal guitarist Page Hamilton.

Beyond his own records, Henry has produced recordings for a number of other artists, and his songwriting collaborations have included work with Jakob Dylan, Rosanne Cash, and Madonna. He also composes music for film and currently lives in Los Angeles with his wife and their two children.

IN THE CAR

Steven Page

The urge to purchase a sport utility vehicle proved to be stronger than the arguments against them. We fought it for a few years, cursing the sudden differences in driving conditions over a very short period of time; all of a sudden, we could no longer see two cars in front of ourselves on the highway. Everyone seemed to be in a minivan or sport utility, and we were dwarfed, craning our necks as if seeing an extra inch to the left or right would help. Emissions loopholes had been found and exploited, and drivers across North America seemed wholly unaware that they were once again driving gas-guzzlers like their parents' Delta 88s. Each truck became a Big Mac, Gap khakis, an Ikea sofa, a Matisse poster with goldfish floating, possibly dead, in a bowl near a window. When we drove off the lot in the shiny black truck, we knew we had become like the rest of the parents at the school. We knew that the beeping key fob that unlocks the doors and disarms the alarm would be the only way we could find our vehicle in parking lots. We had embraced the sameness we thought we'd wanted to avoid. But we caved in, wanting space for a possible third baby seat, cargo room for our Ikea sofa, and four-wheel drive and lots of ground clearance for the once-yearly snowstorm that sends panic through the streets of Toronto.

The snowstorm never really came this year, at least not like last year, when the mayor asked the army to help dig us out of a couple feet of powder. In spite of its uselessness, the truck did seem rugged and attractive, and even possibly enviable as I cleaned up the garage from the damage. One night last week, I'd gone to bed leaving the garage door open, and I guess a raccoon must have found his way in and tried to sleep. I didn't go in for a few days, and when I did, the place had been trashed. It seems the raccoon was trapped and freaked out in there, knocking over bedroom doors we'd never hung, chewing through bits of wood and bags of garbage, and running and shitting all over the truck. Little dirty footprints, four-toed but otherwise unsettlingly human with their fine pads and toes and nails, were all over the hood and roof of the truck like a very advanced dance chart. Fox-trot. No, New York Hustle.

The raccoon made a big mess, and there were footprints on the windows of the garage. Upside-down footprints. I stood for a few minutes trying to figure out from where the animal could descend to run down a window. I then realized as I was hosing down the garage floor that it was entirely possible for him to still be in here. If he had spent all night trying to escape by chewing off the rubber sweep that runs the length of the entire double garage door, then he probably didn't get out, did he? I banged around with a hockey stick—on trash cans, on the rafters. I didn't hear anything. I didn't stick around very long. I am terrified of almost every animal. Disposing of a dead mouse gives me more palpitations than even the fear of a serial killer climbing in a window of my kids' bedroom. Occasionally on the night before garbage day, I will see a coyote who has wandered up from the Don Valley. He peruses the garbage, and I freeze. Do I run in the house and risk being chased inside by a coyote? Do I stand still and watch him sniff my garbage, praying that he doesn't try to sniff me?

Once, driving through the Rocky Mountains in Alberta, we came across a herd of elk standing in the middle of the highway. It was the middle of the night, and apparently this was quite a beautiful sight—the majesty of . . . the serenity of . . . the sheer number (probably thirty of forty or more) . . . but all I could imagine was a charge on my car. Elk so horny for humans or cars that they would hump us. Hooves slapping down on the metal of the hood, tearing through the steel and rubber and glass, spurting elk jism into the night sky. It never happened. The air was still and we just stared at each other, men and beasts. To cut through the calm silence, all I could muster was a panicked "Let's get the fuck out of here," and we did.

I decided to leave an apple on the floor of the garage overnight. If, in the morning, it was still there, I could rest at ease. If, however, it was eaten, then obviously we had a problem. I took the truck to the car wash and got the package they called "The Works," which included hot wax and something called an "undercarriage blast." I thought that the extra cleaning and polishing might get rid of all raccoon memory. I vacuumed the inside. Twice. Just in case the beast had somehow found his way inside, which I knew very well that he hadn't. I drove the truck home, and closed the garage, and repositioned the apple to make it a little bit more obvious for the raccoon. That night, Jonah, our fourteen-month-old, woke up in the night in terror. Not sleeping yet myself, I scooted into his room to give him a cuddle and settle him down. Bad dream. Or he woke up in his bed, alone, wondering if he was alone in the house. Did the family pack up and leave while he slept? What had he missed? Had they forgotten about the newest addition to the family and in some kind of sleepy time warp driven off on some vacation or errand, leaving him alone in his room? I held him and rocked him and told him we were all there, and that it was time to sleep, and that it was very late, and that I love you and Mommy loves you and it's sleep time and goodnight Jonah and goodnight. His feet stopped kicking and he fell limp and very heavy in my arms and I lay him back on his bed and I went downstairs and tried to look out at the garage through the back door. I put on my wife's sandals, three sizes too small but right there by the door, and hobbled out to the garage to take a better look. Wanting to flick on the light but knowing better, I squinted through the window and saw the apple, alone and intact, poised, waiting to be sacrificed. I went to bed and pretended to sleep.

The next morning, the apple was completely gone. I had somehow expected it to be taken by the raccoon, like the tooth fairy, in that moment that I was tricked into sleep. But I think I had expected him to eat it like a human would, leaving the apple core. No evidence was left behind, except for a very few footprints on the truck. No doors knocked over, nothing chewed. Perhaps he has now found a way in and out and just walks on my truck as a way to flex his muscle, as a way to show me who's boss, I thought. I took the car back to the car wash. And then to another one. I watched myself in the rearview mirror and saw the bags under my eyes, the water crashing all over the truck, the flashing lights that were meant to assure me that the wax for which I paid extra was indeed being applied. Tonight I would wait for him.

After the dishes were done, and the kids had their baths and stories and were in their beds, my wife and I took our contact lenses out, and she went to bed with the television on. I told her I'd be back soon, which I knew was a lie. I had decided to sit in the truck in the darkened garage until I could confront the raccoon and remind him that this was a garage belonging to a human, and that humans and their garages and trucks and houses and children and sleeping patterns are not things for raccoons to mess with. I was angry and scared and convinced myself that I was addressing my irrational fear of animals. That we could coexist in the same city very nicely, so long as we respected each other's space.

So I waited in the car. It was still mild outside, and I was just warm enough with a sweater. I had a can of Coke and a bag of potato chips, but what was I thinking? They would be far too loud and give away the fact that I was in the truck waiting. I waited for a very long time and braced myself for him to just drop from the rafters onto my hood and stare me down. I kept hallucinating it, a vague, mushy, sleepy premonition of this beast the size of a Labrador retriever, with its face an inch or so from the windshield of my Toyota. I shivered more out of tiredness than from cold. I was beginning to feel very comfortable in this truck. It was no longer the sellout vehicle that they hand you on the day you wake up, walk out of the house, and realize that you, too, have a job, a wife, and two kids. No, this was becoming the extension of me that I had always craved, like in some race car movie or a show on the Nashville Network about classic cars and the men who love them. This baby could be my lover. I think I can see how men get so attached. This is my car and no one and nothing will ever come between us. I stretched my right arm out over the headrest of the passenger seat beside me, imagining that I was sitting in the driveway with my girlfriend, high school, 1985. Her mom inside the house, knowing what we were doing. But we weren't doing it, I swear, we were only—well, I guess that would be just as bad in her mom's eyes, wouldn't it? The thought of some acne-covered Jewish kid with his hands on her daughter's virgin genitals would presumably be enough to make you steam and pace inside the house. It would make you want to confront that kid and tell him how brazen he's being, and how he doesn't understand what an irreversible change he is making in that girl's life and how he certainly wouldn't be the one you would choose to teach your daughter about sex. But all we were doing was kissing and talking about homework and books and the Clash and how the last two albums were such an aberration, and how we wished we were a little bit older because music had been so much better when we were eleven, but we had been too young to know about it or see it or hear it when it was fresh and meant something. We made out a lot and told each other we loved each other and tried to believe it. The door on my parents' car was screwed up. You had to open it from the outside, so the evenings would always end with me getting out, crossing to the other side of the car, the shape of my erection trying to hide behind an untucked shirt, and my date finally being released from captivity into her mother's house.

Maybe the raccoon would never come. Maybe it had moved on. Maybe it was inside my house, creeping unbeknownst to me as I walked out to the garage. I left the garage at 4:30 A.M. and checked every room in the house. Jonah was lying on top of the covers with his head at the foot of his bed, my wife was asleep with her glasses on, Max, the four-year-old, was grinding his teeth loudly, and there was no sign of raccoon anywhere. I kept watch until I fell asleep on the dining room floor.

In the morning I felt like hell, and the whole family had caught me lying on the floor downstairs, so there was no hiding from what I'd been doing. I'd been trying not to talk about this with them. I'd hate to worry them; the kids are so susceptible to nightmares at this age, and I would hate for them to get upset about this. I figured that I would deal with this myself by confronting the raccoon, and then, well, that's about as far as I ever got, but it was my battle to fight, and now I was ashamed because I had brought my family into this, the very people I was trying to protect. Later, with a coffee, I walked out to the garage to look around and see if I had once again been tricked, but there was no sign of the raccoon at all.

The entire garage, the entire street was still save for the sound of birds chirping and the steady roar of traffic on the Don Valley Parkway. The parkway runs alongside a river that died years ago; local residents are always planting trees and stuff down there, trying to get it to come back, but sometimes traffic roaring like a small river in a quaint valley where fish and wildlife used to be plentiful and kids swam before I was born fools people into thinking they can hear the river rushing. But it's just traffic and there is no raccoon here. I had won the battle in a most unsatisfying way. No blood, no shouting, no throwing a stick or a rake or something, shrieking and running into the house praying that I don't get sprayed or whatever raccoons do. I showered, shaved, ate toast with cheese, and went to work.

I found it a couple of weeks later, as hockey season was about to start. I got out a stepladder to help me pull down my hockey bag from the rafters in the garage. It was time to sharpen my skates, make sure all my stuff was washed, and that everything was there and still working. Basically, I just like to lay my stuff out and look at it for a while before I start playing again. I need to make sure it looks like the hockey gear of a guy who could have been a professional if it wasn't for a bad knee injury from high school, when in fact I didn't even start playing until I was nearly thirty. I pulled the bag down, and it fell to the garage floor with something else. Without even really seeing it, I knew right away that it was a raccoon's nest. It was just some scraps of stuff from my garage and backyard, and inside it were three dead raccoon babies. Scrawny and only about six inches long, dehydrated, looking like papier-mâché raccoon babies and I'd had no idea, and I couldn't even begin to think about what to do with these little bodies who lay there after being trapped for who knows how long.

IN THE CAR

She fed me strawberries and freezer-burned ice cream
I said *goodbye, I guess,* she lifted up her dress
And so I must confess we made out one more time
Before I left for good. She thought I'd
come back, but I
Didn't want to seem like other guys.

A book-and-record love; we sat and read
and our books
between those longing looks compounded by our fear
My tongue inside her ear. My tongue inside her
In the basement of her mother's house where
we once taped the
First three sides of *Sandanista!* for my car.

We were looking for ourselves and found each other
In the car, it was rare to do much more
than simply mess around
In the car, it was mostly mutual masturbation and
though we spoke
Of penetration, I'd have to wait for someone
else to try it out.

Once I had this dream in which I slept
with her mom.
Unless I've got this wrong, a secret all along
Unless she hears this song. Unless she hears it
On a tape inside her car with her new
husband and she
Turns to him and says *I think that's me.*

In the car we were looking for ourselves, and
found each other
In the car we groped for excuses not to
be alone anymore
In the car, we were waiting for our lives
to start their endings
In the car we were never making love.
We were never making love.
We were never making love.

Words and music by Steven Page
© 1998 WB Music Corp. and Treat Baker Music. All rights administered by
WB Music Corp. All rights reserved. Used by permission.

Photo by Ralf Strathman © 2000 Reprise Records

STEVEN PAGE is a singer and songwriter with the Barenaked Ladies. They formed in 1988 and have since produced six albums, including *Stunt* and *Maroon*, which was released by Reprise records in September 2000. Once, his band was nominated for a Grammy Award. He lives in Toronto with his wife and two sons.

IF WE NEVER MEET AGAIN

Jules Shear

Nothing much changed in my everyday life as a result of having written a couple "hit" songs in a short period of time. Yeah, my accountant wasn't worrying me all the time, and I can't emphasize enough the power of, for once, calling him with my head held high. Also, lots of movie scripts appeared at my door so, I guess, two hits and I was officially discovered as a songwriter.

I was never able to predict which of these scripts would be an award-winning, box-office smash and which should never have been made. I made some bad guesses. The one element common to all the scripts I got was a red sticker posted somewhere inside that read, "insert song here." At first, that little sticker thrilled me more than any of the surrounding words.

See, as a kid, I related to popular music through songs

on records, and man, did I ever relate. Sure, I knew the Beatles had long hair, Paul Revere & the Raiders wore Revolutionary War clothes, and Dylan was all Carnabyed out, but I didn't want to leave my room to see any of them perform. In my room it was just the songs and the records that brought them to me. That was my romantic relationship.

My idea of a heart-pounding experience was taking the bus downtown to a rundown store where I'd buy a box of twenty 45 rpm singles for a dollar. The catch was that you could only see the one on top and the one on the bottom. I'd sweat more than I did my whole Little League season divining the right box to buy. Next came the bus ride home with the still unopened box on my lap. All the potential of the exquisite unknown rested there. Then the denouement, back in my room, where I entered all these mysterious three-minute musical worlds one by one. These were songs that seemingly no one but I had heard performed by people nobody knew on obscure labels that were doomed to never sell for the full seventy-nine cents each.

Now this, to me, was alternative music. Some took me to worlds so sad that I couldn't stand to ever go back. With the ones I constantly revisited, I had my most intense musical relationship of all, made all the more special for its privacy. It was just them and me and they weren't even really there.

I thought maybe getting songs in movies would capture some of that for someone. People in darkened theaters were susceptible to musical intimacy. I wanted to give them that moment.

Though I'd never written songs on assignment, I took it all very seriously. After a while, though, it seemed that my work was consistently rebuffed when the filmmakers used a song by someone more famous than me who had gotten the same script. One music consultant felt that my offering was "too orange" for the accompanying scene. How can you argue? When I finally got one song accepted via a circuitous route, it ended up playing out of a transistor radio in a beach scene for about eight seconds. "Well, you made the soundtrack album," friends cheerfully consoled me. This wasn't, however, what I had in mind.

Another week brought another script. I read through, searching for the now familiar "insert song" sticker, but soon forgot all about it as I got caught up in the story of two high school friends in a band. After one commits suicide, the other finds a tape of some of his friend's music, secretly written and stashed away. Now it was incumbent upon the surviving friend to finish the posthumously discovered piece with lyrics. Oh yeah. It was coming. One more page. Yes, the sticker. "Insert song here."

I felt like I knew the music part before I even wrote it. Before it escaped, I captured it on my Walkman, singing the only words I had. "If we never meet again/if goodbyes remain unspoken." I sat on the floor of my apartment, stared out of the window at a tree on East 11th Street, and tried to become this kid.

I was in for a surprise, though, because by the time I finished the second verse, the kid had become me. I worried that I was failing the character in the script, but I kept thinking of the obscure voices on those old 45s that were long ago lost to some landfill. Even I couldn't remember many of the people's names who gave me those secret pleasures. Many of them probably considered their forays into recording to be short-lived failures. Was it sad that they never knew how I loved them or was it beautiful? As a certifiable "cult artist" myself, I had pondered this question from both sides, but I would never give up the path I had made. These thoughts coalesced into the third verse and the song was, all of a sudden, complete.

There was a moment in the script where a girlfriend of the two young musicians stops in the middle of an unrelated performance at school and sings a dramatic a cappella rendition of the song. I got a friend to record it that way with the lead-in line, and her performance stunned me. I decided to do a traditional rock band demo, too, and send both to the film people.

Then I heard nothing. Well, nothing definite. The music consultant called to say he liked it, but the producers had to hear it. The producers then liked it, but the director hadn't heard it. My manager said that I had responded too quickly and they were killing time to see if someone more famous had something.

I've never seen that movie, though it did get made. I've never heard the song they used, though I've heard that it was written by a more famous songwriter who also made a couple obscure albums of his own when I was a kid. I had bought and enjoyed them back then.

No, this song had a different fate. I was playing in a band called Reckless Sleepers, which was conceptually a musical collaboration. We wrote the music for the band in a New York rehearsal studio with everyone playing together. These were the guys I had used for my song demo. Now my band mates were lobbying for the song's inclusion on our album. No one else bought my argument that since I had written it myself, it didn't fit our concept, so I relented and we recorded it.

A record producer whose taste I respected heard it and said, "I'd jump out of a plane holding onto just that song." He wanted to record it with a newly signed act from Philadelphia with high hopes and lots of money behind it. I said sure.

I was again gratified when Roger McGuinn also recorded it for what his label saw as his comeback album. When I was growing up, I loved the sound of McGuinn's band, the Byrds, and that musical influence in the song was clear.

More recently, my friend and neighbor John Hall decided to give it one more rendition with his regrouped band Orleans. I should have warned him that this song wasn't meant to be the big song in a movie. It wasn't destined to be a huge hit on the radio, either. Like Reckless Sleepers, Tommy Conwell from Philly, and Roger McGuinn, Orleans would, too, do a version of "If We Never Meet Again" on an obscure album listened to intently by a small group who found their relationship to the song all the more special for its privacy.

When I'm on the road, playing shows, people often request it, and I sing the song again for them. Other songs that I write come and go, but I don't get tired of this one. Some nights, to sing it, I have to overcome my own fast-flowing, emotional memories of loved ones I will never again meet, at least down here in this world of CDs, tapes, and lost 45 rpm records. It's strange to think that a song that could affect its own writer, let alone others, so deeply didn't really have its origins as a cry against social injustice or even because that woman done left me and I'm as blue as I can be. It was written because a little sticker on a page said "insert song here."

IF WE NEVER
MEET AGAIN

well there's one thing I'd like to rearrange
but after everything's already happened
and there's nothing left to change
they can take their advice and use it all on themselves
cause when all the talking stops
I want to have something else
I want to have a little faith
I want to know what a boy and a girl
can do when they're dizzy cause they're just not
spinning
with this world
ahh, if we never meet again
if goodbyes remain unspoken
I won't glorify our past
but our bond remains unbroken
if we never meet again
well there's one thing that I'll never forget
it's the beauty of a friendship that's not over yet
I know how just one smile
can be planted like a seed

and I want to do that for somebody else
the way it was done for me
I want to have a little faith
there's something better at the end of this path
cause these memories get old and flat like photographs
ahh if we never meet again
if goodbyes remain unspoken
I won't glorify our past
but our bond remains unbroken
if we never meet again
well there's one thing that I don't need to even up
you can be what they've made you into
or you can make your own luck
you can't blindly fight your enemies
you can't blindly follow your friends
I've seen it happen so many times
I guess it's gonna happen again
but I gotta have faith
I gotta know that a boy and a girl
can still make it
even when they're just not spinning with this world
ahh if we never meet again
if goodbyes remain unspoken
I won't glorify our past
but our bond remains unbroken
if we never meet again
if goodbyes remain unspoken
I won't glorify our past

but our bond remains unbroken
if we never meet again

Kate Simon

In a career that spans more than two decades, JULES SHEAR has built a remarkably durable body of work that's established him as one of America's most respected singer/songwriters, with a devoted following that includes the diverse array of artists who've covered his compositions. The Pittsburgh native first came to prominence in Los Angeles, where he was in the country rock combo Funky Kings. Relocating to New York, he launched his solo career with the album *Watch Dog* in 1983. In 1997 Shear released *between us,* a set of original duets on which he was accompanied by an eclectic assortment of vocal partners. He released his most recent CD, *Allow Me*, in April 2000.

GOODBYE SWEET PUMPKINHEAD

Jane Siberry

So the clown was walking along the edge of the ocean with God and he said, "God, I am so sad." And God says, "Why are you so sad, beautiful clown?" And beautiful clown says, "I am sad because I cannot seem to make people laugh."

Let yourself slowly down into the perfumed waters of the bathing pool of the narrative pilgrimage. Don't ask. Just feel. Feel sexy. To feel sexy is, simply, to feel. We will now begin.

(very long pause)

Discomfort changed to comfort at the sound of the human voice. Mine. I'm so sorry. You can trust me. You really can. I'm so sorry. I promise I won't do that again. I'll never leave you alone for so long again. Never. Oh, I'm so sorry, my little Pumpkinhead.

I'll never leave you. Never. I promise . . . and if I do, it won't be for long. I'll come back. I'll always come back. You can count on that . . . and if I don't come back, you'll *always* be in my thoughts. I will always love you. Sometimes they don't let you come back. They hold you against your will, in spite of what you might say. Your protests, at first soft and logical, then alternately desperate and threatening. But they are strong, and they have their rules. So, know that if I ever should not come back that this is why and that I love you and would come back if I could. And, our connection will be . . . will be . . . a pumpkin. Yes, a lovely orange pumpkin that you will find on your back stoop just before Hallowe'en. That will be from me. To let you know I love you and would come back if I could, but I am being held prisoner and they won't let me go, but I love you and you must *never ever* forget that.

fff

What do you mean you have a singing lesson? It's only five in the morning. I know but my singing teacher is really fanatical. And he's very busy and this is the only time he could fit me in. (Ewww! . . . I jump out of bed. Hot hot must find hot water. Oh yuck . . . yuck.) What did you say? Oh, it's a vocal exercise yuck yuck . . . it relaxes the tongue. Must find hot water. I scrub myself everywhere. I run out the door.

When I come home from the next-door coffee shop he's gone. I open all the windows and doors, strip the bed, flip the mattress, burn incense, turn on the fans. Oh . . . oh . . . It serves me right, Lord. I'm guilty. But you can't always tell, Lord. I thought perhaps I had met that one exception. That one person who had the personality of a neanderthal but surprise of all surprises he was fantastically shockingly unbelievably erotic in bed. But . . . I . . . I just couldn't ignore his personality. Guilty. I confess. I confess everything. And I apologize. In advance. For unforeseen sins forthcoming. For unforeseen sins of the forces of the foreskin I couldn't have foreseen they were forthcoming . . . and since him being the only one on the scene for a sin forsooth so lowly on second sight on my part, Lord, just call me Forsythia.

Forsythia, unforeseen, forsaken, and forlorn. Forgive me, Lord, for I have fucked and not loved.

fff

Inappropriate use of the majesty of man. The kind of strength, bodily posturing required when death steps out into the jungle path catching your eye and your eye alone. But no. She must be only eighteen at the most and this is nighttime and I am out for a walk in my neighborhood across from the mental hospital and I forgot to cross the street in time to avoid this alley. And he is her pimp telling her off about something. Sandblasting her unresisting petite frame into the bricks with the force of his manhood. What an inspiring use of masculine power. The power normally reserved for pushing people out of the way of a train maybe. Or defending your life from someone your own size maybe. But she's just teeny. And stoned. And failing. But I guess she was a bad girl. Or he wouldn't do it, would he? I guess she did something inappropriate to the situation. Bad girl. Bad girl. Just for punishment we shall give you this dark alley, and an overamped pimp with the neck of a walrus, and pump some drugs into your personal train tracks. We're so sorry. We'll never leave you all alone again like this. Just this once. And who will push you out of the way of the train? What embodiment of the majesty of mankind will rise to your defense? . . . The blueness of your soul standing out against the paleness of your raggedy veins. Yes, the same veins that miraculously stood out against the translucence of your temple when you were an unsuspecting baby. Oh, what a beautiful baby. Miracle of miracles. She looks just like an angel. What a beautiful baby. But that was then. This is now. Bad girl. Bad girl. And for that we must give you this. We're so sorry. Baby all gone. No more. Come back tomorrow. Baby all gone. Say bye-bye. Bye-bye.

fff

The clown finds the world a place of endless wonder.

fff

Did you work yesterday? No, I had two days off. *What'd you do?* Oh, nothing. I was so bored. Maybe I should redecorate my house. I get so bored. Sometimes I think I should either redecorate my house or just kill myself. *Gee.* Turn up the suction. I don't want to work. Do you want to work? *No.* No. *Why? Do you want to work?* Do you? *Sometimes. Do you want to work?* Turn up the suction. Sometimes I think I should just kill myself. How many more do we have to do today? Has your daughter started the curse yet? *Yes. She told me the bad news a few months ago.*

These are women speaking. Women working with other women day to day within the extremes of life and death and guilt and shame and sadness. No one knows anything for sure. No one tells us. We muddle our way through these situations the best we can, the hounds of grayness mouthing our calves—the sound of drums barely heard or not at all. These are women who have experienced all these things, borne children, buried children. The strange culture that cannot bring this knowledge into our conversation. For we are creatures that learn by watching and listening and no one's talking. Friendships, love based on not knowing who it is we have a relationship to unless there is a crisis. The only way to observe our bottom lines. The trade-off for times of peace. The silt settling until the bones barely revealed. And women . . . when even women cannot heal all is truly lost. One of them notices me listening and turns up the gas. Breathe she orders. Our faces hang suspended one foot apart on this our precious planet. God, you're ugly,

I tell her with my eyes. She can't hear me. I feel like I'm underwater. All gone. All gone. No more. Nice and clean. No more sins. All gone. Baby all gone. No more. Say bye-bye. Bye-bye.

$$fff$$

If this is nighttime I am still walking. When I pass the alley on my way back home they are gone. Who is gone you ask, forgetting. You know . . . the Rembrandt of the two lovers, the Matisse of the maidens dancing around the may-pole, the pale boy gazing into the barely moving river, the mother braiding her daughter's hair. Oh I'm so sorry, I'll never do that again. I mean the pimp and his girl. Instead there are two men standing guard at the entrance to the alley. Standing guard to what? They keep looking back down the alley. I hear a scream and look around hopefully for a tomcat or a baby or someone playing electric guitar. Oh. I'm going to be sick. They look like dogs. Sentry dogs. Waiting for their turn. The girl and the misplaced tribal king. Standing over her like a tank about to pounce. But his neck wasn't thick and red and coarse. And his eyes weren't blue and bloodshot and bulging. And he wasn't snapping his gum as he prowled at the side of the rink watching his team. I think I'm going to throw up. When I got home I called the cops. For some strange reason I sounded drunk but I'd had nothing. She didn't really believe me. "There's something very nasty happening in an alley near me. No, really there is . . . Never mind."

fff

My son came into my room this morning.
He'd had a bad dream.
Hush now.
I can't.
Hush now. Hush little baby . . . (singing)

fff

If this is nighttime I am still walking. I step over the man who has made an agreement with decay. He is lying across the sidewalk. As opposed to the man who has made an agreement to delay decay. Just look at you. Dirty and disgusting. Bad. Bad bad bad. Things coming out of your nose. No love for you. No. Bad boy bad bad. No love. We would if we could but we can't. No love. We're so sorry. But we can't give you any love. No willing physical contact. Not for the rest of your life. Never. Not even when you die. Not until they clean you up and lay you out. There, nice and clean. Filthy, dirty, disgusting man all gone. Oh what a beautiful baby. He looks just like an old man. Miracle of miracles. Baby all gone. Just look at you! Bad boy. Bad bad. Come back tomorrow. Say bye-bye. Baby all gone.

I continued walking. I pass an older man. Hello. Hello. What?

Do you want to work? . . . What did you say? I stepped closer. Do I want to what? I step closer. Do I want to work? I stood close to him staring him down. I didn't fucking care if he had a fucking gun. Our faces hung suspended one foot apart on this precious planet. Finally he said, never mind. I don't know what's got into me. This neighborhood. And I think I might have that swearing disease.

Sometimes people cruise beside me when I'm walking. Calling me from the driver's seat. What? Do I look like a hooker? Does my dog look like a hooker? Does this guitar case I'm carrying look like a hooker? That's right, folks. Step inside this guitar case for the blowjob of your life. Okay I've had enough. This has happened one time too many. I march over to the car and I begin. Are you fucking blind? You miserable measly little blight of a filthy disgusting despicable poor excuse of a two-bit myopic unforeseen blood-shot bulging, thick-necked smelly potbellied pig forthcoming sin forsooth forsythia lowly wouldn't touch your puny filthy disgusting bad bad bad baby all gone, stupid asshole. Fuck.

Then he says, I just wanted to say I like your music.

fff

I'm so sorry. I didn't seem to have a choice. I also stood there at the edge of the ocean while you were watching the little baby mice, the quiet pink apostrophes floating closer and closer to the tops of your rubber boots. The edge of the ocean. The unfathomable interface. And as I gazed upon this expanse my sense of purpose grew until I knew what I had to do and I was not doing it just for myself. It was for all of us. The deep cold sea and the frosty sand beneath my feet. And I went back and stood before your house knowing that you were within. And then I started to blow. And the breath came from my whole being and I huffed and I puffed and I blew your house down. And down it came. Down as surely as the walls of Jericho. The walls dissolving into a grainy liquid that slowly drained into the earth. And I felt a great sadness. I watched you standing there alone. You did not understand what had happened. You stood blinking and uncomprehending in the grainy blue light. You looked so small and vulnerable. So thin, so light. I would have reached out to hold you, my little Pumpkinhead, but it was not the right time or the right place. And you could not even hear my cry that this was the case.

fff

My son came into my room today. Yes, little son?
Mama . . . Mama . . . can you hear me?
Of course I can hear you. Didn't you hear me answer you?
Mama . . . until ye become as little clowns ye may not enter the kingdom of heaven. You can't go yet. You have to laugh first. See the world as a place of wonder for just a second. Against all odds.
I'll tell you a funny story. Clownliness is next to godliness, Mama. Imagine. All that time cleaning the house for God just because you misheard. You were supposed to be finding the world a place of wonder.

fff

So, my friend. I should go now. The grainy blue light is fading and the frosty sand beneath my feet is just a cheap carpet. And my son is asleep on the couch with the dog. I wish I could say everything is all right and like leave it to beaver but it's not. Life is difficult and then just when I'm about to give up the sun comes out and is this truly not heaven on earth. Life is mercurial and changes form just as I become secure. Love is somewhere nearby but I can't quite see it. I don't know if I'll ever trust more than children and dogs and trees. I hope so, though. I haven't given up hope. You know me. I'm always optimistic looking for the sunny side of the street. And I'm slowly becoming wiser. I think of you often. Come and visit. For a short time sometime. You would love these huge mice on the Candy Factory. You can see them from the back stoop. Sometimes flames come out of their ears and this truly ignites the neighborhood. And I think something is wrong with my knees. I keep wanting to kneel and confess everything. O forgive me, Lord, for I have sinned. Or I have not sinned enough. Or . . . something. Just forgive me. And then give me everything I want. And don't take it away. Ever again. I will only accept things under these conditions, Lord.

So . . . Hope you're well. I send you good wishes in the shape of fishes. (Laughs weakly.) Oceans of love from your friend with the swearing disease. At least in this neighborhood. Hugs and kisses . . . Bye . . . (long pause) . . . I sort of

expected to be cut off before now . . . I hope I haven't used
up all your tape . . . well . . . keep on keepin' on . . .
Bye-bye baby.
Baby all gone.
No more sins.
Say bye-bye.
All clean now.
Baby all gone.
Say bye-bye.
Say bye-bye.

GOODBYE SWEET
PUMPKINHEAD

Would you believe me if I said that you're the one
that I've been waiting for for so long?
I've sailed my ship 'cross some stormy seas
looking for my love while my love waits for me

Ah, but what darkness in the hearts of men?
Goodbye Sweet Pumpkinhead

Would you believe me if I said that you're the one
that I've been waiting for for so long?
I've pushed you away and I've pulled you down
but here you still are
your love is so strong

I will never leave you, my sweet Pumpkinhead
And if I do, know that it won't be for long
And if it is for long, now that you will always be in my thoughts
And if I never think of you again, know that this does not mean
that love does not exist between us

Would you believe me if I said that you're the one
that I've been waiting for for so long?

I've sailed my ship 'cross some stormy seas
looking for my love
looking for my love
while my love waits for me

JANE SIBERRY is a singer/songwriter
who has had thirteen records. Previously she
was with Warner Brothers until she started up
her own label, Sheeba, four years ago, which
has released six records and two books. Siberry

has received the Producer of the Year award in Canada. She has collaborated with such artists as Peter Gabriel, Brian Eno, Joe Jackson, and the Indigo Girls.

JOHNNY DREAMS AND THE MIDNIGHT ANGEL

John Stewart

It was one of those flus where every cell in your body hurts. It came on like a wave from hell that moves across your body and tells you that something very wrong is happening to you. I tried to kid myself into thinking: "I can work through this. No annoying little pissant flu is going to get the better of me."

It was all I could do to walk from the living room and down the long hall to the bedroom, where the key word was bed. On the way I barely summoned the presence of mind to pull a carton of orange-pineapple juice from the fridge and a bottle of aspirin and one of Aleve from the kitchen cupboard, which also contains many bottles of vitamins I rarely take and one of DHEA that I take like morning communion, believing it keeps me just horny enough to know that I haven't yet reached the point of thinking about wearing plaid shorts pulled well above the navel with white shoes and long black nylon socks extending halfway up my calf. The uniform of men who have long given up sex. I fell upon the bed with the weight of a small black hole that had been dislodged from a pair of my size twelve Adidas.

I knew that you aren't supposed to take aspirin on an empty stomach, but I hurt to the point of making me feel as if I was exempt from the laws of California and nature.

If I really concentrated I managed the strength to push my thumb on the remote control. The hell of daytime TV flipped by in a merciful blur of color and half sentences. The aspirin was not doing anything, as the pain had now set within my joints as if it would remain there for the rest of my life. It was time for the Aleve . . . a ten-megaton Aleve to be exact, four ten-megaton Aleves. Food was not an option as my stomach was now in punt formation. Orange juice and Aleve were the only items on the menu, along with assorted novenas I remembered from my days in Catholic school.

As the afternoon wore on, my wife Buffy asked if I needed anything and did not think my answer of Dr. Kevorkian was particularly funny. I stumbled back into the kitchen and ingested every homeopathic herb remedy we had in the cupboard, which represented a considerable collection.

Afternoon turned into night as the pain continued, along with my stomach's decision to now actually punt the juice, homeopathic herbs, and Aleve a distance that was, for me, a personal best.

There are many euphemisms for this ritual that for some strange reason I have remembered over the years. My favorites are "calling Ralph in the bushes," "round-trip lunch," "technicolor yawn," "driving the porcelain bus," "the Campbell Canon," and my favorite, "laughing at the rug." I performed all of the above.

By midnight I was beginning to offer a dark mixture of what looked like coffee grounds. I thought that it must be the herbs I had been swallowing. I was now feeling very weak and I had broken into a cold, drenching sweat that had soaked through my shorts and T-shirt as it worked its way through Buffy's favorite Winnie-the-Pooh bedspread.

On my last trip back to the bed that was now becoming my own version of *Seven Years in Tibet,* I dropped to my knees and crawled on all fours to my side of the queen-sized. Everything went black. The next thing I knew, I heard Buffy yelling from the kitchen that she had called 911 and the paramedics were on their way. I was lying on the bed wringing wet and freezing at the same time. I was drifting in and out of a Ken Kesey–like dream state as five paramedics, three firemen, and two policemen entered the bedroom. It's funny how your mind works at a time like that. I remember thinking: "My God, don't they all have something better to do? I mean, did they all have to come?"

A paramedic and one of the policemen were now reading all the labels in the bathroom medicine chest. The cop was reading them with a flashlight. All the lights were on and he's using a flashlight! Policemen do that. We could be in the glow of a hydrogen bomb and they'd be reading with a flashlight. I guess it's part of making good use of your things. One of the paramedics picked up the bottle of Aleve and asked how many of them I had taken. "A lot," was all I could whisper.

The World was going black again as they put me on a stretcher and kept repeating: "Stay with us now, stay with us." I thought, that's what they say on TV to people who are in really bad shape. Why are they saying that to me? I've just got a bad case of the flu. As I was rolled down the long hall to the front door I could see the flashing red lights of the ambulance and the fire trucks. Why did they send fire trucks? Do people with the flu sometimes burst into flames? Spontaneous combustion, I saw it on the Discovery channel one night. They showed some poor guy who now looked like the bottom of an ashtray while the bed he was lying on was untouched by fire. As I was wheeled past her doors, Buffy's mother, who lived with us at the time, poked her head from her bedroom door and asked: "What's going on?" Buffy told her sharply: "Go back to bed, Mother, it's just the ambulance taking John to the hospital." She bought it! Calmly going back to her bed as if she had just been told it was the pizza boy making a delivery.

As they lifted me into the ambulance I now realized that everything was very clear and peaceful. I watched them insert an IV in my arm as they took my blood pressure. I knew this was serious now, yet I had no fear, none at all. I didn't think, what if I die? Will I see my family again? What will it be like? What about all my stuff? All I felt was peaceful acceptance. I heard them radio the hospital that my blood pressure was only eighty over thirty . . . and that I barely had a pulse.

A being appeared in the ambulance, it was all light and had kind of a face. I mean I could almost make out features. It had no legs but showed what appeared to be arms and a definite neck. I remember it was very much like the classic image of a ghost, iridescent and beautiful. It moved about the paramedics, watching what they were doing. It leaned over me; its face almost touching mine. It told me everything was all right. It didn't say the words aloud. It said them more clearly than that. It told me without words. Tears streamed down my face as I felt a great joy and peace unlike I had ever known before. If I was to pass, I now knew there is no dying, all would be all right. I had never felt so unalone in my life. I felt a great presence that filled me and the spaces around me as it was now all one. No separation between me and anyone or anything, even the very air itself. I could almost make out features of the face. The clearer they became the harder it became to focus on them. Then the being was no longer visible, but I could still feel the presence of light. It took only a few minutes to reach the emergency entrance of the Novato.

After I was rushed into the emergency room, the physician on duty took what seemed like an eternity to find out what the problem was and what to do about it. Looking down at me, pale and glistening in perspiration, he spoke for the first time: "You look like Peter Rowan." My God, I'm on death's door and the doctor is telling me I look like another Marin County folk singer who I toured England with years before. I look more like Bette Midler than I do Peter Rowan! I went from my celestial being of light to a replacement for Dick Clark with a stethoscope.

It seemed that I had given myself a bleeding ulcer. The dark stuff I had been throwing up for hours was blood. That's what blood looks like when it's expectorated. A fact that is now forever emblazoned on my memory cells. After three days in intensive care and two days in a hospital room, I was ready to go home.

It was November, the light at dusk was hard and angular as Buffy drove me home and to the scene of the crime, the queen-sized. I've never liked this time of day. It has always felt lonely and sad to me. When I am on the road and driving to the next motel to check in, change clothes, and dash off to a sound check, I find it particularly depressing. The taillights in the long line of cars heading home for me at evening rush hour only magnified the sadness, and home always seemed impossibly far away and long ago.

Arriving at our house, a sprawling California ranch-style built in the thirties, I felt like I was Jimmy Stewart arriving home to Whispering Pines. Usually I'm a daydreamer but I was right in present time. The horseless corral, the long high hedge, our dogs Shirley and Watson coming to greet me were all golden to me. Our son Luke, who was fourteen at the time, opened the car door and gave me a hug; I enjoyed it as if I had been away for years. Thanksgiving, which followed soon after, was a peaceful, thankful day with Buffy's family and my mother, who died a year later. I was able to tell her, when she knew death was near, what an easy peaceful trip it would be.

Thinking back on that moment in the ambulance, I realize that it was more real to me than the keys on which I am typing this story. I now had absolutely no fear of death. I'm afraid of life, losing a loved one, the weight of the day in the morning, or the chance of being incapacitated, but not of death.

I've been asked, if I could sing only one song I have written in a concert, which would I choose? I've never been able to pick just one until now. It would have to be this song. It's the best song I didn't write. It was a gift.

BLACK SKY SHINING

There was a woman I saw on the street.
I swear she was wearing the Moon on her feet.
She said do you know me?
I said I don't know.
She told me to listen
And then I could go

She said I am the course that the river is winding
I am the horse that the angel is riding.
I am the source of the love you are finding.
Do you know who I am
It is blinding?
I am the star in the black sky shining.

There was a boy who I found on the road.
I said are you lost with nowhere to go?
He said no I'm not, I believe that you are.
And he told me to sit on the hood of the car.

He said I am the flame in the heat of the fire.
I am to blame for the tongue of the liar.

I am the same as the bird on the wire.
Do you know who I am
It is blinding?
I am the star in the black sky shining.

There was a dog who had followed me home.
He was not young yet not fully grown.
He said do you know me, we spoke on the phone.
He said I am a King and the World is my throne.

He said I am the cry of the woman who's dying.
I am the wings of the sparrow who's flying.
I am the hope of the child who's crying.
Do you know who I am
It is blinding?
I am the star in the black sky shining.

There was a thief who was tied to a pole.
At his feet was a list of the things that he stole.
He said I am only playing a role,
And asked if I dare look deep in his soul.

He said I am the heart of the warrior child.
I am the moment the beast becomes mild.
I am the part of the soul that is wild.
I am the answers you're finding.
I am the star in the black sky shining.
I come from the light it is blinding.

I am the star in the black sky shining.
I am the star in the black sky shining.

Peter Van Demere

In 1961 JOHN STEWART joined the
Kingston Trio; they recorded "Where Have All
the Flowers Gone?" and "Seasons in the Sun."
During that time he wrote many songs for the
trio as well as for the Limeliters and other
groups. One of his songs, "One More Town,"
was named by Paul Simon as the inspiration for
"Feeling Groovy." He left the trio to sing with

Buffy Ford and they recorded *Signals Through the Glass*, and eventually he went solo. In his solo career he recorded the albums *California Bloodlines* and *American Sketches*. Stewart wrote "Daydream Believer," which was a number one song around the world for the Monkees. His song "Runaway Train" was a number one country hit for Rosanne Cash in 1989. He has had songs sung and recorded by the Four Tops, Harry Belafonte, U2, and Robert Goulet. He continues to write and tour and record.

IRONBOUND

Suzanne Vega

Laura woke up at a quarter to seven, as she always did. Her husband lay next to her and didn't move when the alarm went off. He was a heavy sleeper. She tried to remember what she had been dreaming of, but couldn't think of it.

All she could think of was a feeling of seeing her old boyfriend's face and seeing her hands on his thick black hair. She shrugged it off in her mind. It didn't mean anything. She was married now and didn't fool around. Time was passing, and she roused herself—if she didn't get up now, Tomas was going to be late for school again.

He was a very dreamy child, like her in temperament, not so much like his father. He needed a lot of time to get dressed, to eat breakfast, to comb his hair. Sometimes she was impatient with him, but underneath her severity she loved him more than anything else in her life. Wrapping her robe around her, she went out of her bedroom and into Tomas's.

"Hello, my baby," she whispered into his ear, and rubbed his straight brown hair.

He slept with such a serious look on his face, as though he were commanding troops, or guarding someone's safety, as though it took all his concentration. His eyes opened slowly and he frowned.

"Mmm," he said and tried to turn away and go under the covers again, but Laura wouldn't let him, and began tickling him gently.

"Hey, we need to get up now, or you'll be late again. Get dressed. Your clothes are laid out."

There was no time for a shower, so she put her hair up, fastening it with bobby pins, and put on a dress. She had gained weight since her marriage and since the baby, but her husband didn't seem to mind, and neither did she. It's nice to have some meat on your hips, she felt, and her dress clung to her thighs and buttocks. She smoothed the fabric over her waist and went down to the kitchen.

She thought about making herself some coffee but decided she would wait till after she took Tomas to school, when she went to the market. Then she could really sit down and enjoy it. She liked it sweet and light, and she liked to have a pastry with it.

She liked sitting in the café for a minute, as though she had nothing else to do with her time. It felt like luxury to her and reminded her of her older sister who went to college and spent her time in cafés arguing and reading. Her sister was thin and intense, not like her, who was dreamy and rather soft.

Laura moved slowly around the kitchen, pouring the farina, measuring the water. She thought about Portugal, where she was from, and how beautiful the sky was there. How open and wide, not cut into bits like where they lived now.

They lived in the Ironbound section of Newark, New Jersey, near Avenue L, where people brought their cars in to be fixed. It wasn't bad. Her husband was a mechanic, so it was good they lived here. There was a community of people from her country also, so the smell of food cooking was the same as it had been, and the language, too, among her neighbors.

But there was a word, *saudade*. This meant a nostalgia for something never experienced, and that's what she often felt, a slow kind of restlessness that no one would guess at from her placid exterior. Though some of it was a genuine homesickness.

The hot cereal for the boy was done, and she went into his bedroom to get him, quietly, not shouting for him, as that would wake her husband. Tomas was dressed but seemed to have lost himself while playing with his little trucks.

"Come and eat! Or we'll be late!" she said. He seemed sulky for some reason, but she felt it was just left over from being wakened, and that it would burn off like fog after he was up for a while.

"OK, Mama," he said. Suddenly he looked at her full in

the face. "No kissing!!" He said this, knowing she would grab him and kiss him, which is of course what she did. He looked at her teasingly, and it melted her heart.

After breakfast they began the walk to school, over bits of glass, over the weeds and the grass that poked up wherever it could find the sun, cracking the concrete with its effort to live. Kids in this country are just like those plants, she thought. You give them what you have, and it isn't much. But the good ones will find the light and make sense of it all.

She watched his eyes light up as they approached the Ironbound school yard, where his buddies were already in line. She felt him strain away from her, eager to join his classmates, and she wanted to hold on to him for a minute.

"Come here! Don't run away just yet. Your face is dirty," she said, though it wasn't. He hated her to lick her thumb, smudging off whatever soot had fallen there. The idea of being cleaned by saliva was disgusting to him, but he submitted to it, knowing she would be gone in a minute.

He joined the group of "hot lunch" kids on line. The ones who could afford it brought their own lunchbox, with a thermos in it. The ones with hippie parents had paper bags with peanut butter sandwiches from the health food store or containers of lentil soup, which they threw away. Others like Tomas got the hot lunch from the school cafeteria. Those who were really struggling joined the Breakfast Program as well.

She tousled his hair and let him go. She allowed herself a moment of nostalgia for his babyhood watching him with his peers, but then her gaze turned away, and she thought about her chores for the morning and the coffee she would have first, light and sweet, the way she liked it. She could daydream alone, which was so rare for her now.

Ironbound is a good name for this city, she thought as she stepped off the curb. Iron and metal everywhere. Telephone wires all over the sky. Train tracks. Elevated bridges. Nails and bolts and car parts all over the street. Her husband worked at the Body Shop, which sounded sexy, but it wasn't. More car parts and pieces of metal!

But still, sometimes she wished for something more alive. Maybe we should get a pet, she mused. She knew of some Puerto Ricans in El Barrio who kept a rooster, and one had even kept a goat! Thinking of the rooster made her remember that she had to go back to the butchers to pick up a chicken for dinner. She was in that part of the market now, with animal grease in the cobblestones and blood in the gutter.

She made a note to herself as she walked through the market as to which chickens looked fresh. Should she get a whole one, or would pieces be OK? They weren't such a big family, but you could always use the leftovers. The neck was good for soup. So were the wings.

She didn't mind it so much—economically it was a better life. But something oppressed her, and she didn't know what. So much metal surrounding her from every side. Laura opened her purse to see how much money she had brought with her and fingered her wedding ring. Suddenly last night's dream drifted back to her. She felt that longing again, the *saudade*. But it wasn't for her old boyfriend, or her previous life, or her country.

It was a wild desire to laugh or dance. Or maybe pray. Sometimes she could lose herself while making love, which she enjoyed. She loved her husband. But she still thought of her boyfriend, how he smelled of tobacco and old leaves, and the little name he had for her—"pigeon." It always made her laugh. It was not flattering, but he said it because her hair and voice were soft and her breast was full.

The longing was even more than that, though. It was the craving to be free, in some absolute and pure way, like pigeons were free and whole.

IRONBOUND/
FANCY POULTRY

In the Ironbound section
Near Avenue L
Where the Portuguese women
Come to see what you sell
With the clouds so low
The morning so slow
As the wires cut through the sky

The beams and bridges
Cut the light on the ground
Into little triangles and the rails run round
Through the rust and heat
The light and sweet
Coffee color of her skin

Bound up in iron and wire and fate
Watching her walk him up to the gate
In front of the Ironbound school yard

"Kids will grow like weeds on a fence"
She says, "They look for the light,

They try to make sense,
They come up through the cracks
Like grass on the tracks,"
And she touches him goodbye

Steps off the curb and into the street
The blood and the feathers near her feet
Into the Ironbound market

In the Ironbound section
Near Avenue L
Where the Portuguese women
Come to see what you sell
With the clouds so low
The morning so slow
As the wires cut through the sky

She stops at the stall
Fingers the ring
Opens her purse and feels a longing
Away from the Ironbound border

"Fancy poultry parts sold here
Breasts and thighs and hearts
Backs are cheap and wings are nearly
Fancy poultry parts sold here
Breasts and thighs and hearts
Backs are cheap and wings are nearly
Free"

Nearly free
Nearly free

Albert Sanchez

SUZANNE VEGA emerged as a leading figure of the folk-music revival of contemporary folk songs of the early 1980s when, accompanying herself on acoustic guitar, she sang contemporary folk songs of her own creation in Greenwich Village clubs. Since the release of her self-titled, critically acclaimed 1985 debut album, she has given sold-out concerts in many of the world's best-known halls. With the release in 1987 of *Solitude Standing,* her second album, including the hit single "Luka," Ms. Vega vaulted to a position of prominence in the world of pop music. Vega's most recent album, *Nine Objects of Desire,* was released in 1996. In 1999 she published a book, *The Passionate Eye: The Collected Writings of Suzanne Vega.* She lives in New York City.

LETTER TO
CHESTER BAUM

Loudon Wainwright III

Dear Mr. Baum,

    Thank you for your kind letter and open invitation to visit St. Andrew's. I enjoyed your random observations and vignettes. They were sharp, funny, and interesting. I had no recollection that Dad was visiting S.A.S. on the day of the JFK assassination. Of course, we all remember where we were on that day but it's strange I should have forgotten such an important personal detail. I hope you'll forgive me for using the formal greeting in my reply but starting off with "Dear Chester" or "Dear Ches" somehow doesn't seem right to me. Not only am I writing to my former teacher and the former chair of the school's English department but it's been over thirty years since you and I have seen or spoken to one another. This is my fault entirely since I've stayed away from St. Andrew's pretty much since my visit in 1968, three years after graduating, when I showed up on campus with long hair and a red beard, carrying a guitar case. Mr. Washburn, my old football coach, was friendly that day I recall. Mr. Cameron was more than happy to see me. He seemed genuinely pleased that I had begun to sing and, even more importantly, write songs for a living. "Bull" Cameron, that towering fearsome figure, able to freeze a fifteen-year-old slacker at twenty paces with his deep guttural growling "You boy!" in fact turned out to be extremely kind, even solicitous toward me. Messrs. Schmolze and Hillier were not so welcoming, huffing and puffing, unable to hide their deep disapproval of the hippie I'd clearly already become. Mrs. Schmolze, right out of Dickens with that prissy name and her antiquated bobbed red hair, was especially cold. I suppose I expected unconditional approval from one and all, sensitive and naive young man that I was. At any rate I left Middletown that afternoon vowing to myself never to return, yet determined that one day I'd show them.

Offering up yet another excuse for my long absence let me say that my last year at St. Andrew's was an unhappy one. A recent look at the 1965 school yearbook confirmed that you were away on sabbatical that year so you may not have known this. I did well enough at football and enjoyed being in the school play (starring as Sir John Falstaff in Shakespeare's Henry IV Part 1, replete with bad English accent à la Dick Van Dyke in Disney's Mary Poppins). But almost everything else went badly. Academically I scraped by, somehow managing to graduate. It was a miracle I passed Spanish. I was bored with being a senior and was itching to get out into a world, not the big wide one we were being prepped and groomed for, but the one I'd glimpsed on American Bandstand and at The Newport Folk Festival. It was a world of guitar-playing, truth-telling guys with long hair and sideburns, wearing blue jeans and work shirts, dudes on motor-cycles tightly clung to from behind by the likes of Tuesday Weld in toreador pants or a sandaled and tanned Joan Baez. I had discovered the trouble with a boys' boarding school. There were no girls there. I was fed up fantasizing about Mr. Hillier's fourteen--year-old daughter Patsy or Coach Reyner's wife with her mus-cular calves and Doris Day haircut, and there was next to no excitement anymore at the prospect of my twisting a night away with some poor little rich girl from the Shipley School or Miss Whatever's.

The others in my senior class seemed intent on getting into the colleges of their choice. I didn't even want to go to college. Instead I was "ready to go anywhere" as Dylan (Bob not Tho-. mas) sings in "Mr. Tambourine Man." It was only after unend-ing parental pleading and threats and a long emergency meeting with the headmaster Mr. Moss, during which I remember him telling me about a horrific sledding accident he'd had as a boy (a heavy snowstorm could be seen in progress outside his office win-dow), that I agreed to a compromise. I would apply to Carnegie Mellon where I would study acting, have actual sex with aspiring ingenues, and look and dress as I damn well pleased. In fact, I was accepted there but only spent a year and a half in Pittsburgh. There was something happening in San Francisco involving grateful dead and a jefferson airplane so I dropped out of college in 1967, wriggled out of the draft (psychiatrist's letter), and headed to the West Coast for the Summer of Love. I'm sure my parents wanted to kill me. Mrs. Schmolze undoubtedly would have.

My father once told me the story of how in 1941 or '42 he ran away from S.A.S., sneaking out of his dormitory late one night and setting off on foot for Wilmington, there to get a bus or train up to New York.

Back then this would have been a serious disciplinary offense, punishable by immediate expulsion. However, his adviser and dorm master Mr. Voorhees, who was probably tipped off, took notice of his absence and went after him in a car. He found Dad a few miles down the road and convinced the tearful escapee to return to school. My father claimed he'd always been grateful to Voorhees for this but I never quite bought his cautionary tale with its implied moral.

Now I've come to the last of my excuses. I'm afraid it's another long-held resentment. It was my father's decision that I go to St. Andrew's, which was his alma mater. Like many if not most kids who are sent away to boarding school I felt I was being gotten rid of, exiled from mother and home. Farmed out. In my case it was to my old man's particular farm. When I arrived as a third former in 1961 my adviser was the elderly and soon-to-retire Mr. Voorhees. This couldn't have been a coincidence. We're always in the shadows of those titans, our parents, and there I was at my father's old school, stuck with his somewhat strange name (pretentious Roman numeral III to boot), eating at the same long polished dining room tables he had eaten at, daydreaming and bored as he had been in the same stuffy classrooms. Please don't tell me the faded map of South America is still up on that wall. It's even possible I chucked my socks, jock, T-shirt, and towel into some ancient iron gym locker that he might have used twenty-two years earlier. Maybe my father thought that I

would like going to his school, that I would enjoy the legacy aspect of it all, carrying on the tradition, etc. I didn't. Things were
already competitive enough between us. I suppose your stepsons
and my schoolmates Dan and Henry Smith went through their
variation of all this with the extra added pressure of being faculty
brats. I sent my own son Rufus to the Millbrook School and I
like to think he appreciates my decision now—that and the one
not to name him Loudon IV.

So there you have some reasons why I've stayed away, why
I've never attended a reunion or put in an appearance on alumni
weekend. Now you know why you haven't seen me there, standing outside in a seersucker jacket on a fine mid-June evening
holding a napkin-wrapped vodka and tonic and recapping my
touchdown and two extra points in the Tower Hill game with
some old and frighteningly older-looking teammates. When Mr.
Washburn retired I sent a small contribution for his going-away
present, and more recently I succumbed to your mighty powers of
persuasion, coughing up a few hundred bucks for the annual
fund. But aside from these meager gifts I've ignored every appeal
from the school for money—all because I'm still pissed off at poor
old Mrs. Schmolze! Well, she's not the only one.

In the spring of 1965, my senior year, my father received the
Headmaster's Award, which is given, as you know, every year to
an alumnus and friend of the school who has "made a mark in
the world." Dad, as an editor and widely read columnist for
LIFE magazine, most certainly had done just that, and he came
down to Middletown to receive the award and to address the entire school. I recall the speech he gave as being very straight and
extremely positive. It was full of wonderful things to say about

the old place and how it had prepared him so well for the outside world. As appropriate as that was for the occasion, his seventeen-year-old son sitting there in the auditorium, angry, rebellious, and perhaps a little embarrassed, thought it was a cop-out, a kind of betrayal. I knew my father had been unhappy at St. Andrew's, as unhappy as I was. He had told me so. Perhaps I'm blocking it out but I don't think he even mentioned the Voorhees incident.

Well, I suppose this all sounds rather petulant. I know I'm carping. Maybe it's easier to hold on to these grudges or perhaps it's simply that I've always been jealous of my old man's success. In fact I know I have. For the last thirty years I've been fantasizing about my own acceptance speech, for surely it's just a question of time before I, too, am given the Headmaster's Award. I'll go down there to Delaware on a chopped Harley wearing a black leather jacket and engineer boots with what's left of my hair and a long white beard flapping behind me, and I'll tell it like it was.

All the best,
Loudie Wainwright ('65)

P.S.
I drove up to New York from Baltimore recently and seeing an exit for Middletown I pulled or perhaps was pulled off Interstate 95. Driving the rental car through town I was amazed to see the old movie theater and barbershop were still standing, much less in operation. Now I nose the Caprice toward St. Andrew's. Sud-

denly I'm there. *Aside from the new gym and the even newer science building (neither of which were built thanks to any contribution from me), the campus looks as it did thirty years ago. I park, get out of the car, and walk into the main building. I feel slightly furtive, like a man slipping back into a room to retrieve a wristwatch he's left on a bedside table, not sure if the woman in the bed is sleeping or pretending to. This feels like running away in reverse. It's spring break, so aside from a custodian or two the place is empty. I climb some stairs heading for what was once the third-form bathroom. It's still there. Pushing open the heavy swinging door I belly up to a cracked and familiar looking urinal. I pee, marking this old territory. In 1961 after lights I sat cross-legged and bathrobed on the black and white tiled floor of this can and while finishing a paper or cramming for some exam, suddenly would look up, startled and amazed by the loud cutting blare of the night train's horn. It was a sound expressing everything that was beyond the school, the whole empty world that was waiting for me.*

Now I'm down in the basement which to this day still houses the tuck shop, school store, and school bank. I'm searching the darkly stained pinewood paneling, for somewhere among these hundreds of crudely carved, scratched, and branded sets of initials and dates there should be a "LSW III '65," or "LSW jr. '42." But I can't find us. Maybe we were never here.

I'm in the auditorium now, remembering Saturday nights thirty-five years ago. Watching the weekly movie I was Wainwright then, always insisting on sitting alone, away from my chatty goofball friends, so as to concentrate on the flick, hunkered

down in the dark watching Forbidden Games, Odd Man
Out, Mr. Hulot's Holiday, *and, so appropriate for a boys'
boarding school,* The Great Escape.

*Now I'm standing inside the old gym, scanning the thick
ugly plastered walls. The school's team pictures are hung here in
honor and remembrance. There's "Bull" Cameron in his early
thirties, fierce, martial, and magnificent as he poses with his
young wrestlers of 1935. Among them is a scowling crewcut twelve-
year-old Chester Baum. I find my varsity football team picture.
I'm number 22. Left halfback. Bad skin. Then thirty feet away,
there's a picture of my father standing on the gym steps in 1942
with his varsity baseball team. The word "Saints" is stitched
across the chest of his grayish, scratchy-looking button-up jersey,
and there's a cap perched on the back of his head, its brim pointing up and off at a ridiculous thirty-degree angle. On his left
hand, looking for a moment like a very mild case of elephantia-
sis, the beat up, fat, cartoon-fingered mitt. Certainly you
couldn't call such a thing a glove. He and I, father and son, are
connected by our same sad expressions. We're glum young men,
unhappy Loudons. I don't care much about any of this school
history after 1965. My time and before is what concerns me. It
is interesting, though, to note the few young black faces that begin to pop up in the team pictures of the late sixties and early
seventies. Then, suddenly in 1973, there's proof of the miracu-
lous invasion from the other planet—a photo of a girls' field
hockey team. I go outside and stand in the center of the football
field, recalling the horrific sight of Andy McNair's knee being
driven the wrong way by the vicious clip he received in the 1964
Tatnall game. Then I experience the memory of my father seated*

in the stands watching me play. Now he's up and cheering. I've got the ball. Then I imagine him on that same field in 1940 or maybe '41 in next to no shoulder pads, shod in mud-caked high-topped cleats, wearing an ancient faceguardless leather helmet and searching those same stands for his own father.

SCHOOL DAYS

In Delaware when I was younger
I would live a life obscene
In the spring I had great hunger
I was Brando I was Dean

Blaspheming booted blue-jeaned baby boy
Oh how I made them turn their heads
The townie brownie girls
They jumped for joy

And begged me bless them in their beds
In Delaware when I was younger
I would row upon the lake
In the spring I had great hunger

I was Keats I was Blake
My pimple pencil pains I'd bring
To frogs who sat entranced
My drifting ditties I would sing

The water strider dance
In Delaware when I was younger

They thought St. Andrew
Had sufficed

But in the spring I had great hunger
I was Buddha I was Christ
You wicked wise men
Where's your wonder

Your pharisees one day will pay
See my lightning hear my thunder
I am truth I know the way
In Delaware when I was younger

Ross Halfin 1996

Born in the first half of the last century (1946), LOUDON WAINWRIGHT III wrote and recorded his first album in 1969 for Atlantic Records. His most recent releases are *The BBC Sessions* (Fuel 2000) and a collection of topical songs written between 1990 and 1999, *Social Studies* (Hannibal/Rykodisc). He has also begun working on an album of new songs.

INTUITION:
THE PATH TO
INNER WISDOM

INTUITION:
THE PATH TO
INNER WISDOM

A GUIDE TO
DISCOVERING AND USING
YOUR GREATEST NATURAL RESOURCE

PATRICIA EINSTEIN

ELEMENT

ROCKPORT, MASSACHUSETTS • SHAFTESBURY, DORSET

MELBOURNE, VICTORIA

First published in the USA in 1997 by
Element Books, Inc.
PO Box 830, Rockport, MA 01966

Published in Great Britain in 1997 by
Element Books Limited
Shaftesbury, Dorset SP7 8BP

Published in Australia in 1997 by
Element Books
and distributed by Penguin Books Australia Limited
487 Maroondah Highway, Ringwood, Victoria 3134

Library of Congress Cataloging-in-Publication Data
Einstein, Patricia.
Intuition : the path to inner wisdom : a guide to discovering and using
your greatest natural resource / Patricia Einstein.
p. cm.
Includes bibliographical references and index.
ISBN 1-86204-136-9 (alk. paper)
1. Intuition (Psychology) 2. Success. I. Title.
BF311.E36
153.4'4--dc21   97-13966
                                                          CIP
British Library Cataloguing in Publication data available
First Edition

10 9 8 7 6 5 4 3 2 1

PRINTED AND BOUND IN THE UNITED STATES BY
COURIER, WESTFORD INC.

ISBN 1-86204-136-9

*To anyone who's ever had a hunch or a flash
of inspiration—and just went with it.*

But, especially, to Peter

CONTENTS

LIST OF EXERCISES

ACKNOWLEDGMENTS

Somewhere in this book I note that no mind is an island. Certainly, no book is either—leastwise this one. During the long process of putting together *Intuition: The Path to Inner Wisdom,* so much help of all kinds came to me—sometimes in the most serendipitous way—that I knew this book was somehow meant to be. It simply would have never come as fully into being without the inspiring aid of the following:

My teachers, who've included Louise L. Hay, Alexander Murray, and Phyllis Dahlby, each one providing both a loving beacon and an occasional cosmic kick along my path of growing awareness.

My students, who have been teachers all, no matter the venue. I am especially appreciative of—and this book has been enhanced by—the free-flowing exchange of ideas offered by students and presenters alike attending the Inner Voyage conferences-at-sea.

My colleagues, including James Brennan, Ann Satterfield,

Henry Reed, Mary Ann Riffon, and Colleen Mauro, who, in contributing their professional two cents, have given me many times that worth in insight.

My husband, Peter Einstein, who became a constant author's inspiration and (sometimes nudging) catalyst, as well as a wiz of an editor/assistant (unpaid to boot), by default; and the rest of my family and friends, too numerous to mention by name, each one of whom never ceased in giving me encouragement and advice whenever I needed it.

My organizational angels-in-disguise, including Kevin Jennings and Anthony Bruno, whose structural aid helped kick the project off; Aaron von Solos, whose many ideas helped keep it going; the incomparable aide-de-camp, Deborah Bergman, who gave so unstintingly of her expertise, lucidity, time, and even hardware; Darren Kelly, who made sure all the i's were dotted and the t's were crossed; and Gila Sand, whose word processing wizardry provided the perfect finish.

My enchanted—and enchanting—compatriots Monte Farber and Amy Zerner, talented authors in their own right, who directed me, happily, to Element Books.

Most delightfully, special acknowledgment must go to Roberta Scimone—the best, most nurturing editor I could ever have hoped for. If I'd ever required proof, there it was: Good things really *do* come to those who go with the flow.

To each of the above, my thanks and blessings. You've truly blessed me all.

FOREWORD

Patricia Einstein has written a fascinating and delightful book on the mysteries of the mind. Better than that, however, is the fact that her book is a pragmatic one—a veritable user's manual of alternate states of awareness.

I sense that I'm speaking for a lot of people by saying that I'm sick and tired of all those books of airy speculation about ESP and the paranormal. The media have made us into couch potatoes on the subject. We sit on the sofa and watch television talk show guests relate their own paranormal experiences, after which the alleged "experts" pro and con wrestle to an inevitable draw over the possible "reality" of the experiences. WHAT A BORE!

It's a sad fact that amidst the hustle and bustle of the information age, few of us take the time anymore to go inside ourselves and tap the vast, rich potential of our own minds. We're too busy to take advantage of the simple techniques that great creative geniuses used to make their formative discoveries. Thomas Edison, for example, took self-induced "cat naps" to solve complex problems that perplexed him, resulting in many inventions that we all still use daily!

But, since most of us are in fact now caught up in the supercharged life of an advanced, technological society, how can we get re-acquainted with the surprising powers of our conscious minds? Where do we begin? That's exactly where Patricia's book comes in, and that's exactly why I am so amazed and impressed by it.

She has cut abstract speculation about the nature of intuition to the bare bones, and she goes right to the task of setting out, in plain and simple language, a wealth of engaging exercises that enable the reader to experience the mysteries of the mind directly. I'm captivated by reading through Patricia's exercises, and I'll admit they made me a bit ashamed of myself! I realized that although the study of the human mind is my professional specialty, it's been a long, long time since I just sat down and had a good time re-exploring the mysteries of my own consciousness. I've resolved to use Patricia's *Intuition: The Path to Inner Wisdom* as a workbook. I anticipate I'll make lots of interesting discoveries about myself along the way. I recommend her practical, step-by-step guidebook for recapturing the wonders of awareness.

Raymond A. Moody, M.D., Ph.D.

INTRODUCTION

The other day, I was looking through the *New York Times*, and there it was: another article about a scientific study confirming the existence—and usage—of intuition. In this case, it showed how people are likely to act on hunches—before even consciously knowing they have them. Well, that's always been *my* hunch, but then again, I'm in the intuition business. How wonderful to know that others are beginning to realize the practical power of intuition in their own lives.

It seems that everywhere one looks today, there are signs of an evolution of thinking. The world is getting so complex. More and more people seem to be seeking more enlightened answers to address everything from the day-to-day issues of relationships and job situations to the larger questions such as finding more direction, meaning, and purpose in life. For many, following only a traditional line of logic doesn't seem to come up with enough—or inspire enough—solutions anymore. But where to look?

There is certainly no lack of holistic and alternative help available. Anyone who has turned on a talk show, visited a bookstore, or seen ads all over the media can attest to the proliferation of "experts" offering their advice in any number of formats—from counseling to workshops to books and tapes. Every day there seems to be a new dilemma identified by just the person with just the system that can explain it all—and solve it all—for you. Or can they? How do you know who to trust?

The wonders of technology in this Information Age seem to be adding to the confusion, by fast and furiously churning out tons of information about the ever-increasing options available. In fact, the "facts" just don't stop coming. But what do you *do* with all these facts? How do you know what data to apply to your particular situation? And how do you make a decision when all the "facts" can't possibly be in? In short, how do you cut through the glut to get to the heart of the matter? How do you get the answer that's truly right for you?

That's where intuition comes in. It can be the greatest resource we have as human beings, a natural ability we each possess to perceive far beyond our five senses and logic alone. This incredibly rich reservoir, once tapped, can provide deep insight, knowledge, and inspiration to help guide us through virtually every area of our lives. Of course, the use of intuition is no fad. A powerful inner guidance system, intuition has always been—and always will be—with us to provide the focus and clarity we need to make our own best decisions.

So how do you get to that intuition? How do you best use it? It has long been my belief that just as everyone has his or her own particular path through life, each of us has our respective way to discover intuition and use it. There is no one right way to be intuitive: there are as many intuitive styles as there are individuals, and each of us can easily find his or her own personal intuitive path. Once embarked upon, this path can lead to all the answers and guidance we will ever need and will ultimately lead to our own inner wisdom.

The wisdom of your intuition will eventually allow you to see that finding your answers intuitively is not a linear process. The intuitive path is a journey, that lets your answers evolve from a clearer and higher perspective, as you work on your intuitive ability and continue to evolve your awareness.

The paradox is this: while your intuition can cut through the confusion of any dilemma and provide a usable answer, that answer will continue to grow and evolve as you do. The more you develop your intuition, the clearer your answers can be, all the while opening up options—and even questions—you hadn't previously considered. To this end, you will learn more and more, not only how to apply intuition to answer particular questions and make on-the-spot decisions, but also how to *live* more intuitively. You'll discover that your intuitive path can put you in greater alignment with yourself, the world around you, and whatever new and creative directions your life should take.

Of course, I didn't always know this. I had to follow my own intuitive path to come to this awareness. For me, it started as a child being interested in the unseen elements of life. I took quite naturally to the practice of yoga and meditation and read every book I could get my hands on about Eastern disciplines and metaphysical thought. I didn't know I had any intuitive ability, but when someone told me that an intuitive development class was beginning, I experienced the kind of tingle I feel when something just seems "right." It was the perfect—dare I say "logical"—next step in the continuation of my studies.

I had the great good fortune (or as I later realized, synchronicity of timing) to find myself in the class of an expert and compassionate teacher. Phyllis Dahlby had the gift of being able to give her students all the room they needed to grow, while anchoring them to the real world. We would practice different exercises—some that initially seemed a little bit wacky, or at least difficult. But Phyllis would always cheerfully intone, in her charming English accent: "I don't want to hear the words 'I cahn't.'" And so it was there I discovered that I could easily and consistently access a powerful inner awareness—and, in fact, everyone could.

That first class led to the next and to a network of other students, teachers, and practicing professionals who were involved in a wide variety of holistic disciplines. Practically everyone had something to teach me, and I began to integrate any idea that could add to my growing depth of understanding and ever-evolving awareness. My intuition came more to the fore as I found myself using it in my daily life—making everyday decisions and even taking new directions.

One of the new directions took the form of a burgeoning

career as I became an intuitive counselor and teacher, helping others learn how to tune into and guide their own lives. I didn't immediately recognize, however, the career development that would become the work of my life. It took the repeated requests of friends for intuitive tips, techniques, and guidance before I finally "got it": this was what I was meant to do.

As I continued to grow and expand, so did the services I realized I could offer—giving more specialized intuitive counseling sessions as well as personalized intuition development programs for individuals and corporations. I felt especially rewarded when clients and students alike, from secretaries to artists to CEOs, started calling back to tell me how much the insights and techniques I'd given them had improved their lives. They also asked me to recommend books that would further their own particular voyage toward cultivating intuition.

I've always been on the lookout for anything that could offer hands-on intuitive guidance because I believe the power to guide one's life ultimately should be in one's own hands. However, everyone has to locate this power by following his or her own intuitive path. Frankly, I never found any one book that took into account all the various paths people could take to inner wisdom and the variety of intuitive styles that could get them there.

And so, once again, others prodded me to take my next step: this time, to share in the form of a book, all that I had learned. I decided to write a book that highlighted my philosophy of finding one's way to inner wisdom by discovering one's own way of being intuitive. From the start, I knew the cornerstone should be the establishment of trust in one's own inner abilities. With that as a base, together with a highly personalized program, I was certain I could help anyone—on any level—develop intuition.

In putting *Intuition: The Path to Inner Wisdom* together, I've had to think back on what's worked for me as I have followed my own intuitive path. I've tried to put myself in the state of awareness Zen teachers call "beginner's mind." This is the state of mind that is most open and receptive and the one in which I try to always remain, no matter how far others may think I've come on my personal journey.

I've included many different exercises and techniques, so you can try them on for size to see which ones "fit" best and are the most effective for you. Much of what is in this book has been developed over time through talking to and working with clients individually and presenting my Intuitive Path Workshops in such inspiring settings as the Inner Voyage conferences-at-sea. Each of these situations is an interactive living laboratory, where ideas get put to the most practical test and are tried and honed until I can see for myself what really works.

The feedback I've gotten has been tremendous. Men and women from many walks of life have reported all sorts of changes for the better—from a general increase of intuition, inspiration, and creativity, to more specific benefits that range from greater financial gains and spiritual growth to new and better relationships and more fulfilling careers.

Since I believe everyone has the ability to access intuition,

I've created a program as simple as it is powerful, with exercises and techniques designed to be as entertaining as they are personally enriching. Please try them out. I can almost guarantee the more you practice them, the more intuition and insight will flow to you. You are sure to find some techniques that will be immediately useful in your life. You'll also discover they can reward and delight you for years to come—much as my own explorations continue to excite and nourish me.

It is my hope that as you tap into your natural resource of intuition, you will find and follow your own path to inner wisdom. I know this path will lead you to a more aware, more clearly guided, and ultimately more fulfilling life.

WELCOME TO THE WORLD OF INTUITION

S ome people call it *psychic ability*. Some call it the *sixth sense*, or even *uncommon sense*. Some know it as a flash of inspiration or a strong gut feeling, while others think of it as a little voice that whispers to them. Some feel it is perfectly normal and natural, and others think of it as something otherworldly. You may not believe in it at all, but despite your skepticism, you do have it. We all do. It's all part of what is commonly called *intuition*.

Intuition is an inner awareness and a sense of knowing that is outside the realm of logical thought. Yet it possesses a wonderful flowing logic all its own. A powerful inner guide, intuition manifests itself in the hunches and inspirations that lead you again and again to the added insight, new direction, creative breakthrough, or the ability to be in the right place at the right time. Yet its messages can also be so subtle you might not realize you're receiving them. You may be ignoring them altogether, or you may already simply accept them as a normal part of your everyday life—which is exactly what intuition is.

Each day your intuition can help guide you through everything from mundane matters—such as what to wear, where to find a parking space, or even what card to play—to important decisions, like who to share your life with, what career path to take, who to trust, and, in general, where to find the most fulfillment.

Just as developing your muscles through aerobics, calisthenics, and jogging is a way to physical fitness, developing your intuition through the exercises described in this book is the way to inner fitness. As you develop this sixth sense, you will find it a perfect complement to your everyday stock of common sense logic. Intuition will help you

- Sense what your best choices are—and make them happen.

- Read between the lines and know what's going on behind the scenes at work and at home.

- Reap invaluable creative ideas from your dreams—and be more creative in real life than you ever dreamed of.

- Tune in to the right career moves and make the smartest business decisions.

- Meet your perfect mate—and truly know who's best for you.

- Be more in touch with the thoughts and feelings of friends, colleagues, and lovers—and improve any relationship.

- Respond to any situation with stronger convictions and a greater sense of confidence in your own inner knowledge.

- Experience the sheer joy of discovering and using a talent you never knew you had.

- And much, much more.

Intuition is an inherent trait that we all have. This trait is not a rare gift; it is something that comes to everyone every day.

The telephone rings and you suddenly think of your old friend Joe. You answer it and, lo and behold, it's Joe! That's intuition.

You're dressing for work one morning when "something tells you" to dress a little better than you usually do, and you put on your best tie or blouse. Later that morning the boss calls you to an emergency client meeting. Aren't you glad you "listened" to that early morning hunch? That's intuition.

You're sitting home reading a book one evening, but you

just can't seem to concentrate on it. Somehow you can't stop thinking about your daughter who's away at college. For no apparent reason, you have a feeling that something isn't right with her. You call her at school and her roommate tells you she was admitted to the infirmary just that afternoon. Nothing too serious. But still—aha! That's intuition.

In each of these cases, you were so in tune with a particular person or situation that pertinent, critical information just came to you. By expanding the realm of your intimate inner connections and by getting in tune with a larger source that connects *all* information, you can make intuition work for you in almost every situation.

THE WHOLE BRAIN AND NOTHING BUT THE WHOLE BRAIN

Exactly how intuition works is not known, though science has been working hard to find out. In 1981 Roger Sperry won the Nobel Prize for his theory that the human brain is divided into two separate but equal hemispheres, each governing a different way of thinking. The left hemisphere houses logical, linear thought and is characterized by objectivity, reason, analysis, criticism, and what is generally accepted as adult behavior. The right hemisphere is the home of intuitive, nonlinear thought and is characterized by subjectivity, inspiration, play, creativity, childlike wonder, and psychic ability. Clearly the seat of intuition is the right hemisphere of the brain.

Primitive man was probably much more right-brained in his thinking than we are today. His survival depended on his instincts and intuition. Tuning in to weather changes, geological shifts, and animal habits was crucial to him. He had to hunt for his food not only with all five senses, but with a keen sixth sense as well. It was intuitive sense that not only helped lead him to his dinner, but also told him to flee when he was in danger of becoming some other creature's meal.

As civilization progressed, humans became more left-brained in their thinking. Agricultural societies began to flourish and the do-or-die awareness required by hunting was no longer crucial to survival. Thus man no longer had to depend on his instincts alone. Written language was devised to record knowledge, which meant that people ultimately came to feel more comfortable going by the book than they did living day to day guided by their intuitive sense as their cave ancestors had been doing.

Still, intuition was never forgotten and in many cultures it was revered. The ancient Greeks were the first great logical thinkers, yet they consulted the oracles for guidance. The leaders of ancient Rome, who prided themselves on ruling by reason and order, consulted soothsayers who read the entrails of animals for counsel. Shamans and seers still abound in many cultures around the world. And even in the late nineteenth century, famous American captains of industry like Andrew Carnegie, John D. Rockefeller, and Cornelius Vanderbilt regularly consulted psychics and ran their empires largely by intuition.

For the most part, history and science have discredited

the achievements of intuition with rational explanations. Today, however, we are beginning to realize with a new clarity that the mind has access to information science alone cannot provide. Now that computers are doing so much of our left-brained thinking for us—collecting data, storing it, organizing it, and retrieving it on command—we are free to pursue more right-brained information. In fact, as computers take over more and more of our left-brain functions, our continued success—and survival—depends on developing the kind of thinking that computers can't do.

Nowhere is this more evident than in today's business world. Executives are now relying on their intuition to make business decisions, and studies have shown that those managers who merge intuition with logic consistently surpass their competitors in terms of sales and productivity. The Japanese, of course, pioneered the use of holistic thinking in business management, and their success is now legendary. After much resistance, American business and industry have begun to put their money where their intuitive sense is.

Obviously, the world has not completely converted to a right-brained point of view, and those who operate exclusively on the basis of their intuition are still looked upon with skepticism. Whenever I conduct corporate workshops and seminars, I deliberately avoid using the word *psychic* because of the negative connotations it has for some people. Yet what I teach these clients includes much of what it is that makes for a good "psychic." My clients learn in essence what I learned: how to contact their innate intuition and creative problem-solving abilities.

In fact, there is an increasing demand in the corporate world for developing what is now being recognized as a basic skill, an innate logic that can augment the left-brained logic of analysis and data compilation. From the more creative businesses, like advertising, to the hard facts industries, like high finance, professionals are using intuition to make better deals, improve management and people skills, and evolve their best ideas into fully realized projects.

STEP INTO MY OFFICE

As an intuitive counselor, I look into my clients' lives in order to seek out and uncover any hidden meaning and direction. In so doing I guide them toward seeing themselves from an enlightened perspective so that they can live their lives and make decisions with more self-awareness.

As a private teacher and intuition trainer, I help people discover their own illuminating gifts. My students learn to tap into a never-ending source of information and to see their lives more clearly. In developing their inner potential, they begin to see beyond their preconceived notions of what it means to be intuitive. I get tremendous satisfaction as I see the veil of mystery lifting from their minds. What once seemed possibly scary, extraordinary, or at the very least "out there" is explained and experienced in a way that is open, natural, and far from threatening. My hopes are the same for you as you read this book.

FOR BEST RESULTS

As you continue to read, you will see that the exercises are highlighted and numbered. I suggest that you read through the entire book in the order it is written, doing the exercises as you go along. But if you happen to be drawn to any particular chapter, then go ahead and dip in with the understanding that the more accumulated information you have, the better you'll be at the exercises. By all means, jump to the sections on creativity or prosperity if that's what interests you, but accept them as a taste that will be more fully appreciated once you have given yourself the chance to digest the book in its entirety.

Once you've gotten the whole picture, you'll probably find that within that picture there are certain exercises you favor and can see yourself having fun with. They *are* fun. By all means, share them with your friends. And keep up the fun.

Although you can think of this as an inner fitness book, the goal is not to quickly "pump up" latent intuitive muscles. Instead, proceed at your own pace, stopping and starting as you wish. No one has more intuition than anyone else. We're all involved in the ongoing process of developing our own connection to it, and practice makes perfect.

When you first begin to tune in to your intuition, the information you receive may be subtle. Don't misconstrue it for failure or let yourself get discouraged. If you keep practicing, the messages will come through much stronger and clearer.

Remember: The only thing you need to bring to the task

of developing your intuition is an open mind. Be willing to accept that it can be even more so. Back that up with your willpower to keep the mindstretch going, and you're all set. Now get ready to discover your *own* wealth of guidance and information.

GETTING ON THE INTUITIVE PATH

GOING WITH THE FLOW

Each of us has the ability to connect with more information than we realize, for each of us is already connected
to a universal source of awareness. Think of this source as a
bustling port on an ever-flowing river. The river flows
through every town and village, connecting each one to the
port. So, too, we each are connected to our intuituve
source—a much larger pool of information—through what I
call the *flow*. The flow is everyone's connection to an ever-
flowing, ever-informing awareness.

But if each of us is already connected to this source, why
don't we seem to have all the answers we need? In fact, we
already have the answers we seek, but we often fail to connect with them. Simply put, our everyday awareness is usually not in line with a larger, deeper awareness, which is the

source of intuition. Like the river, intuition is there for us, but to connect with its source, we've got to go with the flow. Following this flow is what gets us on—and keeps us on— our own intuitive path.

Questions seem to pop up almost every day, and we need to connect with their answers. Another company has made you a great job offer, but you don't know if it's too good to be true or too good to pass up. Or else, out of the blue you were handed your pink slip and you haven't a clue what to do. Are you ever going to find Mr. or Ms. Right? Or have you already met him or her and don't even know it? Whatever the question, following the flow of your intuition can help you navigate the uncertain seas of your life, and guide you along the way on your journey to inner wisdom.

In recent years extensive studies have been conducted on the *flow state*, the state in which we sense the universal flow. Commonly associated with the peak performance of creativity, it is actually the state in which we seem to automatically make all the right moves, whether in thought or in action. In the flow state, the thoughts and feelings that in everyday life seem to get in the way suddenly disappear and are replaced by a flowing and powerful mental focus.

Everyone has experienced the flow state at one time or another while reading a good book, playing a particularly engrossing game of chess, or doing anything at all in which it's easy to get lost. It often feels like a state of euphoria during which everything falls into place, and solutions seem to flow to you naturally. How the flow state, which is rooted in the right brain, functions is still largely unknown—despite copious research. Right now science can only tell us that it exists and that it *works*.

The first step in your quest for intuition is to go with the flow, literally. As you enter the powerful flow state, your focus will begin to shift from everyday awareness, and open to a larger sense of knowing and understanding. In the flow state, you'll sense the interconnection of all information and experience, and from this state of awareness you'll be able to draw rich nuggets of intuition.

The flow connects all consciousness, all awareness, all information. Intuition is its perfectly natural product. In essence, the flow state connects you with the source of all your answers. The following exercise will help you begin to get into the flow.

• *Exercise 1: Going and Flowing with the Flow*

To immediately experience the flow, set aside some time—at least five minutes—to lie down and listen to soothing instrumental music. Don't listen to anything with lyrics because the words will distract you.

Let yourself float along with the music, not thinking about anything in particular, just allowing yourself to be carried with it. Don't try to force it. Just relax.

At the end of the piece, come back and take note of the difference between what you felt while the music was playing and what you feel now. Do you see a difference?

WHEN YOU'RE HOT, YOU'RE HOT

The flow state comes naturally during periods of intense concentration and creativity. Many musicians often seem to be lost in their music when they play. Think of the look of near rapture on a conductor's face when he's leading a symphony or orchestra, or the totally into it expressions of a guitarist when he's leaning into a long, bluesy solo. Think of the keenly focused concentration on the face of a world class tennis player. Many athletes talk about the phenomenon of being "in the zone." Whether playing basketball or baseball, for example, their concentration can be so intense they speak of being "one with the ball" when they're "hot" and playing at peak performance. At these moments, all these people are in the flow.

If you don't think you've ever been hot in the same way that a professional athlete or musician is, you're probably wrong. Most likely you've experienced the flow while making love! This particular flow experience is probably best left to the imagination, but suffice it to say that when you are caught up in the act of making love, you can experience intense concentration and pleasure to the point where nothing else, including time, exists.

In this state, you are definitely "on" and moving with the flow. Even the floating sensation experienced before, during, and directly after lovemaking is a part of that all-connecting flow. Try Exercise 3 to get in touch with your own natural flow, but first see if you can refresh your memory (and experience) with the help of Exercise 2.

• *Exercise 2: Flow Recall*

Think of times when you've experienced a state of flow—making love, playing sports, playing music, dancing, painting, getting lost in your work or in a good book.

Next, focus on the experience and what you felt during that experience. Was it a sense of floating? oneness? deep tranquillity or ease? Did you experience other unique sensations or a special, personal state of mind? Let the flow feelings engulf you, and hold on to them for as long as you can. Often we get dreamy when we're remembering a flow experience. Actually, this is just our natural, instinctive attempt to re-enter that flow.

If you have any trouble recalling the flow state, you may do better recreating it from scratch. The following exercise will develop your control over the flow state so that you can get into it whenever you need it.

• *Exercise 3: Creating the Flow*

Take five minutes to express yourself on paper or with a tape recorder. Doodle, draw, think out loud, anything at all, except don't think! Just float along with your stream of consciousness.

After five minutes, see what you have. You may be surprised to find that you have the germ of an idea, a better sense of your emotional state, or a relaxing release as a result of this simple flow warm-up. Repeat this exercise before you start working on a project and whenever you get stuck on something in your work.

LEVELS OF
AWARENESS

Everyone has had the experience of finally solving a difficult problem after simply letting go of it. You may have started off by batting the problem around in your head until you felt like it was batting you. When there didn't seem to be any logical solution, you probably just got up and walked away from the darn thing in frustration and fatigue. Perhaps you actually got out of the house and took a walk to clear your head. Later, when you were relaxed and refreshed, you returned to this problem and, as if by magic, the answer just came to you! The solution may have been so obvious you couldn't quite believe it. "Why didn't I think of that before?" you asked yourself.

Well, the reason it didn't occur to you before is that you were actually *thinking* too much. When you stopped straining your left brain for a logical answer, you relaxed, got into the flow, and let the answer come to you through your own intuition that connected you to a much larger awareness. This larger awareness or consciousness is vastly greater than the awareness anyone can tap from the left brain alone.

In fact, there are many different levels of awareness available to us through our intuition, and many different ways of knowing things. While you were so desperately trying to get the answer to your problem, you were just drawing on the limited funds of your left brain bank of knowledge. But when you relaxed and got into the flow, you were drawing on a universal bank of *all* knowledge. The flow of this knowledge is the actual stream of consciousness—the greater awareness of intuition.

The intuitive state, then, is not the same as everyday awareness. It's a whole other state of mind. Yet, intuition can be used every day.

Many Eastern philosophies, as well as the teachings of Don Juan, have likened this awareness to a warrior's state of mind at the height of battle. Highly aware of everything around him, he is also perfectly attuned to all that needs to be done, and exactly when. Who wouldn't want to face the day armed with that kind of mental ammunition?

In order to enter a state of peak awareness, one must first quiet the part of the mind that constantly categorizes and qualifies. The left hemisphere of the brain, in addition to being logical, is sometimes maddeningly judgmental. An excess of intellectual judgment can lead to doubt and even squelch that powerful, instinctive spontaneity that keeps the warrior safe from harm. It's the part of the brain that wears the editor's and judge's hats and will keep on barking orders until you give yourself a break by allowing *it* to take one, too.

The next exercise is designed to help you give your left brain a break so that your right brain can be heard.

• *Exercise 4: Turning off the Intellect
to Turn on Insight*

Lie down or sit in a straight-backed chair. Gently concentrating on your breath, begin to breathe deeply and rhythmically. Focus your attention on the very center of your forehead and breathe into this area, reinforcing your focus with each breath.

Notice how your focus becomes so strong that your thoughts slip away. If you catch yourself drifting off into evaluation or some other distracting mental activity (and you probably will), bring your attention back to that point in your forehead and keep on breathing into it rhythmically. You may also get ideas or insights in flashes. Make a note of these insights after you've come back. This is your entrance into a higher awareness, the beginning of your increasing intuition.

Start with five minutes. When you feel comfortable with that time period, then go on as long as you like.

THE ONLY WAY TO KNOW IT
IS TO KNOW IT

When you use your intuition, you experience the answers it gives you very directly—you do not feel detached from the very situation you are considering. This means you cannot figure things out with intuition. Instead, you simply allow the answers to come to you and in a very real sense allow yourself to become one with them.

When you use everyday reasoning, you follow a single, commonly accepted line of logic. However, when that sudden flash of knowing comes—knowledge that a certain person will call, that a certain job will be yours, that a certain person is right for you, or that the perfect solution to a taxing problem has been reached—the line you follow is your personally aligned connection to the larger logic of intuition.

You must let the insight come whole, trying not to edit, question, or even intellectually understand it while it's being received. Later your intellect will read it back and register it in your consciousness as a definite piece of rational, practical information that can be applied to your daily life.

But insights themselves are not filtered through the constraints of logical understanding: They are not communicated through the vehicle of the left brain. Rather, they go directly to your experience, to your direct knowledge: territory that belongs to the right brain. It is here that you spontaneously see the whole picture, knowing and experiencing it at once.

Because our minds are normally filled with intellectual, left brain activity, at times we need to be "mindless" in order to avail ourselves of the larger awareness. A public relations director once told me she was a bit sorry that she didn't have to iron as much as she used to, because in the mindless monotony of performing that chore, she'd received a lot of unasked for, but gratefully received, inspiration. Here's an exercise to spark some inspiration of your own.

- *Exercise 5: An Exercise in Mindlessness
  (to Jog Intuition)*

This exercise is a perfect companion for running, swimming laps, using a rowing machine, taking a shower, doing housework, or any rote task.

Before you start the activity, tell yourself that you are now open to your intuition.

Then, open yourself to the flow of the shower or the drone of the vacuum cleaner and "enter" it with your awareness, thinking or saying something like, "I'm opening to my intuition; insights and ideas are flowing to me now." Get into the rhythm of whatever you're doing and flow with it. You may be surprised at the insights that accompany so-called mindless activities.

TAKING A RIDE ON THE TIME/SPACE CONTINUUM

Atomic physics has changed our comprehension of time and space. But what modern scientists have only recently discovered, mystics have known for eons: All comprehension of space and time is only relative. Our understanding of time and space depends on our state of mind or current circumstances. Everyone has experienced a moment when time seemed to stand still and when space actually seemed to change in size—for example, when the walls seem to close in on you or when your home seems suddenly bigger because you are alone. Time flies when you're having fun, doesn't move at all when you're not. Your feelings about the time or space you're experiencing determine how you perceive them.

In the ever-present, ever-eternal flow of intuition, there are no rigid delineations of space and time. It's all part of the same flow, the same continuous whole. When you enter the time/space continuum with the help of your intuition, you will experience a sense of timeless time and spaceless space. When I intuitively "see the future," I'm actually entering the continuum and reading the information that is there in its flow, which is the flow of all time. When you enter the flow, you, too, will sense it as a whole. You, too, will pick up information from all time, including, of course, the future.

We have all had sudden hunches at one time or another, irrefutable moments of insight. These are really the instantaneous results of dipping into the stream of the time/space continuum. When we do so, we shift out of our everyday sense of time, which is defined by a past, present, and future, and into timeless time, where we see a glimpse of the future as part of what it really is—now.

We enter the time/space continuum constantly in daily life with the help of our intuition. An editor friend of mine had the experience of knowing something was up when the air at the office felt "heavy." Everyone seemed to sense an unhappy event was imminent, and indeed some of my friend's coworkers were soon laid off. Before I met my husband, I had recently moved to a new apartment. It was a perfectly fine place, but I sensed I wasn't going to be living there long and so I didn't do much decorating. Sure enough, I soon met my husband-to-be, moved to a much more spacious home, and began to decorate with a passion.

Remembering times in your life when you unwittingly sensed the inevitable will help you begin to read the future on a more conscious level.

• *Exercise 6: Timeless Recall*

Think of times you've had a feeling something was about to happen or sensed an impending change. Perhaps you were playing cards and sensed that an ace was coming your way before you were actually dealt one, or perhaps you had a sudden inkling a friend, aunt, or cousin would be stopping by for a surprise visit just moments before the doorbell rang.

Maybe while working on a crucial business project you suddenly began to anticipate every unexpected development of the assignment before it came up, down to unanticipated reactions from your coworkers and superiors. Maybe you even dreamed about a key meeting, just to have your dream repeat itself in your waking life. Everything about your instincts was "on" and the difficult assignment seemed almost to complete itself!

Try to remember as many of these experiences as you can. Write them down. From now on, keep a log of new ones. You might want to refer to the Appendix (page 214) for learning how to set up your own intuition log. As you remember, try to recall just exactly what it was that made you "know" your hunch was irrefutable. Was it a gut feeling? chills down your spine? an unshakable sense of elated glee? a quiet certainty? Whatever these feelings were, jot them down, too. You'll soon learn to quickly recognize the signals your intuition is sending and act on them with confidence.

THE STUFF DREAMS
ARE MADE OF

Dreams are the best illustration of what you experience when you enter the time/space continuum. Dreams are rarely linear narrations. Events seem to happen outside of time, and one place may seem to be many places at once. The playground behind the grammar school you attended can simultaneously be the Roman Coliseum. Your brother can appear in a dream simultaneously as your brother—and Kevin Costner! You may have a dream about your high school graduation when you are at your present age, your sister is a child, and Ulysses S. Grant is the school principal. While you're having the dream, all of this seems perfectly plausible.

It's only after you wake up and try to analyze the dream by imposing linear left-brain thinking on it that you realize the discrepancies in time and space. The experience of being in the time/space continuum is very similar to the experiences you have in dreams.

In fact, dreams can be a mother lode of intuitive information. Sometimes they seem prophetic; at other times they offer a running commentary on the issues you are working through in your life. In this sense they can provide direction and guidance, whether or not they provide prediction.

Some people do see the future in their dreams. Consider the case of my friend Aaron. When he was a child about to go to Europe with his family, Aaron dreamed about all the places they were going to visit. When he eventually arrived, every church and side street, color, texture, and pattern turned out to be just as he had dreamed them.

Others, myself included, seem to see the future more often *outside* of dreams. This does not make our dreams any less important. Perhaps you, too, through dreaming, have had the experience of getting a sense of what issues needed some looking into in your life. Or perhaps you received confirmation that certain approaches you'd taken to try to solve key problems were the right ones. For example, while working on this book I had dreams that expressed the difficulty of putting all the elements together. Yet they were encouraging dreams, because they gave me the sense that I was indeed going to get through it.

• *Exercise 7: Dream Log*

If you remember your dreams, keep a record of them. Try not to edit or interpret them. As we discussed earlier, the time/space continuum of dreams often is not logical. So keep track of what you remember and see if any patterns arise.

Are you more often indoors or outdoors in your dreams? Are you in any particular place? Does it seem that you're always on some kind of journey? Do certain feelings seem to come up again and again? Do events actually take place after you've dreamed them? Do you see any kind of message in the pattern?

Later on, we'll discuss how to interpret your dreams. But for now, just keep a record of what comes up and see for yourself what you get out of it.

TIME IS ON YOUR SIDE

Psychologist and author Lawrence LeShan calls our experiences in the time/space continuum "clairvoyant reality." Our everyday awareness he calls "sensory reality." Our sensory concept of time is composed of a past leading to a present, which in turn leads to a future. This way of thinking, he says, can interfere with the free flow of information. To get to the unlimited bounty of intuition, we must transcend the bounds of sensory reality, enter the flow of timeless time, and become a channel for its information.

It's not difficult to discover your own inherent ability to channel timeless time. By dipping into the flow of clairvoyant time, you will learn to disregard the constraints of time as it is commonly understood and become your own timepiece.

• *Exercise 8: Time Awareness*

Try to determine what time it is by visualizing the large white face of a clock and seeing the position of the hands. Tune in to the physical details of the clock. Are the hands black? Are the numerals Roman? If the clock were a pie, how big would the slice formed by the hands be? The more detailed your vision of the clock can be, the more informed your guess will be. Check your time against a real clock.

The best time to try this is right after you wake up in the morning. If you always wake up at the same time, try it on the weekends when you're not on your regular schedule. You'll be amazed at how close you can come to the actual time, and with practice you'll get better. By doing this, you'll be overcoming your reliance on the sensory concept of time, while also literally eliminating the need to be a "clock watcher."

As you continue with my program for developing intuition, you will find you also have an ability to see future time in much the same way you have just seen present time. The only difference is that when you're ready to start sensing future time, you'll be looking for the position of the hands of time on the blank face of the eternal now.

HERE, THERE, AND EVERYWHERE

Geographical distances do not weaken your awareness of clairvoyant reality. Not only is all time "now" in the time/space continuum, but all space is "here," too, without any of the barriers that are part of our sensory reality.

In clairvoyant reality, here is there, there is here, and here is everywhere. On the intuitive path it's not unusual to get a strong, accurate feeling about someone who is geographically quite far away.

An actress friend told me a harrowing tale about an all-consuming apprehension she once had concerning her sister, who was off skiing in Colorado. Later she discovered that at the very time she was feeling apprehensive, her sister, who had been caught in an avalanche, was fighting for her life. Fortunately, her sister survived. But it's significant that my friend was able to feel her beloved sister's distress so many miles away. That apprehension came to her through the flow of intuition.

An antiques dealer friend came upon a deal that seemed too good to pass up. It was a guaranteed original Ming vase going for a song, and it looked real enough to his trained eye, but an inner voice loudly told him to move on. Sure enough, the vase turned out to be just about as Chinese, let alone Ming, as his Irish grandmother, and nowhere near as old!

In case you're wondering why the sudden distant call of intuition frequently concerns a deeply emotional situation, there's a simple explanation. Emotions are a right-brain function. The more powerful our feelings are, the more completely they can overcome the strictly rational gatekeepers of our left brain. When those natural intuition barriers are flooded out by our deep feelings, our intellectual back talk gets drowned out, and inner messages can come through loud and clear.

GETTING IN SYNC

We've all had the experience of being in the right place at the right time, and at some point in our lives we've all known someone whom we characterized as lucky. Luck, however, is not a matter of chance. It's really a question of synchronicity.

The renowned psychologist C. G. Jung defined synchronicity as "meaningful coincidence." You might describe it as a string of events that seem to come from out of the blue but in fact happen for a reason. Because the reason cannot be explained in any rational, linear fashion, we tend to attribute it to chance.

Synchronicity is the process of aligning with a larger awareness. Suddenly you seem to be in sync with the fates. We experience the synchronicity of meaningful coincidence all the time. It's that all-so-common occurrence of thinking of John and then running into him or hearing from Jane out of the blue after you'd just brought her name up in a conversation. It's there again when certain words or numbers pop up with increasing regularity and no apparent reason until you decide they might have some kind of deeper message for you.

For example, a model friend of mine kept hearing about Japan and saw references to that country everywhere. Finally, he realized he was meant to go there. His trip was successful and laid a foundation for his entire career. Some might say he just got lucky, but getting lucky in and of itself is really the process of tuning in to your own synchronicity.

Sometimes you can even unconsciously make something happen just by getting in sync with what you want. You don't always have to follow signs like my model friend did to reap the benefits of synchronicity. Sure, you can start listing the symbols that have personal meaning for you, jotting them down when they come up. (There will be much more about this process, which I call using your intuition log, throughout this book.) But just deciding what you want will allow that desire to reach the larger you. That larger, unconscious you, in turn, taps into the even larger awareness of synchronicity, and soon that giant information bank will send what you desire your way.

Not only can you enlist the assistance of a larger awareness in helping you achieve your goals and fulfill your personal needs, but you can also sync yourself with what's going on around you, so you begin to make choices that are most in tune with you and with the flow. Once you've begun developing your natural synchronicity (the following exercises will help do the trick), you'll find yourself the grateful recipient of what many call good timing and lucky coincidences. But you'll know that you've actually gotten in sync with the flow to make the most appropriate (dare we say, in-tune?) choices for your own future.

Here's an example of what I'm talking about: A client of mine in advertising opened to his own synchronicity instinctively, with great results. From the minute he heard about it, he knew he had to have a DeLorean sports car. He started collecting any article and promotional material he could find, and it began to seem that wherever he looked, the DeLorean was mentioned.

Fueled with his own hunch and many seeming coincidences, my client even put down a deposit on a car, sight unseen, long before the first DeLorean was off the assembly line. Many months later, when the DeLorean account was up for grabs and every major ad agency was vying for it, the small firm he worked for won the plum account. Part of the coup had to do with showing off my client's contract in their winning presentation—more synchronicity.

But even that wasn't the end of it. Eventually, my client got to drive DeLorean's own car and went on to write the prophetic line, "Live the dream"—which more or less described what had happened in his own life once he got himself in line with his most exciting possibility. In fact his life exceeded the dream, because flowing with his desire at the right synched time also enhanced his professional reputation. You, too, can learn to recognize and plumb the hidden riches of the meaningful coincidences in your life.

• *Exercise 9: Sync Recall*

Think back and try to remember when you've experienced meaningful coincidences: instances when you happened to tune into someone you were thinking about, when a chance meeting led to your getting something you really wanted, or when you felt you were extraordinarily lucky. Also recall times when you felt you were in perfect sync with your surroundings: getting to the train station just as your train arrived, finding a parking space right in front of the store, being the first to learn of a job opening. Write down these experiences, and keep a log of future meaningful coincidences.

I'VE BEEN HERE BEFORE

Déjà vu is a form of synchronicity. That strong yet inexplicable feeling that you've been here before is a meaningful coincidence that stems from the fact that you have been there before—but not in the sensory realm of everyday reality. In the larger awareness of clairvoyant reality, you are able to be virtually everywhere in space and time. In the clairvoyant realm of intuition it makes perfect sense to feel as if you have, indeed, been there before. When you experience déjà vu, some event, some person, some object is spurring you to recall just a fragment of all you know through your innate connection to other realities.

You can use déjà vu to come out on top in everyday situations. A lawyer I know was having apprehensions about a very important upcoming meeting. When I helped him to get in touch with his intuition, we found he had what he called a "vision" of how the meeting would go. This vision was very detailed. It included what everyone would be wearing and saying—including himself—and ended in a very favorable outcome for my client. When the meeting actually took place, it went exactly the way he'd envisioned it. It was déjà vu. As a result, this lawyer was able to do exactly what he needed to do to get the result he wanted in a highly charged situation. With the help of synchronicity—and the déjà vu in particular—my client was able to create his own good fortune.

A computer salesman I know who works for an aggressive start-up company had a similar experience. Everybody in the company was chewing their fingernails down to the bone, worrying about an upcoming meeting with their biggest prospective client to date. But my friend was the only one who wasn't worried. That was because he'd already gotten a "flash" of the client with a big smile on his face. When the meeting finally came to pass, the client was ready to sign on the dotted line, and did so grinning from ear to ear. My friend wasn't surprised, though, because his intuition had already shown him what the client's attitude would be.

THAT SYNCING FEELING

Good game players and successful gamblers are prime examples of people aligning with their synchronicity. Newspapers are filled with stories of lottery winners who felt the luck of certain numbers and kept playing them until they hit the jackpot. My housekeeper did very well betting on numbers that came to her through the synchronicity of her dreams. And the recent winner of a national poker championship said she felt lucky that day and knew she would be dealt the winning hand.

Those who are good with investments—from penny stocks to megabuck mergers—also allow the aligning forces of synchronicity to inform and guide them. A real estate investor told me he'd happened upon an article about a man who he sensed would be the perfect partner in a deal he had in mind. They met, seemed to get in sync with each other, and are now involved in a profitable multimillion dollar property.

It's important to practice making synchronicity work for you. The next two exercises should prove challenging. Like the old joke about getting to Carnegie Hall, it takes practice, practice, practice. By simply repeating these exercises you'll be toning down the noise of your intellectual back talk and turning up the sweet music of your own intuition.

• *Excercise 10: Increasing that Syncing Feeling*
Part 1—Everyday Predictions

Try guessing at things before they happen: when the telephone will ring, who'll be at the other end of the phone line once you pick up, when a traffic light will turn green. Try to pick the winners at a horse race. While standing in front of an elevator bank, guess which doors will open first. At a train station, try to position yourself on the platform where the doors of the approaching car will open.

• *Excercise 11: Increasing that Syncing Feeling*
Part 2—The Card Trick

Take a regular deck of playing cards and remove the aces and jokers. You'll now have an equal number of high cards (8 or higher) and low cards (7 or lower). Shuffle the deck well and remove the top card—placing it face down in front of you and moving the rest of the deck about 2 feet off to one side—where it's no longer in your direct field of vision but is still easy to reach.

A good place to start is with either the color or the relative value (high or low). See which one you tune into first. If you don't pick up anything right away, try asking yourself: "Is it red or black? high or low?" If that doesn't feel right, try wording it a slightly different way: "Is it bright or dark? Is it worth a lot or a little?"

Go with whatever information comes to you first, and in whatever way it seems to hit you. Then, see if you can graduate to predicting more specific suits and numbers. How close do you come? Don't worry about exact accuracy. You may learn invaluable things about your intuitive style. For example, do you sense things more in terms of color, images or symbols, spatial relationships, numbers or even words?

Of course, the more precisely you try to pinpoint the cards, the more difficult the exercise will be. Keep on trying, though (at the pace and level that feel right to you), and don't be discouraged. As I said, repetition greatly improves your skills. At the same time, these exercises work on your intuitive muscle, developing your ability to access and identify intuition in your daily life. Keep on practicing! Once you start to click with the exercises, you'll be amazed at your own abilities.

As you continue reading this book, you'll learn more techniques that can greatly increase your "hit ratio." Please see the Appendix (page 199) when you're through with the book to try the Card Trick Variation—and see how much you improve.

One last thing to note about the syncing exercises: As you practice both of these exercises, notice how you feel when you're "on" and "in sync." Do you pick up signals from your body—a feeling in your gut or a tingle at the back of your neck or up your spine? Other senses can be involved. A songwriter once told me his songs "smelled good" when they were "on." Other people may feel a slight ringing in the ears or seem to actually hear the answer they seek.

Anything that feels right will express itself through the best and strongest form of communication for you. I personally get a sense of balance versus imbalance—a sense that all the right information seems to fit. Sometimes you just "know." Remember what this experience feels like for you, and try to apply it to your exercises to see if you can determine what's merely a guess, what seems like a hunch, and what's a beyond-any-doubt sure sense of a perfectly nailed answer.

MIND SHAPES MATTER,
OR MINDING YOUR OWN REALITY

To access your intuition, it's crucial that you be open both to the reality of its existence and to the certainty that you can make use of it in your life. In fact, you can't perceive what you don't believe. Simply put, the journey on your intuitive path starts with an open mind.

Nobody reading this book is expected to have the overwhelming belief of a saint, but by maintaining an open mind, having the will to start developing yours, and being willing to believe, you will find intuition beginning to flow through, effectively developing a belief and faith in that reality.

In order to truly open to the wealth of information the intuitive path has to offer, we must begin to examine the system of our own beliefs and cast off the limiting concepts that can block us from receiving the whole intuitive picture.

• *Excercise 12: Belief System Review*

Examine your attitudes about yourself. Has your belief in what's possible determined what has actually happened to you in your life? Can you think of other people whose negative or positive attitudes have determined events in their lives? For example, in every crowd there seems to be one pessimist who walks around with a dark cloud over his or her head. Indeed, disaster seems to be just around any corner this sad sack is near. Likewise, everyone knows a cockeyed optimist whose Pollyanna attitude seems too good to be true, and yet seems always to pull out a plum whenever he or she sticks a finger into any pie.

A MIND IS A TERRIBLE
THING TO CLOSE

A young woman once came to me for a reading, desperately seeking a solution to her career dilemma. She was a not-very-successful success systems developer who ran seminars to help business people excel in their careers. This struck me as rather ironic considering her own terribly negative personality. I knew that before she'd ever be successful in her field we'd have to do something about her gloomy attitude. So I asked her to think back and recall something she really wanted and eventually got—a sweater, a ring, a car, anything at all. She couldn't think of a single thing. "Anything at all?" I persisted. She just frowned and shook her head. "Even a popsicle?" I said. "I hate popsicles!" she exploded.

As we proceeded, I realized this client's overwhelming negativism not only choked the flow of her intuition, but also severely diminished the amount of information I could obtain for her. Her closed-minded attitude about life in general prevented her from making any positive—let alone intuitive— moves. As a result, her negativity was reinforced even further.

I sensed, however, that as a child there had been a time when she felt open to positive possibilities. I asked her to tune in to that time and hold every detail of that memory in her mind. At first she frowned, but eventually began to recall a glorious week on her grandparents' farm. So many delightful, unexpected things had happened: She'd watched a litter of puppies being born, joined a spontaneous moonlit hayride, and had a gorgeous butterfly light and then linger on her hand. As she relived the experience, she could feel herself confidently awaiting the next wonderful event. "Hold on to that feeling!" I cried. Because that was precisely the open, trusting state she needed to be in to start re-experiencing wonderful things from then on.

So I advised her to regularly recall that scene, especially the positive feeling she'd had about herself and her future, and realize that she was, in fact, the same confident girl. At first she felt a little doubtful, but about a month later I received a call thanking me for the advice. "Would you believe," she laughed, "I kept remembering the farm just because it felt good, but my next seminar was actually a success!"

OPENING THE MIND—TO CROSS THE BRIDGE

Your mind's openness to the intuitive path allows it to bridge the gap between the logic of everyday reality and the alternate logic of intuition. This other logic is really just an extension and a complement to what we are already aware of. Intuition not only makes invaluable information yours for the taking, but also can affect actual physical transformation. The mind's openness combined with an individual's will to not only receive but also project intuition has been known to produce spectacular results.

Faith healer Olga Worrel could change the molecular composition of water, actually converting its weight through simple willpower. Instances of psychic healing and psychokinesis (telepathic movement of objects) have been well documented. In parapsychological tests, it has been proven that people will score more psychic "hits" by wishing or willing the outcome. Furthermore, the ability of the mind to change matter has also stood up to the scrutiny of hard science.

Research into quantum physics has proven that the sub-atomic world moves in actual relationship to the thoughts of those observing it. In other words, the reality of what we observe is actually being shaped by our own minds.

The following exercise is a real mind bender. It demonstrates how your thoughts can literally reshape physical reality. Although it may seem to be quite advanced, it is actually simpler than it sounds. The important thing to remember here is patience. Don't rush through any of the steps, and if you don't succeed at first, give yourself time to get it.

A client of mine got it so well he decided to lead his entire office in a mind-bending jamboree. Everyone grabbed the nearest suitable object, with letter openers responding so well that by the end of the week there were no unbent specimens to be found in the whole office. Go slowly through the instructions, visualizing all the way, and be willing to accept your own power.

- *Excercise 13: Spoon Bending—An Exercise in Mind Over Matter*

Find an inexpensive cafeteria-quality spoon and test its resistance to make sure it's not so flimsy that you can bend it yourself with little effort. (Please note: A piece of heavy silverware may be too tough for a beginner to bend, and if you do manage to bend the good family silver, you probably won't be able to bend it back into its exact original shape.)

Using both your hands, hold the spoon out horizontally in front of you in both hands. Hold one end of the spoon inside each fist with the curve in the handle pointing up. Close your eyes and start breathing rhythmically.

Now concentrate and visualize a ball of bright white light over your head. Concentrate as hard as you can on getting the light bright and hot as you move it down through the top of your head.

Once it's in your head, keep concentrating on it until you feel it is as bright as it can be. Then, slowly visualize the ball moving down your neck, into your shoulders, down your upper arms, down your forearms, and finally into your wrists. Focus only on the light and feel the energy of it vibrate as it warms you.

When the light reaches your fingers, say out loud, "Bend, bend, bend!" and try to bend the spoon in one quick motion. Amazingly, the spoon will bend in the middle, as if it were suddenly made of butter, with almost no effort at all.

EVERYTHING
IS ENERGY

With his famous equation E = mc², Albert Einstein proved that when you come right down to it, everything in the universe is energy. Both the physical reality of matter and the abstract reality of the mind are made up of patterns of energy. Connecting with your intuition is the act of tuning in to the never-ending flow of universal energy.

The concept of a universal energy flow is not a new one. The ancient Chinese called this flow *chi;* the ancient Hindus called it *prana.* The disciplines that developed in those two cultures—t'ai chi and yoga, respectively—are based on the art of tuning in to the flow of energy and using it to center the self. When we are centered, we experience harmony—not only with ourselves, but with others, and with our entire environment. Any centering process is actually the act of balancing ourselves with a universal flow of energy.

WHAT'S THE FREQUENCY?

Like other electromagnetic frequencies including X-rays, radio waves, and light waves, the intuitive flow is also an ongoing current of energy. In a sense, tuning in to intuition is like tuning in to a radio station. When we tune in, we're literally on the same wavelength of any frequency we desire.

Just as many light waves on the color spectrum are invisible to the eye, the frequencies of intuition are undetectable to those who are not specifically tuned in to them. But the more sensitive we become to their energy, the more we are able to tap into our intuition. In fact, the term *sensitive*, which is often associated with psychics, was originally used to describe people who could detect the energy surrounding magnets and other objects.

Science has proven that there is an identifiable field of electromagnetic energy surrounding each of us. Through a special process known as Kirlian photography, this field becomes visible to the naked eye. Kirlian photographs of humans, plants, and certain inanimate objects show an aura emanating from each one. This field of energy, which surrounds us all, stems from a larger universal energy field, the flow. We all conduct the energy of the flow, and degrees of this energy naturally radiate throughout each one of us.

STAR LIGHT, STAR BRIGHT

Pregnant women are said to glow. Brides are radiant. Saints are traditionally portrayed with bright halos around their heads. Those whose talent has earned them fame and fortune seem to possess an extra helping of charisma and are known as stars. When a person makes a big breakthrough in his or her understanding of life, we say that person has finally seen the light—or even has been enlightened.

It's no coincidence that when people are in states of high energy, they are described in terms of increased light. Light is the palpable expression of energy, which composes all reality.

You need not bother with expensive Kirlian photographs to prove that you emanate this light flow. The following exercise will demonstrate the energy that you radiate.

• *Exercise 14: Feeling Your Energy Field*

Briskly rub your hands together, working up the warmth. As soon as they feel good and toasty (this only takes about thirty seconds or so), hold your hands palm to palm, lining up the fingers.

Now slowly begin to pull your hands away from each other until you feel a push or a pull (some people feel one, some feel the other) that seems to suggest you've come to the outer edge of a chunk, or field, of energy. Usually this occurs when your hands are four to eight inches apart.

If you don't get it the first time keep trying the exercise until the sensation occurs. I promise you it will. Some people don't feel the edge until they actually play with the field itself, moving their hands closer together and then farther away as if playing cat's cradle with a marshmallow. Try this yourself. Once you get the push/pull going between your hands, you'll get the idea of what the energy field feels like and how to sense it more easily.

The energy field you sensed between your hands is actually your own aura, the palpable, radiant energy that surrounds you. You have just learned to sense one part of your aura's boundary. In the next exercise, you'll learn to explore the parameters of a partner's energy field.

• *Exercise 15: Sensing the Body's Energy Field*

Find a partner and sit down with him or her in a pair of straight-backed chairs. In this exercise you and your partner will take turns being the subject and the sensor.

The subject must close his or her eyes and begin to breathe deeply and rhythmically. Meanwhile, the sensor should warm up with Exercise 14. When you're both feeling relaxed, the sensor stands behind the subject, who is still seated, and raises his or her hands until they are about a foot above the partner's head. Very slowly move the hands down until, as in the previous exercise, the sensor starts to feel the shift in energy that marks the edge of the subject's aura. Again, the sensor can play with that squishy-feeling energy flow until he or she feels exactly where the demarcation lies.

The perimeter of each individual's personal energy field varies widely, and some people have much more prominent and more easily sensed auras than others. So if you don't feel anything, don't worry about it—just try again. You can always move on and come back to it later when you feel more energetically charged.

When you're ready, switch roles and repeat the process.

You've already felt your own aura, but this next exercise will show you your visible light connection to the energy flow of life.

• *Exercise 16: Seeing the Energy Field*

Find a black or very dark surface in your home (a piece of clothing, a tabletop, or even a turned-off television). Turn off any electric lights, pull the shades, and place a single lighted candle behind you.

Put your hands in front of the black surface and examine them. You should see a whitish, filmy glow emanating from your fingers. (Tip: Try focusing on the background.) Try this with a friend and experiment with the filmy shadows. See how close you have to come for your mutual films to touch.

This is what is truly meant by "Reach out and touch someone!" When we feel touched without any physical contact, we are actually experiencing shared energy. When we say a person has an aura of mystery or an aura of contentment, what we are really saying is that we have sensed that person's energy field and are interpreting what that radiating energy represents.

The physical aura is not always easy to see because it can be very subtle. Don't be discouraged, though. When you do begin to see your glow, try increasing it through concentration. Wishing and concentrating will project energy, and you'll see the auric field more clearly.

THE ENERGY LINEUP

Now that you've learned to see and feel your own energy field, it's time to get down to the fine points—the very specific points of energy that line up to form the internal energy system of your entire aura.

Our own energy field is composed of seven major energy centers, also known as *chakras*, each of which is associated with a different key location within the body. Each of the seven chakras contributes a different essential quality to the internal energy flow. Just as white light can be separated into many colors when filtered through a prism, the bodily energy spectrum breaks down into individual hues.

Understanding these individual energy centers, their corresponding colors and how they all interrelate as a whole, remote as it may seem, really helps us to better understand— and make better use of—the whole system of intuition. The more sensitive you become to different colors and the different energies they represent, the more sensitive you'll become to all the energy around you. As you develop your intuition, you may very well start receiving information in the form of colors, so keep the following list in mind, or within close reach. For more specific data on the uses and interpretations of color, you can also refer to Chapter 5 and the Appendix.

THE FIRST ENERGY CENTER: RED

Located at the base of the spine, the domain of the first chakra also includes the reproductive region. This entire area is governed by the color red. No wonder we associate red with raw passion and emotion, physicality, vitality, and sexuality!

Think of the hot sports car that's always advertised in red to get you lusting after it or the shiny red apple a day that keeps the doctor away.

THE SECOND ENERGY CENTER: ORANGE

Moving up a little from the base of the spine and slightly to the left, you'll find the spleen, which is represented by the warming color of orange. The essential qualities here are wisdom, confidence, courage, and strength.

Think of the rich, tawny mane that crowns the strong—and, of course, courageous—lion.

THE THIRD ENERGY CENTER: YELLOW/GOLD

The third chakra is located at the solar plexus right at the center of the body—directly under the breastbone and spilling into the area we commonly refer to as the gut. It's no coincidence, then, that the saying "to know something in your gut" means to know something so deeply and surely that you feel it at your very core—your literal physical center.

The third chakra's governing color, yellow, is associated with intellect, self-awareness, knowledge, and personal power. Why do you suppose that the typical pencil or legal pad is most often colored yellow? The intellectual sharpening effects of yellow make it a perfect choice.

THE FOURTH ENERGY CENTER: GREEN

From the gut, we move up to the heart: the fourth chakra and the literal heart of the energy lineup. The heart's governing color is green. Green represents growth—both physical and emotional—and love and prosperity.

Think of the green shoots and buds that are the first lovely signs of a new spring. Then think of the color of money—the literal green of cash.

While you may not initially associate the color green with the concept of love, can you think of any color that can be more reviving, and more inspiring to growth and expansion?

THE FIFTH ENERGY CENTER: BLUE

At the throat is the fifth chakra that governs both the flow of creative expression and the calm flow of tranquillity.

Blue is the color that represents the energy of this center, and it all makes perfect sense when you think of how peaceful and rejuvenated you feel when you gaze at the ocean or the sky.

THE SIXTH ENERGY CENTER: VIOLET

Smack in the middle of the forehead is where we find the well-known third eye—the sixth chakra and the by-now clichéd but very real passageway to spiritual awareness. Its governing hue is violet. Together, this point and color represent our ability to achieve the highest, most divine knowledge.

Purple has always been the symbol of high endeavors and high connections. Think of the purple robes of kings and religious figures.

THE SEVENTH ENERGY CENTER: WHITE

This point, the seventh energy center, also known as the "crown chakra," is located at the very top of the head and represents our true crowning glory. Its governing color, white, quite naturally caps the entire energy lineup, as it's the radiant hue we most closely associate with the aura. Just think of all those artistic renderings of a glowing halo crowning the head.

White also represents purity, enlightenment, and protection. Think of the quintessentially pure image of a bride in her cascading white veil or the angel that crowns a Christmas tree.

Whenever you feel you need a "shot" of some enlightening energy and even extra protection, try visualizing a white light surrounding you or your environment. This is an ancient trick that cuts through negativity and is helpful—and sometimes essential—in everyday modern life!

LINING UP THE LINEUP

When we are feeling at our best, the seven chakras within each of us are lined up one by one to help create a sense of personal harmony, as well as a growing awareness of harmony with the universal energy flow of intuition.

The more together our energy is literally, the more at ease we feel with ourselves, and the more smoothly we're able to get in sync with the larger awareness of intuition. Just as we wake up in the morning and stretch to get the energy flowing and readjust the body after a night's sleep, we can also add a daily stretch for the body's energy centers to realign ourselves and reawaken our connection with the flow itself.

The exercise that follows could be your key to opening to intuition on a daily basis. Every morning I follow this simple routine of energy alignment. Try it to experience the same benefits yourself. I'm thoroughly convinced that this routine could open you to greater intuitive sense as well as a greater sense of general well-being. My students have all reported back with marvelous results.

Of course, everyone will resonate more or less strongly to different exercises. But please remember, the more you practice alignment, the more quickly your own intuition is likely to get into line with a larger awareness.

- *Exercise 17: Balancing Your Energy
  with the Energy of Intuition*

Find a quiet place where you won't be distracted, and either lie down or sit securely in a straight-backed chair. Start to breathe rhythmically and deeply. Take all the time you need to feel really comfortable and to let your breath flow easily and regularly.

When you feel perfectly comfortable, bring your awareness to the middle of your forehead and visualize a violet light at this point. Using your breath, release and relax into your awareness of this point, and see the light there. The violet light can seem to have a circular form, or perhaps it suffuses your entire third eye area with its glow. Use whatever works for you, breathing into your awareness. Stay there for a little while, perhaps a minute or more.

Next shift your awareness to the center of your throat area, remembering to continue your deep, relaxed breathing. Breathe into the throat area, and visualize a blue light there. Stay with that blue light for a while, until the light is very clear for you.

Move on to your heart area (in the middle of your chest) and visualize a green light there as you breathe and relax into your awareness of this essential area. Take your time; don't rush. Really enjoy this special time for renewing and refreshing your connection with the awareness of intuition.

When you're ready, move on to the solar plexus. The solar plexus is the point under your breastbone that moves in and out when you breathe deeply, as you are doing now. As you breathe into the solar plexus area, see a golden yellow light suffusing the entire area with its glow. Stay with your breathing and your awareness as long as it's comfortable for you to do so, really seeing and feeling that golden light.

Then find your spleen (on the left side toward the back, near your kidneys). Breathe through this area as you visualize an orange light bathing it in its glow. There may be warmth or another feeling associated with this color.

Finally, shift your awareness down to the bottom of your spine and visualize a red light there, heating the entire area with its radiant glow. Breathe and release into this red light as long as you like.

Now imagine a crystalline tube running downward from the base of your spine to the center of the earth. Feel and see a crystalline light in the center of the earth that is at once healing, releasing, and balancing. Now sense that light moving up through the crystalline tube, entering your body through the base of your spine, and working its way up through all the vertebrae and energy centers: healing, cleansing, releasing, and balancing you and your energy.

Feel and see the light move up through each chakra, moving up and out through the top of your head. Now feel and see this light as a crystalline lightning rod connecting you with a flow of infinite energy, the source of all awareness—including intuition.

Try this next variation whenever you feel you need to strengthen your intuition connection.

• Exercise 18: Connecting to the Universal Flow

Lie down or sit up straight in your quiet place and do the energy-balancing exercise (17), breathing through the energy centers as you visualize the various colored lights. When the crystalline light begins to beam out from the top of your head like a lightning rod, think or say out loud something like, "I now connect to a never-ending flow of all energy, all awareness." Keep breathing into the middle of your forehead as you repeat the phrase, and continue to flow with the energy of that crystalline light.

NO MIND IS AN ISLAND

Although your mind is just one small part of the energy of all existence, it contains the totality of all energy, all information: It is a universe in itself. In addition, your mind is already connected with and reflects the other universes of other minds. What that means in everyday terms is that your own thinking has already absorbed the thinking of many others and that you, in turn, have helped form the thinking of the people around you.

Your mind reflects the consciousness of everyone from your parents and teachers to your heroes and even authors who've opened your mind and added a point of view and comprehension that you've incorporated into your own. Those respective mind universes—all minds—keep connecting and reflecting on up to the universal mind of all minds and the universal flow of all information. This mother lode, of course, is what we're referring to as the *intuitive source*. It's also what Jung called the *collective unconscious*. All information is interconnected and your mind contains the potential for knowing it all.

Think of how many artists and designers seem to unconsciously plug into the same schools of thought at the same time. It's the same phenomenon that occurs when a particular movie or book—or even political leader—seems to resonate in everyone's minds, firing and reflecting everyone's own imagination.

When we resonate, we feel identification with information, a oneness with it. This is the natural state of intuition, an all-encompassing state of timeless time and spaceless space. Perhaps the poet William Blake best described this state when he spoke of seeing "the universe in a grain of sand, and eternity in an hour."

The intuitive path need not only be followed to sense such weighty concepts as the universe and eternity, of course. Any object or detail in our lives contains the potential to connect us with a complete world of information. Exercise 19 will demonstrate just how easy it is for one small, everyday object to fully retrieve an entire experience and era for us.

• *Exercise 19: Interconnected Flashback*

Think of one meaningful object from your childhood—a teddy bear, a sled, a cup, a coat, anything—and note the flood of associations it unleashes.

See every detail and really feel what it is you remember. Do you feel the warmth of a childhood bed? Can you see the stripes on your mother's apron? Are you elated at seeing a gold star on your book report? Can you see yourself sadly clutching your sand pail on the last day of summer vacation?

A whole world and a different era can be evoked by one seemingly insignificant object.

ONE FOR ALL AND ALL FOR ONE

We often experience a sense of wholeness with a larger life force. We sense ourselves as part of a larger group yet at the same time see the whole of that group reflected in ourselves—in the workplace, in our relationships, and in our recreational activities.

You'll know what I mean if you've ever played team sports or experienced a team spirit working on a project at school, on the job, in the military, or at camp. Here we see the whole-in-one in motion, as each person contributes his or her personal energy to the group until it begins to take on an energy of its own. Sometimes when a team of any kind really gets going, it's hard to remember who did what, and remarkably no one really cares because the whole is working as one.

Within our families we can see ourselves in the faces and actions of other family members. You may catch yourself repeating a phrase your mother used when you were a child. You may listen to your laugh and realize it sounds just like your father's. In the child, you can see the adult to be and the parent that was. In an adult, you can see the eternal essence of a child.

When we are with loved ones, we sense their moods and

often empathize with them. It's important to take note of the special resonance you feel with loved ones. It's a sensation you'll expand upon to help you tune in to the people you work with or must deal with in everyday life.

• *Exercise 20: Seeing Your Echo*

Recall and record experiences of seeing yourself in others (family members, friends, lovers, colleagues) and seeing your particular situation reflected in those around you.

Is there a new turn of phrase you've picked up from your mate or that your mate has picked up from you? Does your child have a special way of cupping his or her chin in hand that stirs up memories of a long-forgotten habit from your own childhood? Does a friend from another background or part of the world reflect many of your personality traits?

Generate a good healthy list of these experiences in a notebook you designate your intuition log. You'll probably be surprised to see how, after the first few notations, one "echo" echoes into the next almost naturally.

When you have plenty of material to work with, try to construct a composite self-description made up of qualities and traits you see in others. (Example: I have Dan's laugh, but one octave higher. I have my mother's hair texture, although I am blonde. I have my father's dry wit, and my sister's laugh. I have my grandmother's sturdy legs and strong sense of resolve, and my grandfather's high spirits. I have the new baby's dimples.)

To enrich your composite with additional qualities and details, go back to your original list and let it spark new whole-in-one echoes as needed.

BEING A PART OF
THE WHOLE PICTURE

Life is composed of many paradoxes. Perhaps one of the greatest is the fact that when we begin our journey on the intuitive path, what we are doing, in effect, is simply finding out what it is we already know. Accessing intuition is the process of making our own limited minds aware of the presence and resources of an unlimited universal consciousness.

You have already begun this process by balancing your energy with the energy of intuition (Exercises 16 and 17). Now it's time for some firsthand exploration of the difference between your individual mind or self and the "higher" part of you, or your own intuitive self that connects you to universal consciousness. Once you get to know your intuitive self, you'll be much closer to tapping into your natural pipeline to a never-ending source of invaluable information.

• *Exercise 21: Seeing Your Intuitive Self*

Find a comfortable place where you will not be disturbed and where you have access to a mirror. Sit in front of the mirror or stand if you prefer.

As you look into the mirror, focus all your attention on your eyes. Stare into them as though they were someone else's. Study them carefully, looking for the inner face behind the physical mask. The eyes are truly the mirror of the soul, and you are looking for your inner essence, your intuitive self as opposed to your everyday self. Get up and walk around the room, maintaining your awareness of the "higher" you that exists behind your eyes.

Once you find your intuitive self on your own, repeat the exercise. Except this time, use a friend instead of a mirror to find the intuitive self in his or her eyes as he or she finds that self in yours. Discovering the intuitive self this way can often produce an eerie sensation—a sensation that really brings home to you how we are all much greater than the bounds our everyday perception would suggest.

ON AND ON—THE
NEVER-ENDING SAGA

All of our lives and all of life itself is interconnected, continually unfolding and enfolding us. Witness the ocean (long a symbol of universal consciousness) as its waves unfold, rush to the shore, return to the deep, and repeat the same process. Consider the changing of the seasons: fall into winter, winter reborn into spring, spring unfolding into summer, then fall, and over and over again. Notice the continual renewing of families as members are born, die, and live on in the stream of ancestors and descendants.

The development of our awareness follows the same pattern. Our awareness, too, is always evolving and is always connected to the flow of universal awareness. Learn to experience your unique part in this flow, and you'll be rewarded with information that can help guide you through every aspect of your life.

LEARNING THE ABCs

FOLLOWING YOUR
YELLOW BRICK ROAD

Now that you've begun to explore the flow, it's time to go directly to its point of origin—your intuitive source, which is inside you and available at all times to supply you with unlimited awareness and information. Connecting with your intuition is a natural matter of tuning in to your own inherent intuitive source-connection.

By looking within yourself to find the source of intuition, you find, or rediscover, your own center. Feeling centered is really the sensation of being in perfect alignment with your own answers. In the end, the process of finding and connecting with the intuitive source comes down to discovering that you're already there. Finding this source means finding, or opening to, your own inner wisdom. Ultimately, to more readily and more clearly access your intuitive self, you only need to strengthen your connection to it.

In this chapter, you'll be building up your intuitive strength by honing familiar skills you use every day. Get ready to greatly enhance your abilities to focus, to think and speak with intent, and to create clear mental imagery. By whole focusing, affirming, and visualizing, you'll naturally develop your intuition and boost your ability to use it in everyday life.

It's important to keep in mind that strengthening your connection and clear access to intuition is a continual process. You're always connected to your intuitive source, of course, so at any moment you could experience its powerful information. However, becoming aware of this connection and focusing on it more readily takes time and patience.

As you practice the exercises in this book and your awareness evolves, you'll discover that your intuition grows in its own way. Sometimes you'll find your answers are flowing. At other times, intuition and its source seem nowhere to be found. But whether you're aware of it or not, each and every time you consciously connect, you're building up your ability to tune in to your intuitive self at will.

FOCUSING IN

Connecting to intuition is impossible without focusing. If you've brought your undivided attention to any of the previous exercises, you've already used this technique. Focusing, quite simply, is the process of directing your awareness toward the intuitive source. The more finely you hone your focusing skills, the more clearly you allow intuition to come into focus for you. Through breathing, relaxing, and concentrating, you'll learn how to focus like a pro.

THE BREATH OF LIFE

Breathing is more than a way to get oxygen into your lungs. Each breath is a reaffirmation of your connection to the source, and conscious breathing puts you in touch with the force of life itself.

You can actually shift the level of your awareness and your state of mind by changing the rhythm of your breathing. Ever notice how when you're afraid or angry you breathe in quick, shallow gasps? By taking ten deep breaths, as the old saying goes, it's quite possible to let go of those negative feelings. Doing so appeases the left brain's needs by giving it time to do what it does best—think. Then your deep breathing takes you beyond that, on to the intuitive right hemisphere, which has the chance of coming up with solutions that your left brain could never imagine. If ten simple breaths can help ease and open your mind so, just think of how much more you can accomplish once you begin to spend a little more time putting your conscious attention to actively whole focusing.

The first focusing technique, "Breath Charge," is an effective, unobtrusive technique for tapping your intuition during the course of your day.

- *Exercise 22: Breath Charge*

Sit or stand in a comfortable position, making sure that your back is straight and well supported. Close your eyes and fully focus on your breathing process as you inhale and exhale three very deep—exaggeratedly deep—breaths. Really feel yourself release your breath on each exhalation. As you do so, you may start to sense a slightly lightheaded feeling. Once you're completely aware of your breath, continue to breathe deeply and rhythmically—not with the same level of exaggeration, but maintaining concentration on your breathing.

Now place your right thumb on your right nostril, effectively closing that passageway. Breathe deeply and rhythmically in and out of your left nostril. Now release your right thumb, place your middle finger on your left nostril and repeat the process.

Alternate nostrils at least three times, but continue up to twelve repetitions if it feels comfortable for you to do so. By now you should be feeling lightheaded, so take it easy, go at your own pace, and stop whenever you feel it's right.

This exercise clears both sides of the brain. It's a process that has been used with great effect by ancient yogis and modern business executives. Try it at any time of day when you need to clear your head. It will quickly release mental blocks to open you almost immediately to the flow of your intuition.

RELAX!

Focused breathing leads to relaxation—something we all could really use. It's especially important to feel relaxed and to let go of whatever may be physically or mentally inhibiting us from connecting to our intuitive resources. Bothersome mental monologues and persistent kinks in the neck can be equally distracting. We've all heard that the body is the temple of the soul. This translates into the need to keep our spine and neck relaxed because they form an all-important passageway between the body and mind. And the energy of intuition needs as clear a pathway, mentally and physically, as we can provide for it.

Most of us unconsciously seem to know that. Throughout the day we instinctively stretch and roll our necks so we can breathe easier and think more clearly. To consciously warm up for receiving intuitive information, we need to routinely practice neck rolls and spine straightening.

• *Exercise 23: Neck Rolls*

First start to breathe deeply and rhythmically just as you did in "Breath Charge" (Exercise 22). Now start to gently roll your neck. First roll it forward toward your chest. Then stretch it back a few times. Roll it a few times toward your left shoulder and then your right shoulder.

Go slowly. You may be holding more tension in this area than you realize—most of us have hidden knots of tension somewhere in the body, and this area is always one of the prime suspects.

There are two parts to the next exercise—one is more physical, and the second is more mental. Together they combine to relax and release the spine. Try both parts in tandem like a cat stretch first thing in the morning to help you start your day out right.

• *Exercise 24: Spine Straightening*

SHOULDER PULL. Breathing deeply, bring your right arm up and behind your head so that your right elbow is level to the crown of your head. Now touch the center of the top of your back with your right hand (it should be there already).

With your left hand, gently pull your right elbow to the left until you start to feel a very slight pull in your right shoulder. Hold the stretch to the count of six, then relax, dropping both arms gently to your sides. Repeat on the left side.

Keep repeating until you "get" each shoulder at least three times. Feel the difference? I find this tremendously relaxing to do at any time of the day, especially when I'm feeling tight. It's great to know that opening to your intuition also feels so good!

SILVER STRING PULL. This is best done sitting in an upright chair, keeping the spine as straight as possible. Continue to breathe deeply, holding your head perfectly upright. As you breathe, begin to concentrate on the top of your head and breathe into the area, visualizing a silver string at the very center and top of your head that is gently and subtly pulling you upward and aligning both your physical body and your personal energy field.

Now sense your spine, head, and neck gently straightening, ever so subtly "raising" your head. Concentrate on "seeing" your spine straighten, as you continue your deep, relaxed breathing, allowing yourself to relax into this process instead of stiffening with it.

When you feel more aligned, return to your daily tasks, or proceed to the next exercise.

THE RELAXATION/CONCENTRATION CONNECTION, OR IN THE STILL OF THE MIGHT

Relaxation, of course, is also the process of release. When we relax, we release the fears, doubts, anxieties, and even physical sensations that stand in the way of our receiving intuitive messages. Relaxing is really a process of reconditioning the mind, as well as the body. When we relax, we open ourselves to our own intuitive self by letting go of the mental baggage we carry in our everyday awareness.

We can find a good working example of this process in the world of the theater. How many times have you heard about performers who've experienced some kind of trauma right before taking to the stage, only to find themselves caught up in the "show must go on" tradition? Inspired to shift their focus away from their problems by the heat of the moment, such performers are able to go with the flow of their own performance, and not experience a break in that flow until the last curtain comes down. For each of us in all walks of life, some easy daily focusing can provide the same kind of wholehearted release and powerfully directed energy.

CONCENTRATION

After breathing, relaxing, and releasing, which are the "warming up" elements of focusing in, you really need to concentrate in order to complete your shift in focus from everyday awareness to the larger awareness of the flow. Concentration fine-tunes the focusing process—allowing you to tune out everyday thinking so you can more clearly tune in to your own inner wisdom.

Tuning in means stilling your mind, and anyone who's tried to do this for any length of time knows that's not always easy. Thoughts come rushing in, vying for your attention like demanding, cranky children. The harder you try to focus and find peace, the more demanding and persistent they can become. These thoughts can range from mundane reminders like, "I've got to pick up the dry cleaning," to nagging doubts such as, "What the hell am I doing here?" You might recall a recent or long forgotten memory, a lyric from an old song may pop into your mind, or you may hear a favorite melody or recall a scene from a movie or TV commercial.

You may even experience some anxiety as your left brain starts to feel left out. A fear of the unknown may grip you, as you leave the safety of logical left-brain thought, and move into a freer, floating awareness that feels new to you.

If you can relax into this feeling instead of fighting it, you'll experience a pleasant, flowing sensation much like that of drifting off to sleep. Trust it and know you're not entering dangerous waters. Enjoy the trip, knowing you can flow along for as long as you like, and then return at will. Continue to breathe deeply and rhythmically. Allow yourself to experience the flow and the impressions you receive from it without thinking it over or analyzing it at all.

When thoughts do come up, don't fight your left brain. Resistance only gives energy to what you're resisting, creating a vicious circle of mental static. On the other hand, breathing into whatever you're thinking or feeling allows you to simultaneously let it go and open to a higher state of awareness. As you bring your awareness back to your breath, you'll find your thoughts floating to the back of your mind.

WHOLE FOCUSING

Now that you're relaxed and your mind is stilled, you're ready to take in a much larger source of information. Concentration enables you to open to this information, whole mindedly letting awareness come to you without first mentally editing it. Remember, what you're after here is intuitive sense—a flowing awareness channeled through your right brain in a whole new language your everyday awareness must relearn. So it's very important to let the information itself flow when you first tune in—simply, let it all come.

Later you can always bring in the left hemisphere to assess, analyze, interpret, and file what you've received. But the most important reason for developing your concentration is to allow the mind to open and receive without interruption or criticism.

You can easily experience whole-minded concentration with the help of a classic method used by virtually anyone who's practiced meditation, from the most advanced yogi to the beginning student seeking stress reduction. It's a nonlinear exercise that's a natural for opening to the flow of intuition. You may find that one or two experiences with it are quite enough to acquaint you with the experience of receiving information whole and that afterward intuition flows to you in other ways. Or you may discover that this particular way of tuning in to nonlinear language is perfect for you, and you may want to keep doing it on a regular basis.

• *Exercise 25: Whole Focusing: An Exercise in Concentration and Contemplation*

Light a single white candle or select one beautiful fresh flower to focus on. Should you choose the candle, arrange to have a dimly lit environment so you can easily focus on its flame. In either case, the less visual or auditory distraction your environment contains, the better.

Bring your chosen object to your full attention, your full awareness. Really look at it. Drink it in with your eyes, letting any thoughts that arise float away as you concentrate on the candle or flower.

Keep focusing and breathing deeply and rhythmically. Your only goal is that of concentration. Try not to pay any attention to details. Simply breathe and take in the candle or flower as a whole. Continue whole focusing for at least two to five minutes.

After this exercise, you may feel very refreshed. Perhaps you may even have some kind of insight—a new idea, a hunch, or a new approach to a problem or situation. Or you may feel nothing. Never mind. Whatever the results, remember it's all part of the process, and your growing ability to concentrate without intellectual disruption is an important part of your overall developing inner fitness.

To increase your ability to access intuition through concentration—which is really a form of meditation—try the whole focusing variation described in the next exercise. It's an incredible energy booster. You'll probably feel relaxed afterward and perhaps even recharged. I do this exercise myself before tuning in to a client because it opens up the channels almost immediately. I've also incorporated it into my daily routine to continue keeping the channels open and to continue to develop clarity. Try adding it to your routine and see what just a few minutes a day can do for concentration, intuition, and creativity.

• *Exercise 26: Whole Focusing on Energy Points*

Instead of focusing on the candle or flower as you did in Exercise 25, choose one of three energy centers—your third eye, your heart, or your solar plexus—as your focal point. Breathe into the chosen point—again, the only goal being the focus itself. And, as before, do this for two to five minutes.

AFFIRMING THE CONNECTION

Our gentle but heightened focusing prepares the way for the second, more active form of concentration. This form of focusing fine-tunes and gives substance to our intuitive source—connection through words, creating a bridge between the seen and the unseen. The bridge is crossed through affirming, which literally means to "make firm." When we express our intent to connect with the intuitive source, we are "firming up" that connection, allowing it to manifest in the form of intuition flowing to us.

An affirmation can be thought or spoken aloud and can act as both a connector—connecting with your intuition, for example—and as a confirmer—substantiating your own perception of reality. Focused words truly are very powerful in helping to make your ideas and desires not only seem more real, but more fully realized.

Through affirmation you can make intuition more of a reality—and use it more in your everyday life. If you've tried the energy-balancing exercises (16–18), you are probably already aware of the power of verbal affirmation.

FIRMING UP YOUR REALITY

We make affirmations every day, whether we're aware of them or not. Our very lives are affirmations of the way we perceive reality. Just as perceiving the intuitive source hastens our alignment with it, we will positively align or negatively align with whatever we perceive as truth in our daily lives. Say or think you aren't intuitive or creative often enough, and that will be your reality.

Luckily, we've all also been known to make spontaneous positive affirmations when we say things like, "Things have a way of working out." Far from being mindless filler, such seemingly casual affirmations can truly produce creative solutions to sticky problems. For instance, when a marketing expert I know is facing a difficult situation, he often finds himself repeating, "I know there's a way!" To the amazement of his colleagues, he generally pulls a solution out of the proverbial hat—helped by an opening line that has already affirmed his connection to the answer he seeks.

Try the following exercise to make you more conscious of the power of affirmation in your life. Start becoming aware that some of what you've been told, or even say or think yourself, may not be the whole truth, but just a misperceived part of that truth.

• *Exercise 27: Word Power*

Lie or sit in a comfortable, distraction-free environment. Breathe deeply, slowly, and rhythmically, and start to think about your childhood. Recall a time when someone influential—a parent or teacher, or perhaps a friend—said something to you that eventually became an affirmation that you acted out. Perhaps it was, "How bright you are!" Or, "You know, you're not really very athletic." "You're not a joiner." "You're too sensitive." "I can always depend on you." "Your sister's the smart one—you're the pretty one."

Feel the pain of recognition? How close to your personal truth, past and present, are these affirmations? Do you still accept them as your personal truth? Know that you're now ready to accept, or not accept, any definition of your own reality at will.

Now look to your daily life, and observe how current affirmations are informing your sense of yourself. Become aware of statements, direct or indirect, made to you by your boss, loved ones, relatives, or others, as well as statements you find you are making yourself.

Do they reinforce the affirmations of your childhood? Do they represent a need for an improvement in your self-image? The more you can affirm positively in your everyday life, as well as in these exercises, the more powerful the positive reality of your enhanced intuition and creativity will be.

Your ability to create this reality is greatly improved by the positive structure you create for yourself, both in terms of your own affirmation routine and the affirmations of those around you. We all pick up the frequencies of others. That's why many people who are on the path of developing awareness choose to share experiences, and even exercises. In group settings, the positive energy is heightened, rewarding everyone involved with clearer information and increased awareness.

AFFIRMING RIGHT

Be aware at all times of the affirmations surrounding you and those emanating from you. You can probably do these exercises correctly for a few minutes every day, but if you spend the day's remainder in a doubtful, fearful, or otherwise negative state of mind, your earlier efforts will have practically gone to waste.

Think acceptance—of yourself and your connection to the intuitive source. Think acceptance, too, of the process involved in making and strengthening it. Then think repetition—of your positively affirming that connection, and you've got the perfect recipe for "affirming right."

FORMING YOUR OWN AFFIRMATIONS

If you haven't had much experience using affirmations, the concept may still seem a little strange or even a bit silly to you. Please remember, the following suggestions are just that: suggestions. Applying affirmations to your daily life can be so powerfully effective, I encourage you to try. But feel free to substitute the wording of your choice. And while saying affirmations out loud may give them the extra punch of "putting it out there in the real world," if it makes you feel uncomfortable, switch to thinking the words—i.e., affirming within.

It may help you to think of making affirmations as a way of allowing your mind to shift into a higher gear, in order to connect with a higher/larger awareness. This in turn, allows a greater percentage of whatever you seek to actually manifest in your life.

To create your own affirmations, there are really only two simple guidelines. First, remember to keep every statement you make in the present tense, as in the timeless essence of the flow. Second, remember to make every statement positive, for it's positive reality you're seeking to align with. In other words, know and affirm that the intuition, creativity, and inspired guidance you seek is already there, and you'll surely find it.

• *Exercise 28: Do-It-Yourself Affirmation Guide*

As you stay in the present tense and remain positive, you must also keep in mind that you're already connected to, and in the process of receiving, whatever you're affirming. That's why most conscious affirmations start with the phrase, "I am" (or "I'm").

"I am" is the open sesame of affirmation, which is why saying or thinking, "I'm so dumb" or "I'll never figure this out," can powerfully influence the outcome of any situation. Instead, you'll want to follow "I am" with a statement of the most positive and open-ended possibilities. This, of course, is an affirmation of the virtually limitless power of your intuitive self.

Try, "I am now open to" (or "I'm opening to," "I'm now open to," "I open myself to," etc.) an unlimited flow of awareness/creativity/intuition" . . . or whatever it is you personally desire to affirm.

Always remember that the more fully you can accept and affirm your own intuitive source-connection, the more you can avail yourself of your own unlimited awareness. Once you have stated your desire or intent, know that its seed for manifestation has been planted; then—let it go! You've set into motion the powerful mechanics of the law of cause and effect. What you sow, you surely shall reap. You can keep your practice gentle but steady as you allow your intuitive self to process and nurture your verbalized intent. The more willing you are to trust this dynamic, the more quickly your answers will begin to flow from the source of intuition within toward your everyday awareness.

VISUALIZATION: GETTING THE WHOLE PICTURE

Focusing gently opens us to experiencing the intuitive source. Affirmation actively puts our intent into motion. Visualization, the technique that allows us to both receive and project clear mental images, is the final element we need to strengthen our intuition reception. Within those images lies a wealth of information. Although different techniques appeal to different individuals, visualizing is perhaps the most powerful intuitive source-connector of all.

We all know firsthand, from a lifetime of evenings spent in darkened movie houses, the power that words and pictures possess when they are used in tandem. A movie may start from a screenplay, but the experience of words and images working closely together is more than twice as vivid as dialogue alone. Visualization enhances the intent to connect that is expressed by affirmation and multiplies the power of that intent manyfold.

Visualization, like affirmation, is a powerful everyday reality shaper. Just as verbal affirmations determine our perception, conscious mental visualization will also shape and strengthen the way we view our lives. The same bridge between the seen and unseen exists even when we use everyday expressions like "picture this" to describe a plan or a project that is eventually brought to life.

Sports psychology and medicine have known this for decades. In the 1920s a medical study proved that when patients concentrated on picturing a muscle move, it resulted in the actual experience of physical movement. Today, athletes use visualization to improve performance as a matter of course.

For instance, many Olympic skaters have said they may spend the final hour before a competition focusing their attention in from the outer reaches of the stadium to their program, and, finally, to the ice itself. Only when their vision is focused squarely on their best possible performance, and away from the audience and judging panel, are they ready to do their best. High jumpers are trained to substitute the naturally daunting mental picture of the high hurdle with the much more constructive image of themselves sailing over the pole. The success of such visualization methods has been verified again and again in articles about sports psychologists and in the winning performances of the athletes they advise.

Later we'll try some visual tuning exercises to add to your growing repertoire, but first let's examine the important role visualizing already plays in your everyday life.

MEMORIES AND
IMAGINATION

The prospect of visualization can be intimidating to people who feel more kinship with a little voice inside them or with feelings than they do with visual images. Nevertheless, there are two basic sources of visual imagery that naturally flow through your life and that you avail yourself of each and every day.

Their names? Memory and imagination. Who has not conjured up the face of a far-off loved one or the sight of last summer's gentle ocean shimmering with golden sunlight? Remembered visual images are often the most vivid substitute for the real thing, and the daydreams that overcome us in our everyday lives are often as richly visual as reality itself. It's quite easy to see the perfect house or car of your dreams, and certainly any children with imaginary playmates can tell you exactly what their friends look like, down to the last freckle.

Remembering and imagining give us spontaneous visualizing workouts that can clearly tune us in to our own intuition. Every memory you experience confirms your innate power of visualization, and each flight of fancy you embark upon displays your potential for receiving powerful imagery from the intuitive source.

For our purposes the major difference between the ongoing flow of memory and imagination is that memories are images of events that have passed, whereas imagination pictures what has yet to come. In some cases, the imagining process creates pictures that are meant to live on only in the mind. In others, the process unveils events that do indeed come to pass. Within the context of the time/space continuum, the phenomenon of seeing realized experiences in advance is like going back to the future to access a memory of your forgotten past. Never mind if that seems confusing. On the intuitive path, paradox abounds; and certainly no more so than in the process of visualization.

What are you to make of the imaginings that sometimes do and sometimes don't materialize? And how are you to tell the difference between the two types? Don't fear—you'll learn how in Chapter 5 (page 83). For now, simply be aware of the important practical role your imagination may already be playing in your everyday life and of the fluency in visual language you've already developed from a lifetime of remembering.

The next exercise will help you explore how easy it is to access a visual image, to sense all the rich information that initial picture contains, and to see for yourself how closely linked other kinds of impressions are to visualization.

• *Exercise 29: Image Power*

Find a comfortable place that is free of distractions. Close your eyes, and begin to take deep and even breaths as you conjure up a favorite, powerful scene from nature—the ocean, the mountains, the desert at dawn.

See how easily and vividly that image comes to you, and once you have experienced it as a whole begin to explore the richness of its details. What colors do you see? Are there any shapes or visual textures you never noticed before? What particular elements of the natural setting give you pleasure, and what does the light tell you about the time of day? How does the air feel? What other sensory impressions do the details of your picture evoke?

Next, add your imagination. What would you like to be doing in this scene, or what are you doing in it? Get a sense of where things could go in the scene you have created. What do your thoughts tell you about yourself, about this image, or about what you would like to be doing?

Good. You have just used memory, daydreaming, and imagination to give you visually channeled information about yourself. Did you notice any difference between each sensation? More likely both the remembered and imagined parts of the scene had an equally rich reality. As you use visual images and other sensations to fine-tune your intuitive reception in Chapter 5, you'll find that accessing intuition is quite similar to reminding yourself of a particularly vivid memory, and then exploring the insights that richly experienced visual picture has to offer you.

Please remember that visualization, like the total experience of developing intuition, is a process that evolves gradually. Those feelings, little internal voices, and other sense impressions that may come to you more readily are, in fact, what I like to call *previsual visualizations*. They are the stepping stones that will lead you to getting the big picture if you just go with the flow.

As more and more information starts coming into view it also helps to keep this in mind. Intuitive impressions of any kind do not tell us what to do or not to do. They can allow us to see, or otherwise sense, certain events or trends, and then, what is likely to happen if a particular trend is allowed to develop. We, ourselves, must decide what to do about whatever our intuition shows us. Now, on with the show!

• *Exercise 30: Developing Your Own Picture*

Spend a few minutes doing a whole focusing or energy-balancing exercise as well as some deep breathing. When you feel relaxed and open, make sure your eyes are closed.

Then visualize a blank white screen.

Continue breathing into the image as you picture that screen in all its detail. Maybe you're in a private screening room, or in front of your own TV. It is on this screen that your intuitive self will play the "movie of your future."

When the screen is bright and very clear, invoke your intuitive self by saying or thinking something like, "I now open myself to my intuitive self. I allow whatever it wants to show me about my future to appear now."

Now you are ready to put yourself on the screen. First, flow with images of yourself until one particularly meaningful and familiar image comes to mind. If you do not receive a visual image right away, playfully flow with a particularly important feeling, phrase, scent, or any other impression until it transforms itself into a vision. Are you sitting in a children's playroom surrounded by toys? in an office, hunched over a desk? Do you see yourself as a cat, a swan, an oak tree?

When that first image is bright and clear, flow with it, as you did in the previous exercise, and see what new images and situations develop from that first source image. Do children come into the playroom to play with you? Do the piles of papers on the desk grow and grow until you're barricaded behind them? Is the swan gliding effortlessly toward an exciting new shore? Is the cat begging to be let outside for a good run?

Keep on flowing until the vision is complete. Don't edit or judge; just see what images come up. Later you can use the Visual/Feeling Checklist in Chapter 5 (page 93) to interpret whatever symbols your images might present and pinpoint their message.

What did the images tell you about the way you perceive your reality? Can you take any action as a result of what you've seen? How would you like to revise the picture of your life so it reflects your desired reality? Just as you received images from your intuitive self about your life and its future, you can also project images you want to see about your own inner, and eventually outer, reality.

Run the movie again. This time you are the director. Add new images that shift the visual balance so it more accurately and positively illustrates your projected desire. Rerun the movie periodically. What has changed in the movie and in your day-to-day life? What has stayed the same? What visual elements would you like to add? Add them!

Now you've explored the three different means for clearly tuning in to—and strengthening—your intuitive source-connection. For most people, they work best in the sequence presented here. But once you're familiar with the effects of each, you may find that a slightly different—or entirely different—sequence or selection works best for you. Over time, you may also find that you're better at particular techniques and that some work better for you in certain situations or when you're trying to access specific kinds of information. Follow your own guidance just as you follow the flow of intuition, periodically checking in with your intuitive self to make sure you're making that connection as clearly and strongly as possible.

CHAPTER FIVE

PUTTING IT ALL TOGETHER

Now that you've learned the basics, you have all the practical tools you need to begin to receive and apply intuitive information. You're ready now to fine-tune your new skills and put them all together by learning how to "tune in," "get the picture," and interpret what you've got.

How exactly will you accomplish this? Well, first, you'll learn how to develop your natural sixth sense by developing the five you use every day. Next you'll try some easy techniques for learning to use those five senses in an altered—and enlightened—way. Your newly heightened senses will start picking up the pieces of your right-brained puzzle, and your budding intuitive sense will really go to work as you start to develop those little bits and pieces into whole, clear pictures—complete with accompanying story. Bit by bit, whole picture by whole picture, you'll come to know the whole truth of your own insights, creativity, intuition, and guidance.

Sound complicated? Relax! It's easier than you think. Remember to always warm up first (doing some neck rolls, deep breathing, and whole focusing for a bit), and then simply enjoy.

The first exercise, "Mind's Eye Imaging," builds on the visualizing ability you began to develop in Chapter 4. This is a really fun technique, and can be practiced alone or with a partner or even a small group. The technique of mind's eye imaging exercises your intuitive visual muscle, strengthening your ability to receive intuitive information and see the picture clearly in any situation.

• Exercise 31: Mind's Eye Imaging

As always, start by getting comfortable in a tranquil, nondistracting environment, and warm up as suggested earlier. Next choose a magazine or an illustrated book (coffee table books work especially well) from your personal collection. After you've warmed up, thumb through the book or magazine with your eyes closed, and randomly let your hand rest on a page. Then affirm (either to yourself or aloud), something like, "I now open my mind to the picture before me. I now allow the picture to develop in my mind."

In your mind's eye, see the white screen you first evoked in Exercise 30, "Developing Your Own Picture." Some people imagine themselves in an actual private screening room. Others see the white screen as a TV screen. Use whatever works for you. As you breathe into the image, gently allow any critical mental back talk to flow toward the periphery of your awareness and then disperse.

Next focus on the page your hand is touching, and let a picture develop on your inner screen. As always, allow whatever images that emerge to fully evolve without questioning, analyzing, editing, or judging. Explore these images, feelings, or other sensory details and note whatever comes up, paying special attention to your first impressions.

What similarities can you find between your picture and the one in the magazine? Is there a connection between colors, shapes, feelings, or moods? Did you see a fragment of one of the details of the image? Was your picture a simpler, perhaps symbolic version of the magazine picture? Did a feeling come along with your inner image and give you more information about the magazine picture? Remember, the point of this exercise is not to get it absolutely "right."

The kinds of correspondences you perceive will tell you a lot about your personal intuitive language. You'll eventually learn how to fill out flashes using this language and to translate those flashes into fully realized insights and solutions. A look at others' experiences will help give you insights about your own. When one student of mine practiced mind's eye imaging, his inner screen revealed a picture of a lemon grove. The magazine illustration in question turned out to be a group of trees on a sunny day, and my student learned that for him lemons were a symbol for sunshine. In another class, we tried the first group variation described in Exercise 32. This time, the photo was one of a very peculiarly shaped vase of flowers, and one student instantly imaged a picture of a smoked ham hanging from a rafter. We all laughed when we realized that the ham was identical in shape to the flower vase. And my student made an important discovery about how his intuition transmits messages to him.

You may perceive a color, a type of lighting, a feeling, or a sound that somehow represents the picture you're tuning in to, or you may be one of the lucky ones who naturally receives accurate, complete pictures the first time out. Whatever your personal results, don't edit or criticize. Log in your impressions, especially your first impressions, and see what kinds of patterns come up.

If it's at all practical for you to do mind's eye imaging with a partner or in a small group, make a point of trying the next two variations of the exercise. In a group situation you also have a chance to explore your ability to send or project visual images, as well as sharpen your ability to receive them. Secondly, the focused energy of groups greatly amplifies intuitive images and energy for all concerned. The experience can be positively exhilarating!

- *Exercise 32: Mind's Eye Imaging with a Partner or a Small Group*

After you have completed your warm-ups, designate one member of the group as the sender. Have this person select a picture from a magazine or book. Then have everyone visualize a blank white screen in the middle of their foreheads.

The sender will transmit the image to everyone else, just as a television signal is sent out to various TV sets from a broadcasting station. Meanwhile, the receiving partners will be seeing the image appear on their own screens.

Before you begin, make sure everyone's screens are blank. Then have the sender focus on the chosen image first by staring at it and then visualizing it on his or her mind's eye screen. Have the sender concentrate on sending that image out to the rest of the group.

If you are the sender, try breathing into the middle of your forehead, consciously feeling and seeing the image going outward in a beam of light. If you are a receiver, watch what develops on your own white screen, just as you did in the first mind's eye exercise.

Note your impressions, especially your first impressions. Then switch roles until everyone gets a chance to send. Again, don't worry about what you "get," or about who sends or receives more clearly. Everyone has natural strengths, which can only be discovered through exploration.

• *Exercise 33: Nature Imaging*

Choose who will send the image and who will receive it, as you did in the previous exercise. This time, instead of looking in a book or magazine, have the sender transmit a familiar scene from nature to the rest of the group. The natural world could be seen as the ultimate primal picture, and any time you send or receive its vistas you have the bonus of an extra strong and clear energy signal that boosts the vividness of the image.

After warming up, have the projector visualize a blank white screen while the other group members do the same. When all the screens are fully in place, ask the sender to project an entire scene from nature to the rest of the group. This scene could be a house on the ocean, a field of horses, a desert sunrise. Get as creative as you want. Concentrate on projecting the scene in all its detail. Is there an old pump behind the beach house? A bubbling brook running through the field? Are tiny rabbits hopping under the huge desert sky?

As in the previous exercise, the rest of the group will see what appears in their own minds' eye, note their impressions, and then take turns sending out scenes of their own.

It's not unusual in this exercise for each receiver to receive slightly different images—which contribute to the whole picture. For example, when I led one group in this exercise, the image projected was that of a country house. At first, the images the receivers sensed on their inner screens seemed to conflict. One student saw the shade of a thicket of trees develop on her inner screen. Another saw a low stone wall. A third experienced a very happy and serene feeling.

As it turned out, these seemingly different impressions didn't conflict at all. This particular house was shaded and did have a stone wall in back, and it was the source of many fond memories for the sender. All three of these impressions represented pieces of the original scene, and each complemented it quite accurately, without precisely duplicating it. Intuition, it must be remembered, is a language of equivalents. As you learn to go with your own flow of visual, feeling, and other sense impressions, you'll eventually come up with your own equivalent of the big picture.

TALKING PICTURES

Earlier I said that pictures more than doubled the power of your verbal affirmations. Well, it works the other way around, too. Words make intuitive pictures more specific and easier to interpret as a whole. In the process of narrowing and defining a scene, words also deepen and open it up, allowing you to see and understand it more fully.

Spontaneously talking out the pictures you receive helps you to pinpoint their details. And every detail you narrow in on will open your picture up to receive yet another detail, and so on, creating a momentum that will develop your mental picture and your intuitive self-confidence. As a form of affirmation, talking out also vastly improves your ability to interpret developing pictures and make connections between the imagery you perceive and the information it contains.

It's natural to feel somewhat bashful about spontaneously talking out your pictures. At some point, all of us have been told to think before we speak. Now is certainly not the time to give in to those feelings, however. Especially as you're beginning to learn how to develop your intuition, it's very important not to think first, but just go with the flow of describing what you see as you see it, even if the images aren't quite clear yet. This will help them develop more clearly. I promise! Here's how it works.

• *Exercise 34: Talking Pictures*

Warm up in a comfortable place, and try mind's eye imaging, with a partner or on your own. When you reach a plateau in your image reception, spontaneously describe what you are seeing, without wondering whether what you're saying is right or wrong.

If you're working with a partner, ask your partner for confirmation (in the case of the ham and the vase, your partner would have said, "Yes, that's the same shape as the image I'm projecting"). If you are working alone, simply ask your intuitive self the same questions. It will give you the answers that you need, and your own mental verbalization will spark the same focusing and opening process.

Let's go back to the case of the vase and the ham again to watch this technique in action. Put yourself in the place of my student. Now that you've described your initial picture of a ham and know that it represents a shape, your inner screen will open to receive more information. At this point, you might see a shiny white surface or bits of yellow light above the shape. Or you might feel that the shape has a cool smooth surface. You may even put all of these fragments together and develop the picture of a table lamp.

Again, ask for confirmation by telling what you see as you see it, without judging or editing. In this case, your partner might tell you the object is not a table lamp, but that it does sit on a table, and it does have a ceramic base. This specific, focused information might inspire you to revise the image in your mind. Perhaps you'd even pick up a delicious fresh fragrance, and suddenly discover the true identity of the picture.

Always continue this process of spontaneous give and take until any inner image is complete. Record your experience to find more patterns and connections later. With practice, you'll find you can even receive and interpret images and feelings quite fluidly, translating from one idiom to another almost simultaneously in your mind. Even though it takes time and practice to develop this level of proficiency, you may even now experience the occasional flash when symbol and interpretation seem to come to you together.

Once you get good (and it won't take long), try the following variation on talking pictures as you go about your day. It's especially useful whenever you're trying to get more information than meets the eye, say at an auction, or when you're trying to size up a potential date.

- *Exercise 35: X-ray Vision, or
  Seeing Between the Lines*

First, create a blank white screen in your mind's eye and mentally ask your intuitive self to fill the screen with images of the reality of a given situation. You can do this with your eyes open.

Once the fragments and symbols are present, mentally ask your intuitive self, "What else is in the picture?" or, "Show me more." It shouldn't take long to complete an X-ray picture of the situation.

What sort of information did you access? Keep developing the picture until you're satisfied, talking it out with your larger self as you go along. The more precisely you've learned to pinpoint specific images in mind's eye imaging, the more precisely you'll be able to find the practical answers you need.

Here's a fun phone exercise to practice that develops your imaging prowess while providing practical information.

• *Exercise 36: Picture Phone*

As your caller speaks, take a few deep breaths, focus on your mind's eye, and see the inner blank white screen that will allow you to turn your phone into a "picture phone." You may also think to yourself, "I'm now tuning in to the picture and opening to the images on the screen."

See what images develop. For example, try to see what the person is wearing, and look for colors and moods. You may get images or feelings of "hot" or "cold," "up" or "down," for example. These could relate either to the colors being worn or what your subject is feeling at that moment. A color that you see in a flash could also contain a symbolic message. Check the energy color references in Chapter 3 for possible interpretation.

Listen to your caller's voice: What does it tell you? What images does it evoke? Can you sense your caller's physical environment? If it's one you're already well acquainted with, try to tune in to what may be different about it that day. Perhaps it contains a new piece of furniture. Maybe the room is especially clean or untidy, or is in some other way changed. Try to casually obtain confirmation by asking how your caller is feeling, or simply by asking what's new, after you've gotten the picture.

THE VISUAL/FEELING CHECKLIST

By using talking pictures and mind's eye imaging, you've probably gotten to know something about your personal intuitive style. You may have had visual flashes that give you a feeling, or you may hear sounds that tell you something important about what you feel. Intuitive pictures tend to fill in as one sense impression or detail flows into another until the full message is complete.

Checking in on all the different messages a single picture may contain by checking in with all your senses will go a long way toward interpreting those raw bits and pieces of intuitive information. The Visual/Feeling Checklist is an easy, effective tool to use along with talking pictures to develop and interpret your intuitive pictures. Many people find that talking pictures is best to help flesh out those important first impressions, and the checklist is terrific for interpreting and enhancing pictures already in progress. Try it out, get to know it, and feel free to refine it according to your needs.

As you receive images via any of the techniques in this chapter, ask yourself the following questions, each time checking in with your intuitive self for more details.

VISUAL/FEELING CHECKLIST

1. Are there people in this picture? How many people are there? Who are they? What are they doing? Are you there? Is someone or something entering the scene or leaving it? Is this person moving quickly or slowly? What does this emphasis mean to you? Example: If you are in the process of hiring a new employee, you may tune in and see one candidate moving quickly out in front of the pack. This information could help you discover the winning candidate and also indicate that the one you choose will really take the lead on the job.

2. What are the feelings of the people in the scene? If you are in the scene, how do you feel? How do others feel? Is the general feeling of the scene lively, friendly, slow, quiet, tense, staid, youthful? Does it feel—literally or figuratively—hot, cold, wet, dry?

Example: Perhaps you see yourself in the middle of London on a foggy day. Even amidst the cold and wet, though, you feel truly buoyant. This might be your sign that there is joy just on the other side of the big gray cloud you've been living under.

3. Are you seeing an image in the foreground of the picture or in the background? Is this a wide angle image or is it a closeup? What does the focus of the picture emphasize and deemphasize?

Example: If there are adults in the background, and a roomful of kids' toys and clothes in the foreground, that could mean you will soon be spending a good deal of your time with children.

4. What are the colors in the picture? Are they bright? muted? pale? What do these colors symbolize?

Example: A vibrant blue airplane could mean someone's about to take off creatively. For more color symbolism, see Chapter 3.

5. What's the environment of your picture? Is it an outdoors scene? indoors? Is it set in the city? the country? the city you live in? a foreign country? What can you see or sense at the periphery of the image? mountains? a grove of olive trees? ocean? Could the scene itself be a symbol?

Example: As you tune in, you start to see the ocean clearly. The ocean often symbolizes the unconscious, and so could indicate your own process of exploring your personal inner depths or a journey you're about to take to the seashore.

Note: Here, as with other impressions, keep records of the kinds of things that come up in order to find personal patterns and what significance they hold for you.

6. What do you hear in the scene? Are people talking? What

are they saying? Are the voices angry or gentle? Is there any other sound—a whistling wind, a waterfall, bird song, the sound of traffic, a buzz, or a hum? If there is music, what kind of music is it? a traditional war song? a love song? a nursery rhyme?

Example: You suddenly hear the song phrase, "I'll be seeing you in all the old familiar places . . ." It could mean the scene is taking place in the 1940s, or it could be giving you information about a lost loved one who is coming back into your life. Use the other questions on the checklist to tell you which meaning might apply.

7. What are your feelings as you tune in—how are you responding? Are you anxious, joyful, at peace? Are you feeling surprised, helpful, disappointed about the outcome of the situation?

Example: When I was tuning in to one client, I had such a feeling of happiness I almost jumped for joy, and knew the situation we were examining would turn out positively. With another client who'd just been unfairly fired, I felt his shock, and then a slight pain in my heart as I realized he was going to have some heartbreaking near-misses with other work opportunities. But then I felt a sort of calm after the storm, followed by a feeling that clinched a sense of resolution, as I experienced a happy internal explosion, like Fourth of July fireworks. Happily, I could tell him that things would not only calm down—crises usually do—but, in fact, his career would eventually be flying sky high.

Note: It's important when you get any feeling, but

especially a negative one, to see or feel what comes next so you can not only fill out the picture, but come to a better sense of resolution.

8. Are you experiencing any other physical sensations: textures, tastes, smells? There may be a very strong floral scent, or the smell of the ocean, or garbage.

Example: Smelling a fire could clue you in to an incendiary situation. Sensing a bitter taste might deliver an intuitive pun, indicating that an event will leave a bad taste in your mouth.

9. What time is it? Is there something about the lighting in your picture that can tell you the time of day? Is there a clock in the scene? If you get a number, you'll have a great opportunity to pin your intuitive self down. Ask what the number means. Three months? Three days? Three years in the past, the present, or the future? Are there furnishings, clothing, a season of the year, or forms of transportation (horse and buggy, automobile) that give you a clue?

Note: Since time is a continuum, it's one of the hardest types of information to pinpoint and develop. You may find as you log things that certain feelings simply mean "sooner" or "later" to you. The best way to narrow down that elusive time frame is to keep asking your intuitive self specific questions: Ask how many days, months, or years you've moved into the past or future. Continue to ask until you're satisfied.

If you get a picture unaccompanied by a time sense, it may take that first impression a long time to materialize. When I first met my husband I "tuned in" and saw him working on a children's project. For six years I continually saw that project. Ultimately, what I'd seen materialized when he found himself working on both children's television shows and advertising for kids.

After you get familiar with the checklist, you'll notice you get very clear frequent information in some areas and less in others. That's good! Using the Visual/Feeling Checklist not only helps you to fill in your pictures. It also helps you pinpoint your own personal intuitive style. For instance, one of my clients always perceives information as events going on in rooms. Another always perceives information as a movie. Still another habitually hears people talking and develops images to fill out the scene of these overheard conversations.

Eventually, you may want to drop some of the questions from your routine as you discover the kinds of perceptions that guide you most clearly and strongly to more detailed information. You're probably also likely to find that by tuning in to one particular sense or sensation—smelling a particular scent, hearing a certain song, feeling a sense of heat, for example—and allowing it to flow, it will naturally lead you to a picture rich with all kinds of sensory details.

Pay especially close attention to the feelings that accompany any picture: They work hand in hand and can hold the key to the impressions you receive. For instance, a student of mine was talking to his brother when he had the very strong sensation his brother was going to be involved with a nightclub.

He asked him if this was a possibility, and his brother

said that he had been approached to consult in such a business. As my student tuned in further, he began to see a rosy color and started to feel warm and happy, which showed him that this project was likely to happen and that it would be very positive.

Take special note of resurfacing pictures—they're the most likely to occur in your real life. Just as conscious picturing of the same scene or idea will strengthen its reality, images repeatedly making appearances without any effort on your part have a very strong chance of being realized. Conversely, at some point, you may try to receive information about a future project or situation and you won't be able to see yourself doing it at all. There could be a message there for you, too.

Now that you've checked your intuitive perceptions, how do you make sense of them? Here's a perfect example of how the Visual/Feeling Checklist helped one client. She used it to combine the bits of data she received through her different senses into a single clear and ultimately very useful picture.

My client had been trying to determine what was going on with a corporate client of hers. She started tuning in with her intuition when she felt uncertain about her continuing business relationship with the company. The first image she received was of a huge, bright graphic design, which seemed so loud and wild it almost blinded her mind's eye. She had a feeling it represented the general tone of the company, but she wasn't quite sure if it suggested dynamism or confusion.

As she went through the Visual/Feeling Checklist, the phrase "Glory Hallelujah" sprang into the picture. These words didn't seem to go with the picture at all, so she focused on them until they developed into the lyrics of the famous Civil War song, "The Battle Hymn of the Republic."

My client went through an entire verse in her mind in an attempt to find any possible significance. The South had nothing to do with her picture, nor did religion or the Civil War period in history. Suddenly, as she finished the verse, she came to the realization that the song was really pointing to a corporate civil war—the power struggle that was going on within the company itself. The original picture she'd received now made perfect sense. The company she was working with was indeed both energetic and confused. Each piece of the picture really confirmed and helped interpret the information provided by the other.

Note: If you find yourself receiving a multiplicity of images and sensations, and it all seems too confusing, tune in to those which seem stronger and brighter. Those will be your most likely message-providing candidates.

GETTING THE STORY

From time immemorial, we have been intrigued by the details of other people's lives. The ancient, ongoing art of storytelling demonstrates our primal need. With the help of finely tuned pictures, words, and all kinds of intuitive feelings, you can tune in to the true stories of anyone you choose (including your own, of course). Storytelling, intuitive style, will help you fine-tune this skill and develop your overall inner knowledge. You've probably already practiced story-telling whenever you've read a particularly evocative passage in a book. Who can read their favorite authors without mentally filling in the details of a particularly vivid and beloved scene? Furthering the story yourself and taking off from a narrative master's setting is not only fun, it's easy.

If you've ever whiled away time on a movie or grocery line creating lives for the interesting strangers you see around you, and thought, "Gee, I wonder what his story is," then taking that process one step further and creating your own setting for intuitive storytelling will be easy, too.

• *Exercise 37: Storytelling*

Focus on someone who is waiting on line or on someone sitting at another table in a restaurant—or choose any stranger or acquaintance who inspires you. Create your white screen. Obviously, if you're in a public place you can't do the full warm-up. Just breathe deeply a few times and continue breathing into the screen you've visualized in your forehead.

Next, talk to your intuitive self about your subject. A casual question along the lines of "I wonder what her story is?" will affirm your connection with the answer and send information through. Or, think to yourself something like, "I'm tuning in to the intuitive source and getting the whole story." Use the Visual/Feeling Checklist and talking pictures as the information starts to flow.

Once it does, try asking your intuitive self pinpointing questions. For example, "Is this a passionate person, or a cool cucumber type? Is she or he happy or sad? Is she or he cynical or optimistic? liberal or conservative? in a relationship or single? a native or an out-of-towner? a pet owner? a parent? The list of questions is infinite. Let yourself flow with whatever seems to be in the proper line of questioning at the time and continue to flow with the pictures, feelings, or other insights you begin to conjure up.

It's natural to wonder how much of your "story" goes beyond the obvious. It's easy to get certain impressions about a person whose coat is covered with cat hairs or about someone who looks sad and bedraggled. Plain old common sense, you say? Well, the point of developing your uncommon sense is to integrate it with your everyday skills of elementary deduction. When you answer everyday questions you always have the option of going for the most obvious solutions. Developing intuition trains you to see more clearly, both in terms of what's staring you in the face, and in terms of the unseen answers below the surface, to give you the complete picture of any situation.

The ultimate in intuitive integration is realizing that whatever answer you're seeking is already inherent in the question. This bypasses having to tune in to a question or problem altogether and allows you to go straight to the answer or solution. Professional intuitive counselors use this technique all the time.

- *Exercise 38: Finding the Answer in the Questions*
  Part 1

First, warm up. Then have a friend or friends write a question on a slip of paper. Make sure each person writes down his or her own question. Phrase questions to avoid yes or no answers. For instance, instead of asking, "Will I go to Bermuda this winter?" ask, "What will happen with my winter vacation?" Tell friends to concentrate on the question and its desired answer while they write out their questions. This will sharpen your focus and help you to tune in to the information they need.

If you're working with a group, have your friends fold their completed questions in half, so that the handwriting is hidden, and place them in a container from which they can be blindly selected one at a time. If you're working with one partner, don't worry about anonymity. I've even used this technique to answer questions for myself.

By now, we're all familiar with the stereotypic image of a turbaned swami holding a written question to his forehead. Well don't laugh, but you may be employing that technique yourself! Select one of the handwritten questions and hold it to your third eye energy center—or, if you prefer, to your heart or solar plexus. Experiment with all three, because most people find they are more receptive in one of the three locations. Also, you may find that for different kinds of questions you bring the paper automatically to a different chakra.

Don't even try to tune in to the hidden question that is written on the paper. Tune in to the answer instead. Say to your intuitive self something like, "I now allow the answer to unfold." Watch the picture develop on your white screen if you're using the third eye point, feel it developing through your emotions if you're holding the question to your heart, and experience the answer as a gut sense of knowing if you have chosen the solar plexus.

When impressions start to come up, ask for confirmation from your intuitive self and, of course, from the person you're tuning in to. As always, try talking it out immediately, taking off from your first impressions and allowing them to flow into a more complete answer. Then use the Visual/Feeling Checklist to pinpoint information. (Note: Don't worry if the senses you experience are different at various points than those listed here. This is only a general guideline.)

- *Exercise 39: Finding the Answer in the Questions Part 2*

You can use a technique similar to Exercise 38 with questions posed over the telephone. (In this case, the questions aren't hidden from you, but the face of the questioner is.) This is a little more advanced, but there are people who respond intuitively more strongly to the sound of a voice. It's certainly easy enough to try in the course of your day to find out. Again, tune in with and to your white screen, see what comes up, and don't let it bother you if this method produces fewer results. You can also try having someone ask you a question face to face. These last two variations are probably quite similar to what you do when you sit around talking with friends or family anyway. They simply provide a deeper, more informed way of providing people you care about with guided answers and a technique you can really apply very unobtrusively and practically in daily life.

The next exercise offers a way of reading objects and will introduce you to the technique I use as a professional intuitive counselor. The ancient and timeless craft of psychometry uses a very basic technique to achieve powerful results in our contemporary world. Psychometry will provide you with highly guided information about others and should be practiced with a partner or in a group.

• *Exercise 40: Psychometry*

Do your warm-ups. Then ask your partner or the first group member to give you a metal object that touches his or her body constantly: a ring, watch, other item of jewelry, or even a well-used key. A metal watch with a leather band is fine; so is a piece of jewelry that also contains precious stones. It's also best, though not absolutely crucial, to use an object no one but your subject has worn or used.

Hold the metal object in your hand as you instruct your partner to ask you a question that does not have a yes or no answer, just as you did in the last exercise. Next, tune in to your mental screen or feelings and concentrate on the answer as you pick up on the personal energy that has naturally been transferred to the object in your hands. The metal acts as a powerful conductor, as Ben Franklin demonstrated with his famous kite and key.

Talk out the answers you receive with your partner or the group without judging or editing, paying special attention to first impressions. Ask for confirmation, then keep on going until the answer feels complete.

EVERYDAY INTUITIVE OPTIONS

It's easy to check in with your intuition as you go about your day. Whether you need a quick answer to an urgent question or simply want to integrate intuition with your normal work routine, you can do so freely and unobtrusively whenever you feel the urge.

• *Exercise 41: The One-Minute Intuitive*

This technique is specifically designed for sizing up any situation in a flash. Use it whenever you need it—during your work, socializing, traveling, or any other situation where time is of the essence. Warm up by taking a few deep breaths, and focus on your white screen. Quickly ask a question of your intuitive self, and check your very first impression of the answer with the Visual/Feeling Checklist. For instance, before you open the door to an important meeting you might want to ask, "Which tone should I take for my presentation?" This technique will help you to make an uncommonly educated choice in any situation.

Your intuition will always offer invaluable, instant insight on how to gently realign an approach or make a decision that will be just right and just what you need at the time.

There are moments in your life when you have much more time to tune in to an enlightened answer. Do all the warm-ups you need before you visualize your white screen or whole focus on your feelings to see what impressions you receive. In addition to any of the previous exercises, you might want to use a technique that I personally enjoy. Try writing a letter to your intuitive self as though you were addressing an advice column. You're likely to get an illuminating answer to any of your questions—from the most mundane to your most soul searching. Or try talking it out loud—posing your intuitive self a question—then answering! (To save any pearls of inner wisdom, try taping your inner conversation.)

The more regularly you can maintain a balanced program of inner workouts—especially if it includes deep breathing, energy balancing, whole focusing and, of course, a record of your impressions, the more fine–tuned and immediately available your intuition will be.

PROCESSING:
PUTTING IT ALL TOGETHER

Tuning in to and getting your answers on a regular basis, you must remember, is a process. Even when you don't think you're getting anywhere, in fact you really are. For instance, when I first began to develop my intuitive ability, I had a vision of myself as a ballerina spinning merrily. One of my teachers had a telling interpretation of that image: He told me it meant that at the time I was "moving," or growing, very quickly, and I should really enjoy the spin, because eventually a time would come when I would appear not to be moving at all. The time did come, and I indeed felt like I was stuck in molasses.

When your development seems so slow you feel as if you're making no progress, it's important to remember that the process of developing your intuition takes place on many different levels of awareness. So no matter where you think you are, on a deeper level you're still learning and absorbing.

As you open, and continue to open, to your inner wisdom, you'll extend your growing awareness beyond mere data gathering. Slowly but surely, you'll also be evolving empathy—the ability to identify with and find the feelings contained in the facts. Added to your quick-tuning skills, the ability to empathize will allow you to more deeply understand and fully complete the big picture. Developing empathy does take longer and is a more subtle process. But you've already begun the journey to inner wisdom. When you're feeling frustrated, know your empathy is probably strengthening and deepening at that very moment.

Whenever you're tuning in to your own or other people's questions, be sure to look for emotional meaning in any answer you intuit, so that you can apply that answer in a caring way. Think of the difference between a sympathetic doctor and a cold just-the-facts technician. Always ask your intuitive self, as you're receiving impressions, "How can I use this information to help?" Guidance and accurate information received together make for a total picture—wholly and clearly received, and wholly useful in life.

No one has more intuition than anybody else, but we each have an individual intuitive path that unfolds in its own way. Everyone will find that certain methods will reap more accurate answers and certain types of information will come through much more clearly than others. You might be better at tuning into medical information, or you may discover your gifts apply best to counseling, or finding lost objects or people. Similarly, you might turn out to be a better sender of information than a receiver. It's all a part of the process of discovering your intuitive style.

You may also find you have quirky talents. For instance, when I was a child, one of the first signs I had of my intuitive sensitivity was when I began to sense what second language someone spoke. As you read this book, you may also realize that you, too, have a special little talent that could show you an area in which you have a particular intuitive strength—a special intuitive style, or that may show you the way to many more fertile areas to come.

HOW DO YOU KNOW WHEN
YOU GET A REAL ANSWER?

Remember that getting and knowing your answer is part of an ongoing process. You'll get lots of impressions before one develops to the point of certainty. Those first impressions, of course, are the ones that could be the most true and meaningful. Let them all flow, though, without analyzing or editing, and note the strongest, clearest, and most complete.

Do you feel a slight shock of recognition when that right impression comes along? Feel a tingle? or even chills? Do you feel, or hear, the ring of truth? Or do you experience a feeling of perfect harmony or balance when it suddenly feels right? Does your heart beat a little faster? your breath seem taken away? Do you feel it as a gut instinct, or does it hit you in some other way where you live emotionally?

Of course, the ultimate form of confirming your information is to actually see it come true. When an event you foresaw manifests in real life, it's not only proof positive of your intuition, it's proof that what you'd tuned in to was an absolutely correct answer.

You may find certain types of answers you get manifest more than others, or you may get a partial answer that only makes sense when the full answer finally materializes. A client of mine is having a feeling that's very general. She senses that somehow, in some way, she'll be involved with counseling at colleges. No impression other than that first one is very specific right now, but she knows that when the time is right she'll start seeing exactly how it all is going to occur.

It's also quite common to experience what I call the "right church/wrong pew" phenomenon. An intuitive counselor I know once got a flash of a friend looking at slides and kept seeing the word *agency* somehow connected to that image. He thought for sure she would wind up behind an advertising agency desk. Later, she did do a little freelance work in that area, but the slides turned out to be the pictures from her honeymoon—with her new husband, an advertising executive!

You, too, can and will find your confirmation waiting for you—messages are everywhere you look. With practice, anytime and anywhere you'll be open to their guidance. The exercises in this book aren't meant to just give you proficiency at certain times in certain situations. They'll permit you to apply what you've experienced to all avenues of life.

Pay attention to things like subway signs, overheard conversations, movie or TV dialogue, songs, or that fragment of something someone says to you that suddenly sets off an aha! inside your head. Remember the magic of synchronicity? Perhaps you've been thinking about going to France, and suddenly everywhere you go, people keep mentioning France. This could be a form of needed confirmation. Everyone seems to have an area where confirmation suddenly comes in. Some see weather changes as a sign or get a sense of acknowledgment from a song that contains a significant phrase being played "by chance" in a restaurant or on the radio.

WHAT DO YOU DO WITH
AN INTUITIVE ANSWER?

An intuitive answer comes with an inherent directive—apply and integrate it! That means if you get a message during your daily whole-focusing session, or at any other time, put the answer into motion, but if and only if that makes sense for you. Remember, you're going to be using your common sense, too. If your answer isn't meant to be used at that moment, put it on your mental back burner to see what more develops as you continue to clarify the message with your intuitive self. Maybe it isn't meant to be put into motion at all. Only you will know, now or over time.

If you receive information about someone else, use your common sense to decide whether or not you should give it out. Your developing awareness needs to be supported by a sense of responsibility. With your own evolving sense of inner wisdom, you must ask yourself responsibly if the person will benefit from this information. How can you communicate it in a considerate way?

THE SPIRAL
OF AWARENESS

As you continue the process of developing intuition, remember it's not a linear progression moving from one definite point of awareness to another. Instead, all the many different stages of your development, and the many different levels of awareness you experience, are incorporated into one ever-increasing awareness.

Developing awareness has a spiral, upward movement that allows you to see both where you've been and where you are at the same moment, and to perceive the inherent connection between the two. Sometimes the integration process can be a slightly bewildering one. There may be moments when you actually sense the light at the end of the tunnel and at the same time still feel in the dark.

Just remember in those situations there is indeed an answer, but for whatever reason you're not quite ready to see it. You will keep adding to your overall enlightenment as you spiral up in awareness. Soon you'll be able to re-experience a dark moment with a new ray of understanding. This is very much like the experience we've all had as children when our mothers told us, "You'll understand when you're older." Of course, when we matured, we were able to comprehend more from the vantage point of our broadened knowledge and experience.

Rest assured that if you're still a bit hazy about developing intuition, your understanding is guaranteed to clear and widen. You'll gain confirmations and answers to your deepest questions as you continue to develop, to grow, and to—in the truest sense—know.

THE INTUITIVE PATH
TO CREATIVITY

THE CREATIVE FORCE IS WITH YOU

When you access your intuition, you also open up all sorts of creative floodgates. Intuition and creativity are very much related—they're both natural resources of the right brain. In many ways, if you develop one quality, you naturally develop the other. That's why highly creative people are also highly intuitive, and vice versa. You can add flowing creativity to the abounding benefits you gain from developing your intuition. In fact, if you've begun to practice any of the exercises in this book, you've already started to tap your own reservoir of creative expression.

We all have an innate ability to express ourselves creatively. Just as our inherent connection to our inner wisdom makes us all naturally intuitive, it also allows us all to be natural artists.

We may not all be working painters or musicians. But we do each express ourselves creatively in our professional and personal lives when we juggle schedules, put together deals, write speeches or papers, decorate rooms, and otherwise problem solve. Each time we use our wits to complete a less than mechanical task, we're allowing ourselves to be guided by an intrinsic linkup to the creative force.

Creative thinking is whole thinking, and being creative is our way of getting in touch with the whole of creation. We feel balanced or in tune with our whole selves when we engage in any creative activity. Just as the answer is inherent in the questions you ask yourself, the creative solution is already present in the whole of the creative project.

Consider the great Michelangelo's approach to the sculpting process. He felt his task was "merely" to uncover the perfect finished figure that already lay within a block of stone. In the same manner, an artist is already inside of you. You can contact this artist anytime. In fact, unknowingly you already do. The more you consciously open to the creative force, the more your own creative genius will unfold, inspire, and inform you. Try the following exercise whenever you sit down to do creative work or problem solving.

• *Exercise 42: Tapping the Artist Within*

Breathe deeply and visualize yourself surrounded in glowing white, blue, or aqua light.

Next, breathe into the energy point in your throat, heart, or mid-forehead, whichever of the three feels best to you.

Say silently to yourself or out loud something like, "I now allow the creative force to flow and express itself through me."

Remain still and relaxed and continue breathing into the energy point of your choice for a few more moments. Then start to work, allowing your ideas to flow, without judging and editing, as bits and pieces, or whole information, start to come. Keep working as long as you feel inspiration flowing, bearing in mind that you can judge or evaluate what you've got after you've followed that flow.

CREATIVE THINKING IS ALTERNATE THINKING

Now that you've learned how to tap into your natural reservoir of creative energy, it's time to really work out your creative muscle. Both professional intuitives and artists look at the familiar world in a new, or alternate, way with illuminating results. That's exactly what you are learning to do, too, every time you take the leap of faith to open to intuition. Practicing taking the leap of alternate thinking will also allow more of your creative potential to leap forth.

Artists are taught that any picture consists of more than just the subject painted or photographed. The dynamic of the negative space—the space around those subjects and combined with them—makes up the whole picture. The following exercise will help you develop more complete awareness of the negative space surrounding and informing everything, increasing your ability to think alternately and create wholly.

• *Exercise 43: Seeing the Negative Space*

First, choose a highly graphic black-and-white print or photograph from a newspaper, magazine, book, or postcard collection. Now look at the picture as you normally would, concentrating on the generally darker foreground subjects. For example, focus on trees against a sky, people in a room, and so on.

Next reverse the process. Concentrate on everything in the picture except for what you just looked at, as if these parts of the picture were jigsaw puzzle pieces that connected with the parts of the scene that normally catch your attention. Then close your eyes and look again at the whole picture, giving both the positive and negative parts equal importance. Notice how they all interrelate.

Try the same exercise to enhance your perception of the true nature of your everyday life; look at food on a plate, furniture in a room, objects on a desk, and so on. I guarantee your point of view will be greatly enhanced and you'll start feeling more creatively and intuitively informed next time you sit down to read between the lines of one of your own projects.

Humor is another great alternate-thinking creative tool. The best comedians have an offbeat view of the world, which interprets the stuff of everyday life in a wacky, refreshing way. As a comedy writer has said, "Humor is seeing all three sides of the coin."

Laughter itself is like the wholehearted release of focused breathing. It actually changes our level of awareness, lightening it and releasing whatever else is on our minds. So don't forget to laugh at yourself every now and then. Let yourself get into that playful, fertile, alternate state of mind.

Here are some more exercises and games to help you think in alternate ways, and connect with your own natural talent for creative thinking.

- *Exercise 44: Wordspin*

Take a word. (For the sake of an example, we'll use the word *hot*.) Spin off verbally from that original word without using synonyms or antonyms. For instance, you can't use *cold* or *sizzling* to spin off from hot, but you could use *Arizona, salsa,* or *miniskirt*.

Play with a friend or by yourself with the help of pencil and paper. Please keep in mind that this is not a competition. Everyone who finds creative spin-off answers really comes up a winner. The goal is to open yourself to all the alternate possibilities.

Playing games like charades or Pictionary® or working crossword puzzles and other brainteasers all stir the creative juices, too, and make your mind more nimble.

To play charades, divide a group into two teams. Have one team decide on a word or phrase or book title (maple syrup, "come hell or high water," Mother Goose) while the other team chooses one member to be "it." After the phrase is given privately to the person who is it, that person must pantomime the phrase to his or her teammates by using images and gestures to convey syllables or words. Then, switch teams. Pictionary works the same way, except instead of pantomiming the word or phrase, the person who is "it" draws pictures that symbolize the word.

• Exercise 45: Fractured Proverbs

A first grade class was once given the first half of well-known, though not to them, proverbs and asked to make up the endings. They came up with "fractured proverbs" like "You can lead a horse to water—but you can't lead him to fire." And, "All's fair in love—and California." And, "A penny saved—isn't worth anything. You can't buy anything with a penny." The reason the results are so fresh and oddly true is that these kids were not burdened with any established answers. They simply went with what felt right.

Try fracturing some proverbs yourself to build up your own natural alternate thinking power. Alone or with a partner, make a list of the first half of your favorite proverbs or quotations and fill in new second halves. See how freewheeling you can be, and make sure to share the results with your partner, or with an appreciative friend.

Just to get you started, here are some beginning phrases you can creatively finish for yourself:

"A stitch in time. . ."

"A fool and his money . . ."

"We have nothing to fear but . . ."

"Give me liberty or . . ."

"If I only have one life to live. . ."

• *Exercise 46: Likenings*

This exercise will help open your mind to new creative ideas. It could be used to help loosen you up before working on any creative project—from an office assignment to a letter, paper, or proposal you're trying to write.

Create an evocative one-line situation, such as "a day in the park" or "rain on my face." Then add the words "is like" and follow that with a statement or an image that seems to fit. Come up with all sorts of different comparisons, or "likenings," for each one-liner, as in the following example. "Rain on my face is like the breath of an angel. Rain on my face is like . . . a new idea insisting it be let in. Rain on my face is like . . . a gentle joke on me." Once again, let yourself go. The sky is the limit. If your mind draws a blank when you try to come up with workable likenings, try these out for starters:

Sand beneath my feet is like. . .

Children's laughter is like . . .

Having a great book to read is like. . .

Working on a rainy morning is like. . .

"JUMP STARTING"
THE RIGHT BRAIN

The "Breath Charge" exercise (22) from Chapter 4 will help you access your creativity on a regular basis if you use it every morning. But in a pinch, hold your right nostril closed and breathe deeply several times through your left to give yourself an extra shot of right hemisphere input.

You can also initiate right-brain activity through sound. Sometimes when we're faced with a particularly challenging problem or creative task, we instinctively sigh. There are many more refined versions of channel-clearing sound initiators, such as the universal mantra *om*, Tibetan bells, or wind chimes.

For most of us, though, using these options would be highly impractical during the course of a busy day. So let yourself sigh consciously, knowing that instead of emitting a resigned sense of frustration, you're signaling your creative self to get going.

CREATIVITY
IS THE FLOW

Once you apply intuitive sense to creative problem solving, you'll find you're no longer worried about whether or not you have any ideas, but rather about which of your many ideas you can readily use. Just as in the process of accessing intuition, some creative ideas will show up in fragments first.

Others will come to you more fully, but won't yet be ripe for the picking.

Trust is as important to developing creativity as it is to developing intuition. The worst thing you can do is dismiss an idea because it seems crazy—the craziest ideas often turn out to be the most workable, simply because they're the most imaginative.

Keep reminding yourself of this, and remember to keep logging your ideas. (You might even want to create your own creativity log; see Appendix.) The right brain is not a memorizer. That's strictly a left-brain occupation, as anyone who has had a brilliant idea in the middle of the night and completely forgotten it by morning can attest.

You'll soon determine your own best method for collecting and saving your bits and pieces of creative genius for future reference, but notebooks, including a special notebook next to your bed, tape recorders, personal computers, index cards, and even scraps of paper thrown into shoe boxes are all popular, flexible methods. Remember to keep looking for patterns as you log your thoughts, just as you do when you're developing your intuitive messages. Chances are, if it keeps coming up, it's something worth developing further.

Automatic writing, the process of letting words flow spontaneously onto paper, is an easy and enjoyable method of connecting with the never-ending flow of creative ideas. Everyone from French poets to famous psychics to creative writing students have been inspired by it at one time or another. Here's the intuitive path version.

• *Exercise 47: Automatic Writing*

Pick a subject you want to explore—your family, your job, or an actual project you're working on.

To warm up for this creative process, try breathing exercises and neck rolls. Have a pad or notebook and your favorite pen at hand, or use your typewriter.

When you feel relaxed and focused, begin by saying or thinking something like, "I'm now opening myself to all the creativity I need."

Then just start writing quickly and spontaneously, without worrying about whether the output is smart or "good" or even grammatical. Just let yourself flow with your pen and see what comes up. Later, look for patterns or significant fragments.

An oral version of the same exercise is not unlike "talking it out." Get a tape recorder. Follow the same procedure, but instead of writing, just let yourself babble on. This is especially good if you've got one of those minirecorders you can carry around with you.

CREATIVE DREAMING

Dreams are your ongoing flow experience. You're quite likely to be at your most creative right after you wake up from dreaming because that's when you're closest to the natural flow state. Look for clues, cues, messages, and ideas in your dreams. Log them in along with everything else. Pay special attention to the ideas you get when you wake up in the morning or in the middle of the night.

Sting, for example, wrote the song "Every Breath You Take" in a single stroke upon waking up with an inspiration in the middle of the night. An advertising executive I know got an idea about a new product for a major corporate client just after waking up in the morning. When she mentioned her idea to the account supervisor, he was astounded: The client was at that moment thinking of adding exactly the same product to their line. You can also solve problems creatively through your dreams.

• *Exercise 48: Dream Problem Solving*

Go to bed or take a nap with the conscious intent of coming up with a solution. Try drinking half a glass of water, affirming your intent by thinking or saying, for example, "I now open to the perfect solution of this problem." When you wake up, immediately drink the water that's left in the glass and flash on your answer using the white screen technique and referring to the Visual/Feeling Checklist (page 93).

To try an alternative to this technique, avoid finishing the water in the morning and, in fact, be careful not to move your head upon waking. Research has shown that moving your head can act like a reset button—mentally starting your day anew, so see what you can flash on before "resetting."

You may get a complete answer at that moment, or a fragment you can develop over time. The answer may come later that day or week. You may need to repeat the process, to get a clearer answer. This is one of those exercises that work much better for some people than for others, so don't worry if it doesn't work for you.

CREATIVE CYCLES

As you concentrate and focus, you'll also want to tell your right brain how long you'll be creating. Research has shown that the brain seems to work at peak creativity for ninety-minute cycles, so you may find ninety-minute creative periods help you work at your best. But you may also find you have a personal creative cycle or an optimal creative time of day. I personally prefer to sit down for a long period of time, but I take frequent breaks during that extended period. Some people can work at their peak for four hours; others work very quickly and intensely for one.

Once you discover your own personal work pattern, stick with it and try to build your schedule around it as much as possible. It sounds obvious, but many people worry they "should" be creating a certain way. If you work at peak productivity for the two hours right before sunrise, do it! Get ready to dig in your heels if you find, as a stylist friend found, you have long two-week creative cycles that alternate with two-week fallow periods.

We all know some people who are early birds and others who are inveterate night owls. They simply already know and respect their creative rhythms. Cycles are also known to change, so try to go with the flow if you find that your once up-'n'-at-'em morning peaks turn to after-the-late-show creative highs.

CREATIVE FILL-OUT

Creative ideas often come to us in fragments—just like other intuitive information. Applying the Visual/Feeling Checklist and white screen techniques will help you expand on your creative flashes. These tools help you decide which of many ideas to go with and boost your inspiration or focus as you go about executing a creative project.

When he is trying to decide which among many creative ideas from a brainstorming session is best, my husband white screens each possibility to see which idea, as it develops and plays in the movie of his mind, seems the most full, detailed, and workable. He describes it as seeing which image literally has "the most future."

I know a photographer who talks about getting an "escalator" of ideas while he executes a project. For instance, first he will envision a model for a proposed shoot (stair 1). Once the model is literally in the "frame" of his mind, he'll see what she should be wearing (stair 2). Then, with that physical image in front of him, he'll fill in the background atmosphere (stair 3), and so on, until he comes to the top of the stairs—a richly detailed and imaginative whole picture.

Picture your own ideas on your mind-movie-screen. See what images seem to fill out more naturally to discover which ideas really have more life. Then talk through those pictures to develop them even further. Even as you're creating, the picture can evolve, filling in with ever-richer ideas and information.

You can also picture the future of a creative idea the way you picture the future of an everyday situation. Just flash forward a week, a month, or six months with the help of your inner white screen, visualizing a calendar or the changing seasons if you have to. Then use that information to make decisions or gain focus in the present.

LOCATE THE ESSENCE; FIND THE FEELING

The ability to tune in to feelings will aid your creative work as much as it sparks your intuition. Emotion is at the heart of an idea, and it's also what usually communicates that idea to others. Think of the movies, where a tone or a feeling is often the force that really tells or sells the story. Consider French Impressionist painting, which was motivated not so much by a feeling as a concept: a revolutionary new method of interpreting light. Still, when you see a finished Impressionist painting, your response to its beauty is probably an emotional one. In other words, you've felt the essence.

Anything you do creatively has its own essential feeling. Finding that feeling is often the key to releasing the full potential of a project. So when you're getting new ideas and trying to tune in to them to see if and how they could be developed, always ask yourself, "What is the main thing I am feeling?" just as you do when you use the Visual/Feeling Checklist (page 93).

Locating the essential feeling is also a good way to salvage an idea that isn't quite right. Before you automatically discard a creative approach that didn't pan out, ask yourself if there isn't really a spark, an essence, or a feeling in the idea that is worth saving. When you have that essence, work it in with new creative ideas or put it back in your sandbox of creative bits and pieces to rework at a later time.

The following easy-to-practice exercise will develop your ability to hone in on essential feelings.

- *Exercise 49: Going for the Essence:
  Finding the Feeling*

Remember this party game question: "If you were a tree, what tree would you be?" Well, it's really just a variation of this next creative exercise. Not as silly as it sounds, it helps you to think in nonlinear terms and, more specifically, to think in a way that quickly reveals the heart of the matter. Both Part 1 and Part 2 will greatly help you develop your ability to locate your feelings when you evaluate your own ideas. The more you practice, the better and more confident you'll become.

PART 1: QUINTESSENCES. You can do this exercise on your own or in a group. Either way, start by picking a broad category of things that contain a lot of different members: trees, movie stars, birds, flowers, cartoon characters, musical instruments, books, or even pastries.

Then consider each member of your group (or a group of people you know, such as family, office companions, friends, or roommates if you're working alone) either by putting each in turn on your white screen or spontaneously and literally, from the top of your head, assigning your subject the category member that seems to best express that person's essence.

For example, if your category is pastries, a rather thin and proper friend might suddenly become a cheese straw. If your category is musical instruments, that majestic-looking teacher with the great voice might become a violoncello. Have fun with this and try not to think at all while in the process. Later you can analyze why, for example, such "species" as Bucky Beaver, an elm tree, and a skylark are the quintessences of your boss.

PART 2: FEELINGS. In this variation you will associate an essential feeling with an object or a person, or vice versa. Pick an essential feeling (happy, sad, tired, cold, hot, etc.) and, following the quintessential technique, match that feeling with a person or with a member of a category. What flower best expresses "sad" to you? What tree, "tired"? For people, choose strangers when you're standing in line, dining out, or in a park, and locate their essential feeling.

Note: Choosing friends probably won't provide you with enough creative stretch because you are most likely already fairly aware of their feelings.

EMPATHY IS CARRYING FEELING
A STEP FURTHER

Sometimes you can actually personalize a problem to solve it creatively. Remember, when you're in the flow you're in a state of oneness. This creates a powerful empathy that you can apply to creative assignments. When you wholly empathize with a particular problem or challenge, you can feel, from the inside, what it takes to solve it.

Advertising has made a science out of understanding products and consumers by creating personality profiles of both. If you write, be your characters. See how you would feel if you, yourself, were each of them in a given situation. If you're writing or talking to someone, try to empathize to the point at which you can really feel what they're feeling. Is your audience reacting to what you're saying? What does he or she need to hear?

Whether you're gardening, cooking, writing, organizing your office, taking a photograph, or working with any other kind of creative project, you can tune in to find out what your project needs. A TV director friend has such a finely developed sense of empathy, he is constantly saying, "The camera wants to be here." There will be more on how to explore the gold mine of this technique to improve your success and prosperity in the next chapter. For now, you can adapt this concept to your particular creative projects. Follow the next exercise to help you develop and use your own creative empathy.

• Exercise 50: Creative Empathy

Use the white screen technique to focus in on the person, product, or problem, in order to find a creative solution. See the object of your interest on the screen in full and living detail. Then put yourself up on the screen, actually becoming what you're picturing.

It may help to see yourself superimposed over the other image until you meld together and become one. Perhaps you find you don't need to see yourself on the picture so much as to send your full awareness to the image of the project and feel that awareness literally entering your subject.

Let's say you're trying to come up with a creative idea, and then a creative plan to sell it. Take turns becoming both the problem (say a shoe that needs to be comfortable but stylish) and your target consumer (who needs to be comfortably styled). If there's a middleman involved (say a manufacturer or an investor), use the technique to empathize with his or her needs, too.

Once you feel you're there in terms of becoming one with your subject, ask your intuitive self, "How do I feel?" "What do I need?" Pay special attention to visualization and feeling as you tune in to your own responses.

For a truly enlightened creative solution, try problem solving with a variation of the technique just described. See yourself on the white screen as your favorite role model, the one most appropriate for solving the problem at hand. Your chosen role model could be anyone, from your mother or mentor to a great leader, artist, or scientist. Then ask your role model/intuitive self what to do in this particular situation. If you're the sort of person who sees all sides of a situation, try choosing a very decisive role model for balance. And if you're more of a black-or-white person, choose a model who you think would have empathy with everyone involved.

TALKING IT OUT

Once you've gotten creative ideas or are in the process of developing them, it's good to talk them out. Conversation itself is a form of the flow. When I'm writing, I often find myself deep in conversation with myself, talking out and talking over different creative options.

Here's a technique that will help you release and loosen your creative muscles. This exercise is especially good for filling in the details of any abstract concepts and is useful in many creative situations, from writing an essay or speech to creating and selling a product.

• *Exercise 51: Free-Form Free-for-All*

Brainstorm to come up with three words that describe the essence of your idea, the feelings that best describe it, or the feeling you want it to convey.

Using pen and paper as your own personal Etch-a-Sketch, take each of the three words in turn and create a flow of associative word leaps.

For example, in one of my business workshops we created

a make-believe product called Fruit Chewies. Then we used this technique to establish essential ideas to creatively market it. The three words the group came up with were *fruit, chewy,* and *fun.*

For fruit my workshop's examples included "fresh," "natural," and "tasty." For fun, we got "joke," "giggling," "laughter," and "bouncy." Don't worry about whether the words make sense—for instance, we got the word "dentures" for chewy. Just let the words and associations flow.

When you've explored all possibilities, look at the words on the screen of your white paper and see what kind of whole picture you've gotten, or can get. Perhaps you can make more associations from this picture or create a meaningful story by putting certain words together. Tune in to your inner white screen to see if you can develop the picture even further and to see if certain ideas feel right. You'll probably come up with some interesting concepts and maybe a surprising answer. You could suddenly visualize the essence of your project, or at least gather enough information to go on and finally solve it.

FOLLOW-THROUGH:
UNBLOCKING AND PERSISTING

In order to be fully creative, we often need to have a burning desire. New York artist Mary Boochever says, "My ideas spring from necessity." Songwriter Doc Pomus said, "Why does anyone write? Because they have to." Unfortunately, we all don't have that burning drive to draw on every time we must create. Often, necessities are not self-imposed: We have a deadline to be met, or a client or friend who needs a creative solution—now! Or perhaps we have the time to create, but are in need of a creative energy boost to completely carry through our ideas. Here is an exercise you can use to unblock your own creativity flow and muster up that feeling on demand.

- *Exercise 52: Fire in the Belly*

Sitting with your back straight as you did in the energy-balancing exercise, imagine a great warmth at the base of your spine. Feel that warmth fill your abdominal region, moving up until it fills your entire stomach with its radiating glow.

Now run that fire up through your spinal column in whatever color it shows itself to you—perhaps a white light, or a deep red flame—without worrying about focusing on the colors of each individual energy center along the way. Simply see and feel your spinal column as a long, firm, glowing column of heat.

Finally send the energy upward and outward through the top of your head.

The original creative unblocking force is the flow itself. Whenever you're feeling stuck, try the following tricks to help you get into the creative flow and be reminded of its constant presence.

FOLLOWING THE FLOW OF WATER. Water has long been the symbol and conduit of the flow. Try to consciously use water as a creative stimulant. Drink lots of water to help get your creative juices flowing again. Take a peaceful pause by a fountain, pond, or riverbank if you can for creative refreshment. But in lieu of that, simply go wash your hands. Silly as it sounds, it really helps.

Take advantage of a most natural mundane activity to gain a literal shower of ideas. As you jump into the shower or take a soothing bath, see what ideas or germs of ideas come to you as the water stimulates your senses. After you towel off, write down anything that came to you, even if it seems incidental. Many times you will find yourself receiving the seed of a creative breakthrough.

FOLLOWING THE FLOW OF MUSIC. Mystery fans will remember that whenever Sherlock Holmes was on the verge of breaking a case, he'd whisk Watson off to a concert, or run off to one himself. Listening to the music, Holmes let his mind flow, and in the process he'd subconsciously pull all his clues together into one seamless, highly creative, and wholly singular solution. Elementary! Try giving your left brain up for a moment to the powerful flow of music. Put something highly melodic on the stereo or tape player, and let creative inspiration take over.

LETTING GO

Letting go, like releasing so that you can whole focus, is a very important part of the creative process. In order for creativity to be actively expressed, it must be passively received and accepted by you. When you completely let go, you allow the process itself to regenerate you so you can nourish and harvest new ideas.

You've probably already experienced this yourself if you've ever spent time straining and straining to solve a creative problem, only to have the solution percolate into your awareness after you've finally given in to the urge for a break or nap. We've already seen how dreams, another instinctual method of letting go, are a tremendous source of information. That's why we get so many ideas right after we wake up or come out of a daydreaming session. Often ideas leap to mind when we're thinking of nothing at all.

In this sense, letting go is as much the first step of the creative process as it is the last. Think of all the new ideas you get when you're thinking about nothing at all. Then think of all the creative techniques you have at your fingertips and all the ways you can use those techniques over time to develop your ideas into fully realized projects.

Relish the luxury of being able to let your ideas bubble up slowly, even as you pay more active attention to what's on the front burner. For instance, an artist friend keeps seeing the image of a certain number hop out onto her mental screen, apparently begging for her to produce a painted rendering of it. She's looking forward to the time when that image will become a literal hot number and be ready to be filled out into a completed work. For now, she's enjoying the leisurely process of letting the picture develop—right before her eyes.

CHAPTER SEVEN

THE INTUITIVE PATH TO SUCCESS AND PROSPERITY

YOUR ABUNDANCE CONNECTION

Just as following the intuitive path naturally leads you to more creativity as well as intuition, it can greatly help open you to more overall abundance in your life. Abundance can take the material form of prosperity and success, but its whole picture includes everything from love, energy, creativity, intuition, and wisdom, to a sense of fulfillment—professionally or otherwise. Ultimately, abundance is anything at all you need to support and nourish your whole self as you follow your path through life.

You have the innate potential to manifest more and more wealth of every sort in your life, just as you have the ability to increase your intuitive and creative skills to better fulfill your path. In fact, while you've been learning to connect with your intuitive self, you've also been in the process of discovering your successful self.

Your successful self is the part of your intuitive self that already knows how to create and connect with your most successful possibilities. Easily accessible, it's ever-ready to receive and perceive all the answers and opportunities you need to manifest your greatest abundance—whatever form that takes for you—from a fat bank account, profitable deal, or fulfilling career, to a happy marriage, million dollar idea, or radiant health.

By sharpening your intuitive skills, you'll naturally increase your potential for greater success and prosperity. You can use the techniques you've already developed—whole-focusing, affirming, and visualizing—to more powerfully align yourself with your intuitive connection to abundance.

You'll discover an interesting paradox, however, as you continue your way along this path. The more you "do the right things"—consciously tuning in to where you need to be going and what kind of answers and guidance you need to get there—the less you'll need to constantly make such a conscious effort. Just as you found in connecting with your intuitive self, you'll find that in order to plug into your greatest success potential, you only need to be in the flow.

This awareness, in turn, will allow you to reshape the way you are realizing all the success available to you in your life. Remember, as you grow and evolve along the spiral of awareness, your success path and your perception of it, will evolve as well. Whenever you feel frustrated, know that your intuitive self can put you more in tune with the course you need to take and how you need to take it.

As in the process of developing awareness, even when you think nothing is happening, your inner wisdom, in fact, can be kicking in. Eventually, you'll be allowed to see—and reap—new and better opportunities, possibilities and outcomes.

As you affirm your inherent intuition and keep developing it, be aware of how your successful self is coming into play. Let your intuition be your guide as you tune in to the best goals to shoot for and how best to achieve them. Then let the process of manifesting your most successful guidance and solutions flow and evolve naturally.

• Exercise 53: Connectiing with Your Successful Self

PART 1: Try this whenever you need a general reminder of your intuitive connection to abundance.

Take a deep breath and close your eyes as you bring your awareness to your heart, and continue to breathe deeply and rhythmically. Keep sending your breath and your awareness to your heart and start to remember a time you felt successful—perhaps when you won that raise, got that job, graduated school, even successfully performed any of the exercises in this book. Begin to feel what it felt like then. What does that feel life? Do you feel a warmth? a tingling sensation? Do you seem to be smiling and glowing? Do you have a more quiet sense of "rightness" and "balance"?

Keep remembering this successful feeling in as much detail as you can, for as long as you want. Know that you can return to this feeling anytime you want to reconnect with your successful self.

PART 2: Try this whenever you need more direct guidance from your successful self.

Begin by doing Part 1 of this exercise. When you're ready, shift your awareness to your mental white screen as you focus on the topic you wish to tune in to (asking for a raise, brainstorming for a new business project, deciding what option would be the most successful, etc.). Keep sending your breath and awareness to your white screen and allow your mind to shift into a higher gear by saying or thinking something like: "I now open to all the guidance and information I need to lead me to greater success and prosperity."

Keep breathing as you let yourself experience any thoughts, feelings, pictures, words, etc., that come up. You may receive a complete message, a fragment, or nothing at all—now or later. But by continuing to connect with your successful self, you're more likely to receive successful guidance when you need it.

PUTTING IT ALL TO WORK

As you continue to develop your intuition, ideas for creating more success, prosperity, and abundance will naturally occur to you. You can really put these ideas to the test in the workplace. Doing good, successful business requires far more than knowing and applying facts. Whatever your line of work may be, it can only be enriched, and you can only be made richer, by using intuition to fill in the facts and get a jump on getting the big picture.

We've all seen dramas about street-smart detectives and savvy lawyers who followed their hunches to fill in the blanks before all the facts were uncovered. It's the nature of intuition to provide you with a "vision" before you have the facts or figures to back it all up. So don't dismiss ideas or strategies just because you don't yet have the data to support them. This is something I really stress in my business workshops, where many of those attending are required to think creatively but still "have their butts" on the (bottom) line.

In day-to-day business dealings, there's a tendency to take only the most logical steps instead of allowing for some powerful intuitive leaps. Purely logical minds tend to come to the same kind of logical conclusions, and in the business world, doing the same thing everyone else is doing is a sure-fire ticket to mediocrity. Creative solutions in any line of work require creative thinking and intuitive leaps of faith.

On a very practical level, going for the intuitive vision first and working backward from that vision to prove its viability is often a whole lot easier and more productive than blindly following logic or hard data. Following logic step by step without a vision of the big picture to guide you can often lead you in the wrong direction and eventually leave you at a dead end.

A few years back, two companies were planning on entering into the wholesome snack business with virtually identical fruit snacks. One company's product was stalled in test market when they took the logical approach—promoting their product's wholesome benefits. The second company knew they had to take a more creative approach or they would get stalled themselves. Their research told them they had to communicate to moms that their product, Fun Fruits, was a wholesome snack, made from real fruit. But they also had to convince kids that the snacks were fun to eat.

The problem was this: kids thought anything that was wholesome enough for their moms couldn't be fun for kids to eat. How could one commercial make both moms and kids happy—and sell the product?

Everyone was so hung-up with trying to logically solve this inherent contradiction, they couldn't see the forest for the trees. But an intuitive creative director had a vision that resulted in a very successful solution. While working on the problem, he kept seeing an image of laughing trees, and instead of discarding it as nonsense, he tuned in to how he could possibly use that image productively.

Though it didn't seem logical at first, he soon realized that the laughing trees were the key for communicating both the fun and wholesomeness of Fun Fruits—while appealing to both moms and kids. An entire series of highly imaginative commercials were created in which Fun Fruits fell from giggling trees—making kids think the products were fun and moms think that they were naturally healthy.

Working from a vision instead of trying to solve the problem head on resulted in a highly effective campaign—and record sales for the company. Remember, intuitive thinking is whole thinking. It solves business problems by seeing them in a broader perspective, in which many solutions are possible, including solutions that might never have been revealed by following logic alone.

When you make business decisions based largely or even partly on your intuition, you'll find that you naturally keep closer tabs on the ways in which those decisions play out. This instinct will naturally give you the opportunity to make adjustments in your intuitive decisions by going with the flow and righting the course of your vision with your common sense. As the right brain leads the way, this give-and-take between the left and right hemispheres will guide you toward the absolutely best solution based on both approaches to the problem.

Remember, business projects tend to develop over a period of time. Whenever a consensus is required, little is instantaneous. The direction of the flow, however, can change suddenly midstream. In cases like these, your intuition will always give you a jump on the competition and help you avoid practical, bottom-line-oriented pitfalls way before the facts and figures would indicate a problem is coming up. Your reward will be a reputation for business savvy, good instincts, and creative problem solving.

On the other hand, if hard reasoning and research is your bread and butter, you don't have to completely forgo the help of your intuition: Just reverse the process and let the left brain lead the right. A product researcher I know uses his intuitive and creative thinking to make more sense of the numbers that he's getting. Numbers are subject to interpretation, and a strong intuitive sense is the key to more deeply integrating and understanding hard data.

Many prestigious figures in the business world made it to the top by going with intuition despite the figures. Allen Neuharth, who launched *USA Today*, commissioned tons of market research to determine the potential viability of his national newspaper—but it was all inconclusive. He went with his gut, however, and three years and multimillion dollar losses later, the test results were still not definite. But Neuharth was definite about continuing and the paper today is a national success.

The marketing people at Nike didn't even bother with research testing when they came up with the "Just Do It" campaign. They intuitively knew their theme line would be a "slam dunk" with their potential customers and, in effect, "just did it" themselves. Their results made marketing history, rocketing Nike to the top of a highly competitive field.

A recent study has shown that CEOs of major companies use their intuition in 80 percent of all decisions they make. So why not you?

No one is advocating that you throw caution to the winds and act only on your gut, but unless you use your instincts too, you won't have all the very helpful details of the big picture at your disposal. Psychologists have pointed out that there is a correlation between entering high risk/high finance fields and being open to intuitive guidance. In such ventures, one must come to expect the unexpected, and try to see ahead as far as possible to take advantage of trends. Maybe that's why so many achievers in so many risky areas from Wall Street to politics, show business, fine arts, advertising, and sports take advantage of the information a good intuitive counselor or astrologer can offer them. Every year I see a greater percentage of these "success types" myself in my private practice and intuition workshops.

To steadily increase your own intuitive business instincts and overall prosperity quotient, just keep following the flow, practice your intuition exercises as regularly as you can, and check in with your intuitive self for confirmation as you go along. Developing your intuitive skills in general will enable you to more clearly tune in to that sometimes subtle confirmation process and help you make the very best business moves and decisions.

For more specific ways to tap into the flow of intuition to develop greater success, read on. Use both your common and uncommon sense to see what best applies to your own field and how to use it. Then get ready for opening to intuitively successful guidance of your very own.

SELLING WITH EMPATHY

We're all involved in selling at one time or another, whether it's selling an idea, getting a point across, selling ourselves to a prospective employer, or actually holding down a sales position. In any of these situations, your intuition can go a long way toward helping you to accomplish your goal.

A story about my father-in-law will show you just what I mean. The man was what is commonly known as a "born salesman." He sold so many storm windows during the housing boom of the sixties that he had to move his business to another county to find people he hadn't already sold to. He was so well known in the last town he settled in, he was called its unofficial mayor. The secret of his success was the very caring way he had of intuiting and filling his clients' needs.

Just as he had an instinct for knowing when to close a sale, he also had a knack for knowing how much his customers could afford. He often found himself "unselling" certain customers on some more expensive features, costing himself initially on commissions, but creating an invaluable reputation for himself as an honest businessman. His intuitive sales approach paid off handsomely as his grateful customers referred scores of new customers, whom he treated in the same caring fashion.

Having empathy for a client's needs helps to strike a balance between buyer and seller and also helps to find the sales solution inherent in the sales problem. Inevitably, the better salesperson is the one who's most caring. The winning sale is made by going with the flow of the situation. In that flow you can intuit a client's needs and know when to press on, when to back off, when to try another approach, and when to close the deal.

A boutique owner friend of mine adds creativity to that blend. Whenever I visit her store, I find her making truly inspired suggestions to her customers about how to creatively adapt or even alter the clothing she sells to fill many needs. One day when I complimented her about this, she said, "Oh, when I come to the shop I just turn on the program." In other words, she instinctively affirms to herself that she'll go with the flow to help her customers make inspired choices and help herself make some wonderful sales.

Marketing is another aspect of sales that requires good instincts and the ability to empathize with the consumer. Ken Hakuta, also known as Dr. Fad, has an uncanny ability to take offbeat products and turn them into overnight success stories. Hakuta specializes in finding items people don't need but are going to fall in love with anyway, like Wacky Wallwalkers, those little plastic creatures that crawl up and down your walls by themselves. Hakuta was introduced to them when he opened a package from Japan a few years back. He didn't need consumer research to tell him he had a hit on his hands. He just knew it.

The secret of Hakuta's success lies in the fun he has with his work and his terrific knack, or empathy, for knowing which items people are going to go mad for. You, too, can use empathy to help you come up with the best business ideas and solutions.

• Exercise 54: The Empathy Connection

Next time you need to create or market a product, devise an organizational system, write a presentation, or fill another kind of business need, try imagining that you are that end product or goal. Find out what it needs. You've probably already used this technique whenever you've said to yourself while in the process of working out any problem, from decorating a room, to writing a paper or presentation, "It needs something . . ." You've definitely used it if you tried the creative empathy exercise in Chapter 6 (Exercise 50).

First, breathe deeply, and see the white screen form in your mind's eye. Sometimes it helps to start by seeing the project you're working on and then to picture yourself super-imposed over it, literally fusing and becoming one with the task at hand. Or after getting the picture of that project on your screen, breathe into both that image and your third eye energy center. This will fuse the two together and give you a mind's eye view of your project's personality and needs.

If you are dealing with a product, be that product and try sensing both your needs and how you fit into your consumers' needs. If the product is used on a part of the body, be that body part. If you are devising a new filing system or computer program, be that system and sense what you need to function smoothly and efficiently. If you're preparing a presentation, use the empathy system to feel what tone or wording you need to get your point across. This technique can be applied to people, too. What does your client need? your boss? your organization? Find out by using your intuition to be that person or structure.

In the very early 1970s the company that made Arm & Hammer products asked their advertising agency to develop a name and image for their new nonpolluting laundry detergent. Although similar products sported bold graphics and cutesy names like "Ecolo-g," the young creative executive on the account used his intuitive sense to put himself into the box and to identify with the product on a primal level.

As the product, he felt that to fulfill his needs he needed to go against the tide of accepted detergent imagery. In fact, he felt he needed a definitely less-than-flashy name and a package that looked like the old Arm & Hammer baking soda box—which consumers had always associated with simplicity and purity. His co-workers considered the idea half-baked since it defied conventional "detergent thinking" and would probably confuse consumers. Fortunately, the agency president was more of an intuitive type himself and recommended the "simple solution" to the client—whose product is still encased in a package that looks like a big box of baking soda and is the only one of its original competitors still around today.

LITTLE VOICES, LITTLE FLASHES, LITTLE FEELINGS

Developing the ability to follow our little flashes, little voices, and little feelings can certainly help us on the job. Eloise, a personnel director, says she's always using her intuition to read between the lines of the résumés she receives. Once she found a job applicant who looked perfect on paper, but something told her he just wouldn't work out. She passed along this information, but it went unheeded. The candidate was hired, and a few months later he got the company in trouble, costing them a lot of time and money.

Eloise's intuition also helps her to discover the perfect

candidates even when their credentials are less than perfect. As a result, Eloise has got a great track record for filling positions with the right people as she follows and develops her flashes of insight and strong gut feelings.

Dick, a brand manager, was in charge of renting a car to get his team to a big meeting. The rental company said everything was fine, but Dick had a gnawing feeling he should change his plans and get to the lot no later than twelve noon even though the car wasn't needed until somewhat later in the day. Not used to having such a strong feeling, Dick acted on it and ended up renting the very last car on the lot. As a result of that successful intuitive experience, Dick has started to trust and follow his hunches a lot more often than he used to, with very beneficial results.

REVELING IN THE OBVIOUS; "STUMBLING" ON THE LESS THAN OBVIOUS

A schoolteacher client of mine found she had a knack for buying houses that quadrupled in value over a very short period of time. She describes it as just getting a "sense" of their potential, and finds the process quite obvious.

Intuition can be so natural, it indeed feels obvious, which may only be the effect of the irrefutable power of intuition. Entire fortunes have been made by people following the "obvious" directions and making the "obvious" decisions with the "obvious" clarity of their own inner sensing.

Sometimes, your intuition may also see you through a situation that seems less than obvious. Dorothy, a literary agent, was contacted by a team of authors who were offering what she felt to be a very timely project. These authors only had a limited amount of time to see many different agents. Normally a very deliberate person, Dorothy suddenly found herself canceling a whole day of appointments to meet with them on the basis of a strong hunch. Even when they called and told her they'd gone with another agent, she was confident she hadn't heard the end of it. Sure enough, a few days later, the authors called back to say they'd decided to go with her after all.

Whatever your business decision, obvious or otherwise, your intuition will help you make the best choice possible. Consciously tap into its power by checking in with your intuitive self, following the Visual/Feeling Checklist, and using empathy to get that literal inside track.

(INTUITIVE) TIMING
IS EVERYTHING

Good timing is an absolutely wonderful business benefit of following the intuitive path. Dorothy sensed the timing was right for her book project. I recently heard a story about Clint Eastwood having an intuitive timing experience while he was shooting the film *Pale Rider*.

Eastwood had carefully worked out a filming schedule to include a sequence of some dying autumn leaves that would open his film but would be shot later on in the schedule. Yet suddenly he woke up one morning and decided to shoot the dying leaves that day in place of another scene. So at great potential cost and inconvenience to all concerned, the lineup was changed and that sequence was completed. When the cast and crew woke up the morning after doing so, every tree was absolutely bare—every last leaf had fallen during the night. Eastwood's unsettling and seemingly oddly timed schedule change had suddenly saved the day, and a very important part of his film.

As a director, Eastwood is famous for going with his intuition. During production, he changes schedules constantly. Yet his pictures always come in on time and on budget. He has said, "You have to wait out fate; you can't meet it head on." That really means that you've got to go with the flow to achieve the most success. When you do, you'll be able to shift your focus as it becomes necessary to maximize opportunities, and be rewarded with the fruits of perfect timing.

YOUR NATURAL FLOW OF COURAGE AND CONFIDENCE

Let's face it: In order to really make it, in the material world or otherwise, it takes plenty of courage and confidence. Being in the flow gives us confidence as we begin to experience an unerring sense of knowing. In turn, we begin to develop courage to keep going forward with the flow. Having courage and confidence together allows us to take the risks we often need to take to truly realize success. When we're really going with the flow, those courageous leaps of faith somehow don't seem that risky at all.

Take the example of another of Dorothy's clients. This author sent Dorothy and many other agents an unsolicited manuscript. Months later, as Dorothy was straightening her office, she discovered the work hidden under a pile of papers. It was totally battered and covered with dust, but she cleaned it off, took it home to read, and decided she was interested.

When she called the man's office, his secretary immediately said, "He's not here right now, but he said if you called to tell you to just go right ahead with it." Even though the odds were very slim and much time had already passed, the author, with striking certainty, knew that Dorothy and Dorothy alone would eventually be the one to successfully represent him.

Your intuition will surely guide you onto your path toward success and prosperity. You know you're in the flow when you suddenly possess the uncanny ability to run across the very resources and information you need. Not only does this phenomenon help you out practically, it also confirms the appropriateness of a chosen project.

I know a graduate student who is writing a dissertation that's a real research challenge. To complete it, he constantly has to use his wits to ferret out obscure bits of information. As if by chance, or so it seems, he keeps on running into people who have whole boxes of the specific kinds of papers he needs. This kind of experience encourages him to continue the risky business of this challenging project.

Sometimes you just get a powerful hunch about a path you should take, but that hunch is very short on the loads of information you think you need to follow it through. Never mind. If a hunch is so strong you can't ignore it, try following it anyway. Many of the most successful careers have been built by those who recognized and seized a good idea when they got one. For instance, I know a TV producer who felt a persistent desire to go to Chicago, a city where she did not know a soul. She finally had to act on it, and when she arrived, she quickly connected with a project that was perfect for her talents. As she started developing it, ideas and favorable circumstances started pouring in, and kept on pouring in, even though she had no tangible resources or contacts in the city. To her, clearly, the signs were right. This pattern confirmed to her that she was on the right track, while it also provided her with a wealth of practical resources.

Courage and confidence seem to come together effortlessly in the phenomenon known as beginner's luck. This type of success results from an unjaded openness to the concept of limitless possibilities. How many times have you heard a story about a smashing success that began with some version of, "I didn't know any better so I just jumped in—and made it!" Adding a burning desire to that open-minded approach can often make beginner's luck close to inevitable.

I know a normally shy, but very competent, woman who decided she wanted to do research for a prestigious national news show even though she lacked a media background. New to that world, she was naively oblivious to the odds against her. She wanted the job so badly that she pulled out all the stops. After sending the show's producer a telegram that extolled her virtues and a newspaper that headlined the illustrious addition of her talents to the staff, she landed the job for real. One giant step on her success path and one more beginner's luck story for mankind!

No matter where you are in terms of your own prosperity or career path, treat each effort you make toward success as a fresh beginning with unlimited potential. You'll release the doubts and hesitations that block you from a greater flow of prosperity, develop the confidence and courageous risk-taking instincts of an energetic up-and-comer, and open yourself to beginner's luck every step of the way.

Not everyone has that all-consuming, emboldening desire to follow a definite career-related path. Sometimes you may not know what you want or you may be ambivalent about which of several paths to take. In these situations, get support from the fire in the belly technique you learned in Chapter 6, which will provide you with courage for creative risk taking in your professional life and help you to see your unique career path as it lifts you into the flow.

For a special boost, try the next exercise whenever you want information about your path and for helpful guidance along the way.

- *Exercise 55: Tuning in to Your Success and Career Path*

Do your warm-ups, including deep rhythmic breathing, energy balancing, or focusing on a chosen energy point, if you wish. Put up the white screen as you affirm by saying or thinking something like, "I now open myself to the perfect unfolding of my career path. I open myself to words and feelings that will show me that path now." Keep breathing into your white screen and see what emerges in words, pictures, or feelings.

Keep checking with your intuitive self for explanation and further guidance. Are you seeing a complete picture or a fragment of one to come? Ask for a sense of time. Is there a message concerning direction about the way you should approach your career at the moment? Is there any new idea to develop, or a plan to be put into action, or is your picture showing you what will evolve in the future?

Always ask your intuitive self how you can apply this information as you develop an overall awareness of your career path and plan. In addition, always check in with your intuitive self for any possible cues when you hear about new investments, peruse the classifieds, and read business books and biographies of illustrious business people.

BEING YOUR LIFE'S ENTREPRENEUR

Entrepreneurs are famous for the sort of courage and determination we've been talking about; that is, the sort of courage that allows them to forge ahead and follow their desires against all odds. Most often, they do so without the security of a fully detailed map to steer by or seemingly any tangible means with which to manifest their plans.

Consider the success story of two IBM researchers in the 1970s. Like many other scientists of the day, they happened to hear of something called *superconductivity*, the theoretical possibility that electricity could travel through a ceramic compound without creating any friction and without any loss of energy occurring at all.

At the time, there was no such ceramic compound, but imagine what the world would be like if power were as unlimited and inexpensive as running water. The implications were, and still are, incredible.

This is exactly what the IBM scientists thought. However, IBM had given express orders not to pursue this endeavor, which they thought was impossible, practically speaking. The scientists, however, had a strong hunch that the company was wrong this time. That hunch was backed up by the common sense of their scientific training, and it was so compelling that on nothing but a wing and a prayer, they defied company orders and for two years spent every spare minute conducting experiments on ceramic compounds, at great personal inconvenience and professional risk.

Two years later, they made the first crucial discovery about the practical version of the compound their superiors had called impossible, and opened up a whole new branch of the electrical industry at the same time. Today superconductivity is becoming a reality, and those two scientists are now patent holders at the forefront of the industry. So now, not only do they have a very exciting position in this brand-new market, but they also have the satisfaction of having made one of the greatest modern scientific discoveries. Now there's an example of following instincts all the way down the intuitive path to success and prosperity.

Then there are the stories of Myra and Colleen, each of whom had an intuitive flash to start her own business and each kept following intuition from adversity to success.

Colleen had been between jobs, after years of working in the magazine business. One day, while raking leaves, she had a hunch to call the Center for Applied Intuition, even though she didn't know why. After asking them to send information, and subsequently looking at the center's publication, a lightbulb went on over her head. Why not create a newsstand-quality magazine on the subjects of intuition and creativity? She wrote a proposal, the center's director loved it, and the next day she was in business!

Her magazine, called *Intuition*, was an immediate success, but after two issues the center folded. Although future prospects looked bleak, Colleen held to her vision. She received offers to have the magazine taken over and be made part of some other organization, but despite having no money, Colleen felt strongly that that wouldn't be good for her—or the magazine. At times she even considered getting another job, but each time she seemed to hear an inner voice telling her, "no!"

Eventually a wealthy individual, who'd seen the magazine and loved it, contacted her and offered funding to allow her to continue publishing. So *Intuition* hit the newsstands bigger than ever, and it continues to thrive largely due to Colleen's determination and trust of her own intuition.

Colleen's hunches really pay off, for example, when it

comes time to do promotions and solicit subscriptions. With reams of expensive direct mail lists to choose from, she uses her gut to make the most productive choices. She must be doing something right, because *Intuition* has become the fastest growing alternative magazine on the market.

Myra, a talented chef, got the idea to start a gourmet Mexican prepared food business with her husband. New to this end of the field, she received plenty of advice from supposed experts, but her instincts often told her when it was wrong. Many times she was offered "help" in exchange for pieces of her business, but each time she refused—even though she was totally broke—knowing she had to do it her way.

When a huge supermarket chain wanted to sell her products—but only with its own name and label—she insisted on keeping her own company's name, knowing instinctively that they would go for it despite all evidence to the contrary. On the final day of the offer, her products received a rave review in the *New York Times*. An executive of the supermarket chain saw the review and told the buyer to carry Myra's products—with her company's name intact.

Today, Myra's company is growing faster than ever, as she continues to trust and use her intuition on a daily basis. As a matter of course, she relies on her gut to create new products and marketing plans, approach new clients, and hire the most productive employees. She recently reminded me, however, that in her frustrating first year, she almost let her business go—but I had advised her to keep following her vision and her instincts. I'm glad I was able to help her, but it was her risk taking, inner drive, and intuition that made her dreams a successful reality.

If any of these stories ring even a faint bell with you, that's good. Basically, we should all be entrepreneurs of our own lives, going with the flow, and taking charge of our careers with courage, confidence, and self-esteem. No matter what the particulars of your situation may be, always remember that on your path you are the captain of the expedition. Your intuitive self will help you navigate your life to your greatest abundance, whether your path leads to the reward of being the head of a happy household or the head of a powerful company.

When you're musing over long-term moves, keep tuning in to your career path to see what patterns and details come up. Like any intuitive information, some pictures will seem to have more life than others. Keep developing them until the time is right, adding common sense to the mix until you come up with an abundance formula any entrepreneur would applaud.

FLEXIBILITY

By now you've probably gathered that the common thread in all of these success stories is the ability of each person to go with the flow, following his or her intuition even when numbers, schedules, hard data, or popular opinion might indicate otherwise.

Imagine what chaos might have ensued on Clint Eastwood's set if he had stuck with his original schedule, or the opportunities Dorothy and my friend the TV producer might have missed if they had shrugged off their hunches. In the short term, going with the flow can be of great help in your business dealings, but in the long term it will do much more than that—it will really let success and prosperity flow. Many, many long-term successes are built on the ability to sense the way things are flowing, and then to move along with them.

Consider the story of a translator I know. She had an overwhelming intuitive sense that she should travel to Spain directly after graduating from college, even though she didn't know a lick of Spanish. Once there, she found herself taking to the language like a duck to water, sailing her way through an intensive Spanish program, where she heard about a school that hired American English teachers. She was not looking for that sort of thing, but on a whim she went to inquire about the position, and it turned out to be the very day they were hiring for the next semester. Following the flow of her intuitive path, a career had suddenly been born. Within months, clients were asking for her to do some translation work. Once back in the States, her intuition led her to more translation opportunities, including a chance meeting that resulted in her work being featured in a prestigious magazine.

All the experiences my friend has had in this "surprise" field have met with great success, and together they help form and keep developing the big picture of her career path. Some of her moves are more spectacular than others, which might seem like common sense. But you really know you've gotten the knack of applying intuition to your career life, or the rest of your life for that matter, when each move seems to flow naturally into the next, without a lot of fireworks or fuss.

In this sense, there is really no such thing as a detour on your career path. It's all part of the whole. Building your prosperity on a literal wing and a prayer means affirming success in your life, and then going with the flow of your unfolding success path. Just check in with your intuitive self along the way. Let the flow of your own intuition lead you to investments, clients, jobs, and whole new careers, and help you make the most successful decisions.

It also helps to be aware that you're developing a flexibility that will continue to help you meet and make choices that come your way as you move along your path. Don't worry about the details—they'll evolve and fill in naturally as you develop your intuition and as your course evolves. The fear of details, which I like to call the "what will happen if . . ." syndrome, is very common. Know you will have the flexibility and awareness required to deal with those details as they come up, and you'll be that much more able to be open to your own unfolding prosperity/success path.

CHAPTER EIGHT

THE INNER WISDOM
OF INTUITIVE ADVICE

As your inner awareness expands, the time may very well come when you feel the urge to broaden or vary your methods of developing your intuition. Yes, all the answers you ever need are inside of you. From time to time, though, you might want to seek the input of a professional intuitive counselor or take instruction from an expert in one of the many intuitive arts. This is really just a way to continue the process of developing your own awareness by expanding it with another unique, empathetic, and finely tuned point of view. A talented professional can readily tune in—and actually help you tune in more—to your own intuitive self.

By the way, intuitive pros may call themselves anything from sensitive, psychic, psychic advisor, psychic counselor or intuitive, intuitive advisor or intuitive counselor (which is how I refer to myself). Throughout this chapter, the terms are used interchangeably. But beyond titles, I'll explain how these professionals can help you.

TO GO OR NOT TO GO...
TO A PRO

These days, the variety of intuitive counselors available to us is exhilarating—and confounding. If you live in an urban area, you've probably noticed signs and ads for everything from personal readings to psychic fairs, gypsy tea leaf readings, astrological consultations, and even things like psychic energy balancing and psycho/spiritual therapy. If you live in a less populous part of the world, no doubt you've heard a story about someone who's gone to see a psychic counselor even if you haven't been exposed to one yourself. And, of course, just about everyone has seen one of those seemingly ubiquitous psychic hotline ads.

The most important thing to know about intuitive counselors is that they're not all that different from you. They're simply individuals who have made a commitment to develop and use their own intuition to help others. When you go to see any intuitive counselor, you are really boosting your own intuition by getting a dose of a professional's more powerfully developed abilities. The best intuitive counselor is one who truly acts as a catalyst for others' insights. A counseling session can help you to see your present much more clearly, and it can also highlight major upcoming trends in your life so that you can take advantage of them in whatever way you think best.

Perhaps the best motivation for seeing an intuitive is for what I like to call a psychic tune-up. Periodically checking in with a pro to heighten your awareness about what's going on in your life can accelerate your own understanding and spiraling growth process. Basic maintenance like this helps you to keep your own intuitive equipment in top shape. Refueled and well oiled, you can then go on yourself to handle rough spots or unexpected shifts, and even learn to steer clear of avoidable problems altogether.

You may also feel the urge to visit a pro when you reach an important crossroad in any of the seven major life experience categories: romance, work, money, creativity, health, family, and spiritual development. If you experience a significant loss or setback, an advisor can help you expand your understanding of the situation and counsel you on how to best deal with it. The perspective is unique, but it can also help support the counseling offered by ministers or psychotherapists.

Any reason, no matter how frivolous, can be a valid one for taking advantage of the opportunity to speed your inner growth. Remember, though, a professional intuitive counselor cannot make life decisions for you, just as a minister or psychotherapist could not. Like the ghosts of Christmas Past, Present, and Future, professional counselors will use their abilities to tell you what they see coming in your life. And by the way, even the best intuitives see in terms of probabilities—

that is, they see what is most likely to happen based on the situations, trends and undercurrents they perceive at that moment. As on the tote boards of Las Vegas, probabilities can change—just as you are subject to change many things yourself. Don't expect to leave your consultation with all the answers. Hopefully, you will leave with invaluable information that can help you tap your own rich vein of awareness and understanding and that will ultimately lead you to your own best conclusions.

HOW TO PICK YOUR ADVISOR

The first step in picking an intuitive professional is hearing or seeing that person's name. You might pick a name off a bulletin board or out of a newspaper with the help of your intuition. Or you may read about an intuitive counselor in a publication you esteem or see the name mentioned in a magazine or book interview with a writer you especially admire.

Someone you know and trust may mention a wonderful session he or she has had. If you come across an advisor's name this way, use your intuition to sense if your friend or acquaintance is someone whose taste is likely to be similar to your own. If so, this is another good sign that the counselor in question may be one who resonates with your needs. Many of my own clients come to me from personal referrals because they've felt they were more or less in tune with the people who referred them.

A note to those who may feel inspired to call a psychic

hotline: please don't. While there may be the occasional talented professional working at the other end of the line, the probability is not likely.

Once you have a name you feel comfortable with, the best way to find out if the advisor is right for you is to give the person a call. Everyone has the right to call and ask about the sort of counseling a psychic offers without feeling obliged to make an appointment. Feel free to ask as many questions as you need. You might start out by asking the counselor about his or her method and specialty. All counselors have specialties, both in the methods they use and in the kind of information they're especially good at providing. For instance, the method I use is psychometry. (You read about psychometry in Chapter 5, and I hope you can practice it yourself.) My specialty seems to be providing an enlightening overview combined with practical perceptions and guidance. I help clients to see the overall purpose and themes of their unique path in life, which allows them, in turn, to get at the meaning of present events in their lives, as well as what the future may hold—and what they can do about it.

There are almost as many valuable methods of getting intuitive information as there are intuitive professionals. The method you opt for should be a fairly accessible one, but don't let it become a deciding factor. It's far more important to concentrate on the vibes you get from the counselors themselves. Trust your own intuition and remember the Hindu saying that advises, "When the student is ready, the teacher appears." My feeling is that you really just need to tune in at the right time, without worrying too much about your methods.

As you talk to the counselor on the phone, try to tune in further. Ask yourself, "Do I feel comfortable with this person? Does he or she sound like someone who will understand me and my path? What does the person's phone style tell me about his or her counseling style? Is the person very professional and clear? warm and flexible and slightly more informal? Is he or she especially curt, or brusque, or spacey?" If the person you're talking to is the counselor's representative, the same information applies.

Ask yourself how that style meets your needs, and whether it makes you comfortable. Someone can be the best possible counselor for your best friend, but only so-so for you. It all comes down to what I call personal resonance. Some intuitive counselors will warm your heart and spirit, while other, equally competent advisors will leave your awareness out in the cold. So don't be shy about asking questions, and try to really tune in to the answers you get. Use the Visual/Feeling Checklist (page 93) to fine-tune your reactions.

Use your common sense, too. Do you feel comfortable with the attitude and language of the counselor? Feel free to ask what kind of space the sessions are held in, if it's important to you. Does the counselor work behind a desk in an office, or in a more casual kind of space where you could kick off your shoes if you wanted to? Each of these environments could have an advantage for you, depending on your own responses and tastes.

If you have a particular social or sexual orientation, you may want to find out how an intuitive counselor feels about it before making an appointment. Although a counselor doesn't have to share your orientation to do good work for you, you certainly wouldn't want to go to see an intuitive counselor who is homophobic if you are gay, or an intuitive counselor who is only keen on traditional family values if you have a nontraditional family decision to weigh.

Also, when you call, be sure to ask if you can tape your session. Remember, the right brain is not a memorizer, and it's the very hemisphere you're going to be activating during your reading. You need to really let yourself flow during a reading and must not let yourself be distracted by the worry that you'll forget what you've learned.

Taping is invaluable because it releases you from that worry. Some counselors provide a labeled tape with your name and the date of session as a normal part of the service they offer, but others will ask you to bring your own. You might think twice about seeing any counselor who doesn't allow you to tape. There may be an intuitive out there who does have a valid reason for this request. However, there may be those who ask their clients not to tape to prevent them from comparing notes and discovering that they've all received suspiciously similar readings.

The fee for the session is something else you should find out during your initial conversation. You can turn to the guidelines section at the end of the chapter to help you determine what a fair session fee would be for you.

IN THE BEGINNING...

On the day of your appointment, there is some very important preliminary work you can do to make sure you have the most productive session possible.

First, spend some time focusing on what you want to get out of the reading. Many prospective clients ask whether they should bring a list of questions with them. My advice is always the same: Really focus on the questions you want answered, whether this means making a physical list or a mental one.

However you want to collect them, it's good to have within easy reach specific questions you want answered. They will serve as a wonderful focusing point for the session itself. As one of my favorite bits of ancient Chinese wisdom advises, "It furthers one to have somewhere to go." That certainly goes for intuitive counseling sessions, where your questions can become the starting point for receiving crucial information.

On the other hand, if you're too finite about what question you want to ask and what answer you want to get, you may very well limit the full potential of your session. If you go into a consultation only looking for specific answers, you'll close yourself off from potentially invaluable information.

Any question is great for getting the session started, but open yourself to answers that could possibly lead to other questions. Sometimes clients who come to me concerned about finding the perfect mate have only one type of question and answer in mind. They never stop to think that maybe they need to learn more about themselves before they can learn about their future spouses. If you can go with the flow of the session and stay open to potentially new lines of questioning, you may receive information far more profound and influential than your original questions warranted.

So even as you make that original list, be prepared to flow with the session and the answers you receive. Anything may happen during a reading. An area of your life that is very much in the background may come into the foreground. Or the answers to your questions may be entirely different from what you'd expected them to be, but even more appropriate than the ones you'd originally considered.

It's also essential to do some whole focusing by yourself before you go to your session. You'll be greatly helping yourself to get the most out of your reading by tuning in to the flow of your upcoming session. This isn't to say that an intuitive counselor just throws out whole information, leaving you to interpret as much as if you had to decipher your own intuitive messages. But the flow of your consultation could, and may, go anywhere, so the more focused and tuned in you are, the more you can follow potential, intuitive leaps from one area to another. The higher your awareness is during your session, the more you'll click with the higher awareness of your counselor, and that, from my experience, yields a much more open and informative consultation.

Some counselors, myself included, start each session with some whole focusing with the client. Here is my routine, which you can use in any quiet place before your session.

- *Exercise 56: Presession Warm-up*

As in whole focusing, breathe in and out deeply three times, really feeling the release as you exhale. It helps to close your eyes for deeper concentration and release.

Now keep breathing rhythmically as you visualize a bright white light circulating through you and around you, literally illuminating you.

Affirm to yourself or aloud something like, "I now open to the guidance and knowledge I most need in my life. I allow the information I need to flow to me with perfect clarity from the person I'm seeing. I accept only the highest, most loving, and most useful information."

Keep whole focusing for as long as you like before going off to your session.

Also do yourself a favor and don't schedule your appointment with your counselor on a day when you know you're going to be extremely busy. Sometimes you can't always plan to be calm, but do your best to try.

Along similar lines, realize that intuitive counselors get tired and frazzled, too. You may even want to ask before making your appointment what time of day your potential advisor is most relaxed and "on." You may not have a choice, but if you do, wouldn't you rather get your guidance from a rested source? (For that reason, if for no other, don't even think about calling a counselor at 5 A.M. with a burning question.)

OPENING UP AND
GETTING DEEP

Some readings are very structured; others are more free-form. Your counselor may have prepared charts and graphs for you based on your name or your birthday. He or she may look at your hands during the course of the reading, consult cards, or hold an object that belongs to you, as I do. Other counselors have no visible tools or don't need any other kind of information to do their work. The only constant is this: When you go to a professional intuitive, you're going to see someone who's a specialist in obtaining and interpreting non-linear information. So the answer you'll eventually get will be translated from the language of intuition. Think of an intuitive counselor as an enlightened middle person, tapping into right-brain wealth, inspired by the left-brain question-and-answer process you, the client, initiate.

Some counselors prefer to deliver their information first and then have you ask questions, whereas others prefer a more free-form, conversational reading. Ask your counselor which kind of feedback he or she prefers. Or, as most of my clients do, let your advisor take the lead. Always make sure you ask all the questions you need to in order to really understand what your counselor has to share with you. The reading is for you. Therefore, the most important thing is for you to have as much understanding as you can when you leave.

Try to strike a balance between listening carefully and

asking pertinent questions. During an intuitive counseling session, the information is being filtered through a different awareness, but it is still your information and your reading.

Don't think if the intuitive counselor asks you questions that somehow it's cheating. You are not giving yourself away or giving your counselor too much power if you answer questions or give out information or confirmation as the session goes on. Use your intuition to tell if your counselor is, indeed, fishing, but generally your counselor needs to find the same balance between asking and receiving that you do. If you trust that you've already used some intuition to choose your advisor, you'll flow better with the information you're receiving and contribute more to your own session.

Ideally, the whole intuitive consultation process gives you the ball so you can run with it. Think of your advisor as a catalyst, a professional whose job it is to help you help yourself. What really warms the collective heart of professional intuitives everywhere is to hear from clients that something they were told allowed them to see things in a new way, or let them find their own inner power to make important changes. Speaking for the pros, I can say that kind of thanks gladdens us more than hearing we were right about a future event. One of my clients even told me, "I learned more in one session with you than I did in five years with my shrink." That's perhaps the most rewarding kind of feedback any professional intuitive could hear.

WHAT KINDS OF RESULTS
TO EXPECT

Whatever the method, much of intuitive counseling consists of tuning in to the many thoughts, experiences, and insights you already have about a question and bringing them into clearer focus for you. Think of a photographer who picks out the most telling or interesting image in his or her lens and focuses the whole shot around it, letting everything else fade out a little. As you look at that finished photograph, its focus helps you see what is most important and what is merely background information.

You can look at intuitive counseling the same way. What an intuitive counselor does, in one way or another, is to find the perfect focus or most important theme of a certain moment in your life. By sharing the present picture with you, the counselor can then intuit upcoming trends—the way the picture of the same scene might look if it were taken in a few months. The counselor is not the photographer, though, you are. You're creating the scenes of your life, and an intuitive counselor is simply more practiced at seeing them in the most illuminating focus and light.

Since the professional intuitive is tuning in to your picture now, you're probably going to be familiar with many of the issues raised. So you might say that, as far as intuitive counseling goes, no news is good news. If everything your counselor brings up is news to you, it's a pretty good sign that you're at least a little out of touch with your life.

Your session will probably include a lot of confirmation of the rightness of thoughts, ideas, and feelings that have already crossed your mind at least once. As your counselor confirms what you've envisioned by singling out or acknowledging certain approaches, hunches, and feelings you've already had, the confusing thoughts that have been battling in your mind's foreground will fall into place around your newly confirmed right-focused picture. You'll be able to really concentrate on what's most crucial in your life at this very moment.

Let's look at an example. One of my clients, a writer, came to me for a session on her novel in progress. She was close to finishing it, but had suddenly run into an unexpected twist in the writing process. Instead of wrapping itself up neatly at the end, suddenly many different, unexpected endings were presenting themselves to her. In the course of her work sessions, various approaches to this new dilemma had occurred to her, but when she came to me she simply asked me to tune in to see what information I, myself, would receive about her book and her finishing it.

As I conducted the reading, several things came up. First, I sensed she might need to write out all the possible endings and choose the best elements from each. When I mentioned this, she smiled. She explained to me that strategy had crossed her mind, but she had been afraid that it was just a way of procrastinating, or that, worse, it would lead to a dead end. Then more information came through to me about the book. I asked her if she had changed the name of her main character. Again, she smiled. She said she hadn't, but that she had been thinking about it and had even talked over the possibility with a friend, keeping the option in the back of her mind. But now that I'd mentioned it, she continued, she'd go ahead and do it.

Finally, I got a strong impression of the essence of the book in progress. When I mentioned it to her, she looked surprised. She said that was part of the book, but an unexpected part, and one that had been troubling her. As it turned out, the fact that I picked up on its strength and relevance confirmed its importance and allowed her to concentrate on it, brushing away all the distracting doubt and worry.

Confirmation is easy to apply to your life, since, in general, you've already considered the solution before it is confirmed. By enhancing your awareness of a situation, your counselor empowers you to deal with it. If you are already trying to listen to your intuition, you'll probably find yourself saying things like, "Oh, I was feeling that way but I was wondering if that was really happening or if it was just my imagination."

An intuitive counselor can also confirm more general feelings that you are having, and transform those feelings into practical information. Take the case of a client of mine who came to see me when he was feeling ambivalent and apathetic about his position at a PR agency, but didn't know what else he felt like doing. When I tuned in, my intuition told me it was really the right time for my client to leave his present position. I was able to tell him I didn't see any future opportunities and challenges in his job.

I confirmed what his intuition was telling him, and I

provided him with some practical information to boot. I was also able to reassure my client that I didn't see a dramatic ending, such as being fired from his present situation. As he confirmed the larger pieces of the picture that were falling into place, I was able to focus on smaller, more specific details of the issue. In his case, these details had to do with job opportunities. I gave him the name of a company to pursue and the first name of a man he didn't know at the moment, but who might prove helpful to him in the next three to six months.

These specific details were not meant as foregone conclusions. The point was to prepare my client for the opportunities that were going to present themselves to him in the near future. As the reading developed, I confirmed each specific detail I saw with my client to see if it seemed to make sense for him. If it didn't, I'd try a new twist on the same intuitive information until we came up with something that was useful to him. You may have tried this yourself in the psychometry exercise in Chapter 5 (Exercise 40). Certainly other counselors who use different methods can offer practical information that pinpoints and confirms a client's needs and feelings equally well.

Remember, along with confirmation, much of what an intuitive counselor illuminates are upcoming trends in your life so that you can take advantage of them. Lurking behind the most specific and practical detail an intuitive counselor can suggest is the sure conviction that a personal trend is coming around the next corner.

If you are the slightly nervous type, and we all are from

time to time, an intuitive consultation can really soothe your nerves about taking the initiative in any area of your life. Anyone becomes more confident when their inclinations are supported by a little evidence.

Of course, confirmation is not always so straightforward. Since it reflects the flow of life itself, intuitive counseling is full of twists, turns, and surprises. Your advisor may intuit that the flow is not moving in the direction you'd prefer, and will advise you on how best to turn the circumstances around in your favor.

He or she may also give you a ballpark estimate of how long it will be before certain plans you have begin to bear fruit. We're all trained to think short term, but if we're truly to progress along the spiral of awareness, we also have to think long term. Gaining long-term insight is like developing your vantage point from the spiral of awareness—it can help you see, accept, and get the most out of what's going on right now. Remember, you have free will. Your advisor is only giving you trends based on the current situation. Your knowledge of those trends can help you change the projected picture, and that new picture may well be the one that accelerates your growth.

While we're on the subject of twists and turns, your intuitive counselor could sense that the issue you came to consult about is related to another life issue. That is to say, fear of leaving your job could have something to do with fear of leaving your parents. Or a lack of trust in one of your children could have something to do with your lack of trust in your own creative or business talent.

There may be something very primal that comes up in your session—for example, an unresolved and resentful relationship with your family—that you realize will never be completely resolved within the structure of an intuitive consultation. It may be time for you to go with the flow of working through that situation by contacting a trained psychological therapist.

Don't be surprised if a compassionate intuitive makes that kind of suggestion or recommends any other form of release or therapy, from isolation tanks to meditation to energy-centering massage. The flow is not particular about the methods you use to gain the results you want. There are infinite solutions to any one problem, and getting at the roots of problems intuitively, psychologically, physically, or by any other route is just another way of easing your way toward a greater sense of resolution and abundance.

HOW YOU CAN
HELP THE PROCESS

All different kinds of information will probably be part of the flow of intuition provided for you as an intuitive tunes in to your questions. Anything from advice on your path through life and personal challenges to childhood events, names of loved ones, and estimated dates concerning when certain events will take place, can all be part and parcel of a reading.

The way you respond to this information influences the kind of reading you get. The choice is yours. You can either focus on the straight facts or go to the very heart of any personal problems you have.

Clients are often impressed by their counselor's ability to come up with names and initials or to predict mundane events, like leaking pipes. Accuracy like this is useful if it enables you to trust the deeper, less verifiable insights your counselor shares with you.

However, try not to focus so intensely on this kind of dazzling surface information that you miss out on the more lasting meaning of the counsel being offered to you. It's my belief that information for information's sake does you and your awareness little good. It's how you apply that information or how your counselor can advise you to do so that does the trick. Always remember to ask, "What can I learn from this?"

There is no such thing as a dumb question. A professional intuitive counselor is in the business of compassion. During your reading, he or she is attuned only to you and to your awareness. Any kind of personal judgment your advisor may have should be left outside the office door.

You'll also probably be interested in any information your advisor can give you about the timing of certain events in your life. Although once in a while you may happen upon someone who's a real time prediction whiz, generally speaking the best time estimate is a ballpark estimate. You can reasonably expect a counselor to advise you that he or she sees an event coming your way within six months. However, don't count on being told that an important event will transpire on March 3, 2010. Or tomorrow. Or next week.

In fact, if you focus only on the exact time and place something is supposed to happen, you may miss out on a much more significant piece of information. Since time is a continuum, both the past and the future come out of now, and what happens now will shape both past and future events. (Remember, too, probabilities can change.) Simply sitting on your hands and waiting for March 3, 2010 to come down the pike probably won't accomplish much at all.

Don't be surprised if your counselor uses phrases or words that have special, private meanings for you, which he or she couldn't possibly know. For instance, if you are examining a relationship, your counselor may mention a typical phrase your partner uses. Once you've focused on that phrase together, this may open your counselor to shed further light on the feelings or patterns that lie behind it. Or an intuitive may suddenly use uncharacteristic language, which turns out to be very revealing, to describe the person in question. In a recent counseling session I found myself describing a client's relative as a "gay blade." As it happened, gayness was both an issue concerning the relative and an issue my client was trying to deal with. The strange expression that popped out of my mouth, seemingly out of nowhere, actually opened a discussion that my client immediately felt comfortable with. Every intuitive counselor can have seemingly magical moments—this is only one of many. So look forward to receiving forms of confirmation that are often as unexpected and revealing as the results of the session itself.

GOING WITH THE FLOW
OF YOUR SESSION

If you are feeling doubt or uncertainty during a session, try to express it in a nonresistant way. It's an unwritten contract that when you come to see an intuitive counselor you've accepted that they can intuit. So try not to challenge your counselor on his or her intuitive ability, just as you wouldn't challenge a psychological therapist on his or her credentials during a therapy session.

For instance, asking an intuitive counselor how many children you have, just to see if he or she knows the answer, isn't helpful to you. You already know how many children you have. But asking your counselor to give you more specific information about a particular problem your youngest child is having is perfectly valid and quite helpful as well.

If you don't feel a session is working for you, try and go with it anyway. Later on, when you listen to your tape, you may very well find that you get something out of it you did not understand at the time. This happens to almost everyone at some point. You may even discover that a part of the reading that seemed off was actually right on the money and that you just weren't aware enough at the time to absorb and understand the information it contained.

Despite all your careful screenings, it's possible you'll have to leave a session while it's still in progress. If an intuitive counselor asks you for more money than was mentioned on the phone, get up and walk out. Call the Better Business

Bureau while you're at it. A reputable intuitive will not ask you for more money. Furthermore, if an intuitive counselor starts talking gobbledygook about evil spirits around you, you should make an immediate exit.

HOW TO READ A READING

When the subject of intuitive counseling comes up among a group of people, there is sometimes one person who says, "I went to see X, but X can't be a very good counselor because he only told me good things." A variation on this is the one who says, "Y is a terrific counselor. She tells it like it is. She makes me feel really uncomfortable, and that must be good."

How a professional intuitive delivers the reading is an important issue. It's my personal belief that most people focus on the negative side of life much more than on the positive. Instead of seeking the help of an intuitive counselor to anticipate and plan for a positive growth experience, many regard counseling sessions as "reports from the front," or bulletins that can alert them about upcoming battles, so that they can duck the bullets and head for the nearest foxhole. Ironically, by keeping that negative reality on their minds they align themselves more closely to it and can actually end up bringing it into their lives instead of avoiding it.

To correct for this, sensitive intuitive counselors (myself included) try to help people rediscover their connection to a more positive supply of inner wisdom and growth potential.

This doesn't mean we're Pollyannas. It simply means that a dedicated advisor feels a certain responsibility to deliver information in a way that is helpful, which generally means showing what good can come out of any situation that's been intuited.

If I see a potentially difficult situation coming up for one of my clients, I don't necessarily view it as a total negative. Instead, I see it and express it as a growth opportunity. If a person is already going through a painful experience, they certainly know it. My job is to show them how to use the information they receive to deal with their pain more effectively, avoid future distress if possible, and, in either case, show how they can go on to improve their lives.

Intuitive counselors should never let their egos interfere with their work, especially if a client could be hurt. For example, a friend of mine went to see an intuitive advisor who seemed to specialize in financial consultation. This consultant told my friend she would never have any financial security, because as soon as she became solvent, something would always happen to relieve her of her funds. As a result, my friend was advised to spend whatever money she had on things she wanted, so that at least she would be relieving herself of funds in a constructive way. Constructive? This advice certainly wasn't! A compassionate advisor who perhaps had picked up similar information wouldn't have presented it in such a way that the client was left with no alternative but to assume her life was a financial disaster.

The moral is to beware of any advice that doesn't leave room for a growth opportunity. Basically, you should be wary of someone who interprets your reality in an absolutely negative or judgmental way and who offers no chance for self-improvement or the exercise of your own free will.

Be responsible. If you feel as if something's wrong with the way your advisor's handling the situation, don't ignore it. It's well within your rights to say, "Wait a minute. I don't accept that and don't want to be talked to that way." On the other hand, if your counselor flatters you more than the fox flattered the hen, take that flattery with a grain of salt and probe more deeply into the information that's being offered. Finally, if you find your counselor picking up on some good upcoming trends for you in a sensible and grounded way, while also pointing out the occasional area where there's room for growth, just sit back and enjoy the ride.

THE INTUITIVE ART OF MIX AND MATCH

You may go to more than one intuitive counselor over time and find they give you conflicting information. This is just one more reason to check in with your own intuition. One of your advisors isn't necessarily wrong, because as we've seen, the picture of your life can change over time, sometimes over a period as short as a week or a month. If one counselor tells you you're going to be a business-person and another sees you writing poetry, use your own inner resources to look into the whole of what, together, the two advisors have offered you. You may find that none of the information applies to you, or it may be that everything else about the reading made sense to you except for this one piece of information.

Perhaps, for example, the information referred symbolically to the poetry within you or to the fact that you should be more businesslike about your career as a poet. Or maybe you'll be happiest as a business executive who writes poetry on the side, or have a thriving career in arts administration. Use your common and uncommon sense to find out. Situations like this one are all the more reason why the state of your awareness, and hence the state of your life, is ultimately up to you.

It's also important to be aware of the phenomenon I call *intuitive slants*. A talented and compassionate intuitive counselor may have occasional blind spots or subjects about which information doesn't come through quite as well or as objectively as it does in others. For example, I tell the few clients who ask that I'm simply no good at predicting the outcome of sports events.

As for objectivity, I know of an intuitive counselor who sometimes makes overly negative predictions concerning careers. One reason for this may be that her own career is full of fitful starts and stops. Nevertheless, she's quite wonderful with other kinds of advice, and people who consult with her learn to take any predicted career chaos with a grain of salt.

The comparative worldliness of your advisor can also slant or tint information, which you may be required to reinterpret. Just last month, a colleague of mine highly recommended a telephone intuitive counselor who works out of her kitchen in California. "This woman's wonderful," my friend said, "and gives uncannily accurate readings. But just keep in mind there may be some corrections you need to make to allow for her frame of reference. You know, she saw me taking a trip to California, when really she was seeing my house in the Mediterranean. She was right on the money about everything—the warm climate, Spanish style, blue-green ocean. But she just assumed it was California because she's never seen the Mediterranean."

Also, the closer you come to areas not related to your own direct experience (such as past lives and some information offered by trance channels), the harder it's going to be to validate that information. Only your feelings can validate the information you receive. For the sake of example, let's say you've explored past life therapy because you believe that for you it has either psychological or spiritual benefits.

A specialist in this area focuses in on one lifetime, or more, that seems particularly resonant for you now. Depending on how many times you go to such a specialist and on whether or not you go to different specialists, you may find yourself getting what appears to be contradictory information. Ask yourself why that information might be coming at this particular time and what the essence of its message could be.

There's clearly no physical library you can reference to see if this kind of data is right, so check with your intuitive self to see if it fits. While you're checking in, ask how you can apply it to better understand and improve your life. For instance, if a counselor believes you were a musician in another lifetime that was cut short, that may help you to understand why you are a musician now. Or if your career choice seems impossible at every turn and you are advised you had a long and happy career in this area in another life, it may be that you have no need to repeat the experience.

A final word on the subject of multiple advisors: It's good to be sensitive to the changes in your own flow, which may make you resonate to different methods and specialties at different times. If you find yourself being disappointed with advisor after advisor, however, consider the possibility that maybe you don't know what it is you're looking for. Use the opportunity to take some time to tune in and center yourself by yourself. A rule of thumb: Three intuitive advisors, and that could be pushing it, should really be the limit at any one time to consult on any one issue.

SOME GUIDELINES AND ANSWERS TO COMMONLY ASKED QUESTIONS

There is no American version of the American Medical Association to give accreditation to intuitive professionals—another reason why it's important to get good referrals and/or use your own intuition to seek out the best intuitive counselor for you.

Some people prefer to bring a friend along to sit in on their session. If this is your preference, be sure to ask the counselor if that's okay. Some do mind. Unless it's a specified couples session, many intuitive counselors often find they are limited in what information they can divulge and feel hindered by the presence of a second person. Also, you may be less focused when a friend is present. Remember, this is your time for you.

Please don't assume that just because your counselor gives intuitive advice, his or her schedule is nonlinear, too. If you show up late, you may not be able to extend your session to make up for your lateness. And when you're making the appointment, ask how long the session will be.

As far as fees are concerned, basically you need to let your intuition and your location be your guide. In major urban areas intuitive counseling sessions, like much else, tend to be more expensive. In general, if you are considering a low-priced reading, you're probably talking about a consultation with some kind of limitation. You may receive only ten to fifteen minutes worth of information or not very good information. Or perhaps the counselor in question is not 100 percent terrific, but is very good on certain issues.

Don't assume, however, that the more you pay the better the counselor. Whether a one hundred-dollar consultation is twice as good as a fifty-dollar reading depends entirely on the quality of the reader. Other factors to consider when tuning in to an appropriate fee are these: the part of town your advisor works out of (high rent affects intuitive counselors, too); how "hot" he or she is at the moment (the law of supply and demand works here as well); and experience (if I had to go for one determining factor, this would be it).

The only real rule of thumb here is to make sure you're intuitively working in the best way for you. But a corollary to that rule is, the more expensive the session or the more esoteric the method, the more questions you should ask, both of the prospective counselor and of your intuitive self, before committing to a session. Ask yourself, "Would the reading have the same value without all the snazzy packaging?"

WRAPPING IT UP

When your session comes to a close, you'll want to feel both a sense of completion and a sense of continuity. There are a few simple ways of making sure you got what you came for and of keeping the avenues open for further communication.

Like many intuitive counselors, I'm often asked, "When should I come back?" The answer is that only you know the answer to that question. You may never have to see a professional again. You may want to come back in a year or, as I do (yes, intuitives do go to other intuitives for information), come in for regular tune-ups. If you're going through a lot of changes, you may even want to come back as soon as the following month. Whatever feels right is right.

An unanswered question about something you discussed in your session may percolate up through your awareness a few days after your reading. If you feel confused or incomplete, by all means call the counselor. Many counselors, including me, even make a point of letting clients know this is okay at the end of each session. Certainly try to have respect for an advisor's time, but if you need a little more clarification about something that came up, do give a call.

The best way to get the most out of a reading is to take

it in whole, let what needs to stick stick, and release what doesn't seem appropriate. You may prefer to review your tape to clarify things. You may also want to listen to that tape every now and then to see if something new catches your attention in a way it didn't before. You'll find listening to the tape also helps you to discern patterns of information that can invaluably point to patterns in your life.

Here is a focusing technique that will help you get the most out of your reading after it is completed. Do this exercise before you listen to your tape.

• *Exercise 57: Postsession Wrap-up*

Repeat the breathing and white light visualization you learned in the presession warm-up (Exercise 56).

Then say aloud or think to yourself something like, "I now allow myself to hear the deepest wisdom and highest guidance. I know I will learn and use what I need to achieve my greatest growth. I let go of anything that does not apply."

Keep whole focusing for as long as you like before turning on the tape.

Listening to your tape once in a while will also help you develop your own intuition. You're going to be hearing how a pro really works, and you could easily pick up some professional techniques to apply to your own tuning-in process.

CONCLUSION . . . THE PATH CONTINUES

Now that you've traveled this far down the intuitive path, you've undoubtedly gathered that having—or using—your intuition means a whole lot more than just getting "psychic" flashes.

In developing your intuition—and, in turn, deepening your inner wisdom—what you've really been evolving is a highly practical philosophy of life. Intuitive thinking is whole thinking and should be applied to your whole life. That means you can really use your intuition to explore all the avenues of your life path, ultimately gathering a much larger sense of its context and purpose. With intuitive sense you can put your whole life into perspective and gain a sense of where it is as well as where it's going.

Remember, though, that intuition isn't an all-purpose magic wand. As your awareness grows, you'll come to keenly realize and accept the paradox that although sometimes the power of your intuition is so great it can seem almost magical, at other times it will simply seem to have vanished. Always keep in mind that intuition, like your personal path, has a unique flow of its own. Try to go with that flow as far as you can when it feels "on" to you. Remember this during those seemingly off times: Intuition is often so subtle and so natural that, blissfully unaware, you may actually be using it as part and parcel of your everyday thinking.

In general, however, you have been consciously learning how to use and apply your intuitive sense. And you'll become more and more familiar with how intuition works for you personally (and how you can make it work) as you continue to develop it. For your ongoing inner development, here's a list of basic do's and don'ts that should enlighten your process and keep you pointed in the right direction.

INTUITION DO'S AND DON'TS

- Don't "inflict" your developing intuition on others—don't be a know-it-all and a show-off. (This, of course, becomes less of a problem as you develop empathy.)

- Do help others to tap into their own intuition by asking them, "How do you feel about this situation (or person, or decision)? What does your gut say?" This way, you can guide others to experience their own intuition without inflicting your particular beliefs and abilities on them.

- Do have fun with intuition, especially with other people. Humor, we've seen, immediately raises anyone's awareness. Have fun trying out some appropriate intuition-developing routines with friends, family, co-workers, and mates. You'll allow them to find and use their own intuition, further develop your own intuition skills, and have a lot of laughs in the process.

- Don't turn intuition into another "should" to hang over your head in life. For example, don't berate yourself because you should be better at it or you should use it more often.

- Do let intuition flow to you as it comes, and let yourself go with that flow as you need to. And do let go of that mental tape that tries to tell you otherwise!

- Don't try to analyze why your intuition works sometimes and not others, works in different ways, or even why it works at all.

- Do understand that by its very definition intuition is really beyond analysis. Enjoy that refreshing angle, and flow with your intuition.

You'll be surprised at how much you can integrate it into your life in a very commonsense way
after you let it all flow—minus the analysis.

- Don't consider anything here to be written in
  stone. This book is really intended to serve as a
  guideline that shows you how much you, in fact,
  already know and how easily you can tune in to
  and go with the flow of your own life—in the
  way that's right for you.

As you keep going with the flow and cultivate your intuition,
you'll naturally develop a sense of wonder toward your own
virtually limitless potential. To experience all of the fulfillment our lives truly have to offer, we need to maintain that
sense of wonder, and we need to keep exploring every potential of our paths. We each must do this in our own way, of
course. But watch a child engrossed in observing the tracery
of veins on a new green leaf, and you'll get a sense of exactly
the kind of wondrous, exploring attitude you need.

An almost childlike curiosity will allow you a chance for
fulfillment, even as you weather some very adult self-
questioning. In those times when you are uncertain about
making the right decision, use your instinctive sense of wonder to show you the possibilities—especially when the
answers you seek don't seem black or white.

Sometimes, no matter how much you allow yourself to
flow with your life and your intuition, you find yourself
caught in an uphill battle or even downright stalled and stuck

in difficult situations. Think of these as growing pains which, as the name implies, can accompany many of our most valuable life (and growth) experiences. The pearl needs an irritating grain of sand to manifest its perfect form. You yourself gain perfection and develop your own grit when you learn how to grow from each potential life catalyst. Using your intuition to try to better understand and move through each of these growth stimulators, you can gain a greater sense of resolution and find the contentment you can only know after learning such difficult lessons.

Take advantage of your progress along the spiral of awareness and look to the state of fulfillment that exists beyond any current difficulty. Above all, the main rule of thumb is the same as the one you go by in developing any aspect of your intuition: Trust yourself. Through your ongoing connection to the intuitive source and to your own inner wisdom, all awareness is flowing to you right now through every situation you encounter. And each one presents a precious chance to grow, to know, and to truly experience contentment with the flow of your life.

You've embarked on a wonderful journey. You'll encounter many interesting developments as you continue to follow your intuitive path to ever-increasing wisdom. I'd love to hear all about them—whether it's in the form of sharing your intuitive discoveries, your questions, or certainly your responses to this book. Write to me!

Yours in love and loads of intuition,

Patricia Einstein

MORE INTUITIVE TRICKS AND TECHNIQUES

FINDING LOST OBJECTS

First, take some deep breaths to relax into the receptive state that will help you get the information you need. Anxiety definitely chokes up the flow. When you're ready, put up your inner white screen.

Now slowly widen your mental focus, gradually zooming your awareness out like a camera to bring the area immediately around the object into this mental picture.

Look for visual clues that might tell you where you are. For example, if your screen reveals the inside of a drawer, what other objects do you see in the picture that might tell you in which drawer the missing object will be found? You might even try asking your intuitive self, "Where am I?"

If you need more clues, try zooming out a little wider until more of the surrounding area comes into view. Or try mentally flashing backward in time from the lost object as it sits alone on your white screen. Imagine going back to where the object was right before it was lost. Look around. What do you see? What does the scene tell you about where your lost object may be now? If you're missing a watch, what time does the watch say when you look at it?

If your first few attempts don't help you locate your object, try again a little later, perhaps when you're not trying so hard. Finding lost objects is a lot like trying to remember someone's name—it's the sort of thing that doesn't always come to you right away, but often pops up unexpectedly later on. So be on the lookout for brief mental images that come to you later in the day, particularly when you're going to bed or right after you've just woken up.

My husband used this technique to great effect. He'd lost a watch and was very upset, but then he started to visualize the watch on his white screen. He checked for clues of what could be surrounding the watch, and he started to sense that it was in a dark place with some objects near it. A few moments later he realized that those surrounding objects were paper clips and the dark place was a hidden portion of a bookshelf. He went to the shelf, and sure enough, there was the watch, hidden under some papers and lying right next to a pile of paper clips!

CARD TRICK VARIATION

See how much you've improved your intuitive skills by adding visualization and breathing techniques to this synchronicity exercise.

Start by preparing your deck of playing cards as you did in Exercise 11. Now close your eyes and visualize your white screen. When you're ready, visualize the card in front of you slowly lifting up from the table and tilting to one side to give you a quick peak at the front. What kind of impression do you get? Is it high or low? red or black? Was it bright or dark? dense or airy? Is it worth a lot or a little? If you're drawing a blank, try "breathing in" your answer with each inhalation as you ask the questions to yourself. If you still don't get a sense, a feeling, or a visual impression, just blurt out the first thing that comes to mind—either the color or the relative value (high or low).

Before you turn over the card, see what your next impression about the card is. If your first impression was the color, try tuning into the relative value. ("I feel it's red . . . and it's also low.")

Are you any "hotter" than you were before? Now try predicting the suit or the value of the card. Even though the odds are much tougher, some people are relatively better (versus pure chance) at making precise predictions on things than more general predictions. And, as always, practice makes perfect!

READING THE "PSYCHIC" BAROMETER

You've learned how to tune in to your intuitive self for ongoing guidance and information. For quick answers to yes or no questions, however, nothing beats trying one of the following.

THE PENDULUM

This technique is adapted from an ancient tried-and-true method. Use a pendant if you have one or create your own by taking a three-to-six-inch piece of string and attaching a little ball of tinfoil to one end so there's enough weight to allow the string, when held, to swing.

Holding your weighted string or pendant in your hand so it can swing freely from three to six inches on its chain, think of the question you want to ask. Now address your pendulum as you would address your intuitive self (think of the pendulum as an intuitive middle person).

The first question to ask your pendulum is what kind of movement will indicate a yes answer. Now begin to breathe deeply and rhythmically, and wait for the pendulum to start moving by itself. It will! Note whether it moves around in a circle or back and forth. Next, follow the same procedure to ask which kind of movement will indicate no.

Now ask your question, making sure that it can be answered by a yes or no (see "Finding the Answer in the Questions," Chapter 5, page 103), allowing the pendulum to move freely on its own.

Note: If your pendulum seems to move in a dramatic fashion (i.e., if it moves very surely in an unusually wide circle or arcs more dramatically than usual to the left and right), interpret it as a psychic exclamation point at the end of the answer that's been given you. Sometimes it really will seem like your pendulum is sending you a very loud message of "Oh yes, yes, yes!" or "Oh no, no, no!" At other times it may seem as if your pendulum's not moving at all or is moving too subtly to register a definite answer. In these cases, try again later or try the following technique.

THE SPLIT SCREEN

Visualize your inner white screen and divide it in half. It, too, will function as your intuitive middle person, so ask it which side of the screen will indicate a yes answer and, by default, a no. Your intuition may register these yes and no answers on the screen in any number of ways. It may do so by way of a flashing light radiating from the appropriate side. Or perhaps the correct side will move toward you, or signal you in some unique way. It may not even be visual: You may hear or feel an answer via your screen or have a sense of which side of the screen seems right. Whatever works is right for you.

Again, as in the pendulum exercise, ask yourself a question that can be answered with yes or no, and note which side of your white screen responds. Here, too, a more intensified response means a more emphatic answer.

You can use the split screen technique very quickly in practically any everyday situation. Use it to test your business options, creative ideas, intuitive judgments, and so on, especially when you have to make an immediate decision. When you have the luxury of more time, add this technique to your review and decision-making process to give your comprehension an intuitive boost.

To quickly see how you really feel about whatever you're considering, try literally tuning in to your gut.

GUT-TUNING

Once again, ask yourself a question that requires a yes or no response. Take a deep breath, close your eyes, and continue to breathe deeply and rhythmically—directing your breath and awareness to your solar plexus. Keep breathing as you silently focus on your question, and pay special attention to whatever feelings come up.

Do you feel a sense of warmth? Do you tingle anywhere? Do you feel yourself tighten or relax? Do you get a sense of balance or imbalance?

Any of these experiences could indicate a sense of rightness or wrongness of the option you're posing to yourself. If you're not sure if the answer is yes or no, silently ask your intuitive self for confirmation by asking to be allowed to feel strongly—either positively or negatively.

DEVELOPING INTUITION WITH OTHERS: SUGGESTED WORKOUTS TO SHARE

One of the wonderful bonuses of developing your intuition is being able to share the fun and benefits with friends, intimate partners, and even business colleagues. You can quickly teach others whatever mechanics the two of you or the group need to learn collectively. You'll see mutual results in no time, and in the bargain you'll get to know each other and yourself much better as a result of developing your intuition together.

Following are the exercises that I've found to be the best for sharing, many culled and adapted from this book, as well as some new ones that are especially good for specific situations. The suggestions are divided into two categories: groups (which can include friends, office colleagues, team members, fellow musicians, students, you name it) and an intimate partners category.

The following suggestions are meant to be just that. Since every group is as unique as every individual, use your common and uncommon sense to choose the most feasible techniques for the people you know and the most workable order in which to practice them. You may find you have a group of people who want to meet on a regular basis to "work out" their intuition. Remember, you can also spontaneously whip out any exercise that seems to be appropriate whenever any working group or team is at an impasse to get the ideas and energy flowing again.

While you're at it, whoever you're working out with, don't forget to have fun!

GROUPS

SPOON BENDING (EXERCISE 13). This gets folks into the swing of things by discovering hidden abilities and developing more trust in the intuition process itself, which helps open them to try more exercises afterward. Even the most literal-minded individuals (or especially the most literal-minded) seem to thoroughly enjoy this one. As mentioned earlier, at the office you can try bending letter openers, too.

SYNC GAMES (EXERCISES 10 AND 11). Adapt these exercises to suit your needs. Suggestions: Try syncing with elevator doors, tuning in to the colors that friends, colleagues, or clients will be wearing on a given day, what time people will arrive at the office or at a party, when traffic lights will change. Keep track among your group, and exchange experiences and insights.

Designate a "sender" who chooses a card, then projects it—staring at the card, breathing it "in" and then "out" with each breath—while you (or partners) try "breathing it in" through your white screen. You can even try using playing cards with a partner or partners to help improve your hit percentage.

Don't forget here and in all other exercises to cue others to clue into their own personal sync signals. Also take note of how your friends and colleagues begin to sync with each other, by wearing the same colors or saying things at the same time.

RELAXING/RELEASING. The exercises that helped you start to relax and open to intuition will help a group do the same. Try practicing "Breath Charge" (Exercise 22), "Neck Rolls" (Exercise 23), or "Spine Straightening" (Exercise 24) together.

IMAGING PRACTICE. Almost everyone responds to imaging exercises, and they're perfect for groups. Try any of the mind's eye imaging exercises (31–33). Show your group how to talk out what they're receiving with "Talking Pictures" (Exercise 34) and how to develop X-ray vision with Exercise 35. You may also want to photocopy the Visual/Feeling Checklist (page 93) and distribute it to everyone in the group so all have an easy reference guide.

STORYTELLING (EXERCISE 37) is fun to do in a group almost anytime there's someone around to tune in to, for example, a new colleague or boss, a new client, people in line or in a restaurant, and so on. Try going around in a circle to build on to other group members' stories. This will give you an even richer narrative with even more to build on as everyone's details and insights are tuned in to and developed by the entire team.

FINDING THE ANSWER IN THE QUESTIONS
(EXERCISES 38 AND 39). If you feel your group is ready for a more "advanced" tuning-in exercise, this is a good one to try.

PSYCHOMETRY (EXERCISE 40). This exercise is a great crowd pleaser. Try passing around a dish of different guests' jewelry at a party. The results will be surprisingly good. In other group situations, start out by practicing with each other's jewelry or other objects. Then try a group tune-in on metal items belonging to a boss, co-worker, or client (use papers if you can't get anything metal, or try photographs or any other item belonging to the subjects in question).

OTHER GROUP SUGGESTIONS

Demonstrate the split screen technique (from the "Reading the 'Psychic' Barometer" tip described earlier), and get your group to tune in to questions of mutual interest. For instance, at the office, ask how certain projects will turn out, and with friends, ask how certain issues concerning one particular friend will be resolved.

If you're interested in developing group creativity, try "Wordspin" (Exercise 44), "Fractured Proverbs" (Exercise 45), or "Likenings" (Exercise 46).

You can also have fun showing how to jump-start the right brain by doing the alternative nostril technique in the

"Breath Charge" exercise (22). Silly as it looks, people really enjoy this one. They get a regular charge out of it!

For a change of pace, try a group experience with "Dream Problem Solving" (Exercise 48). Pick a single creative problem and send everyone home to literally sleep on it. At the next group meeting (preferably the next day), put together a composite picture from those remembered dreams and you'll get a picture with some interesting similarities and guidance. Use the Visual/Feeling Checklist (page 93) for interpretation.

Locating the Essence/Finding the Feeling (see page 127) is a great morale and team spirit booster. Make sure to try both parts of the exercise. Believe it or not, the metropolitan staff of one of the nation's leading news services had great fun casting each other as pastries!

Especially good for business situations is the "Free-Form Free-for-All" (Exercise 51). Try it with a colleague to right-brainstorm marketing plans, new ideas and solutions, and so on.

At the office again, it's most helpful to try "The Empathy Connection" (Exercise 54) to increase your group's creative problem-solving ability when the well seems to run dry.

INTIMATE PARTNERS

For more intimate intuitive development, you can certainly adapt any of the exercises from the above suggested group workouts.

OTHER INTIMATE
SUGGESTIONS

The sync games are especially good ones to try. Since you are probably already at least somewhat in sync with your intimate partner, start with sync games, but go further with the exercises. Sync with phone calls, words, even thoughts.

Try "Psychometry" (Exercise 40) and "Finding the Answer in the Questions" (Exercises 38–39).

You'll find that answering each other's questions can sometimes be easier than answering your own. You'll also be pleasantly surprised to find that when you tune in to an intimate partner you gain the bonus of receiving insightful information about yourself as well.

Also try using the white screen technique to tune in to your partner's present, and then his or her future. Once you've got a clear picture in place, add yourself to the scene. Where do you fit in? Is there a message for you as well as him or her?

To stimulate your mutual love flow, here's a new exercise to share.

LOVE JUMPS. Place your left hand on your partner's heart. Have him or her do the same to yours. Take hold of each other's right hands, and breathe deeply and rhythmically, looking deeply into each other's eyes.

Whole focus in this position for as long as you can. Feel the flow of energy between the two of you. That very palpable current could be seen as the literal "love flow."

Contacting it in this way together will not only put you in touch with its powerful energy, it will also clear the way for greater love to flow between you both—as well as help establish a stronger intuitive connection.

This is an especially good technique to practice after experiencing some kind of problem. It helps you both get back on the literal "love track." And, it's got another wonderful function: At the proper place and time, it serves as an incomparable prelude to an evening of deep lovemaking!

BINGO—
INTUITIVELY CHECKING OUT YOUR
"LOVE-CONNECTION"

Once loving prospects start showing up in your life, you'll want to use your intuition to help determine their rightness for you. When tuning in to a new love potential or relationship for that "bingo" sense of rightness, from the start pay special attention to the following signals.

Feelings. Remember to essentially "feel out" the person in question. It may seem obvious, but some people look so good on paper—and in person—you may ignore some basic negative intuitive feelings you have about them. This works the other way around, too, of course.

Follow up on any negative feelings you may have. As in some of the greatest romantic comedies, initial tensions can eventually lead to true romance. So, keep tuning in to see what other feelings and images come up until you reach a sense of potential resolution.

Images. Try putting your new love interest on your white screen as you've learned to do when checking out creative/business options. Does his or her image seem to stay on the screen, or does it fade away or flicker in and out? Is it richly detailed or barely filled in? Do any personal symbols or images come up that tell you something? If you are tuning in to several different potential interests, which seems to have more life, more future?

Put yourself into the picture with the person in question and try the same techniques. Does that double image fare as described here or does it change? Try flashing forward. What are the two of you doing together? And, in all cases, what is the general feeling of the image or scene?

Synchronicity. Check the flow of the relationship the way you do when you're checking out the rightness of ideas, jobs, or projects. Are things falling into place? flowing? Do you just happen to run into him or her on a crowded city street— near where you usually never find yourself? Are there interesting, personal patterns that relate this person to the flow of all your love relationships, or do you intuit a sense of evolution from past relationships to this one? Is there a sense of harmony or attunement between the two of you? Do you find yourself saying the same things at the same time, or do you seem to immediately sense what the other is saying or thinking?

Remember, don't analyze while you're in this whole checking-in process, because a lot of what you discover won't make logical sense. Love, like intuition after all, is a nonrational phenomenon. But if you find, by following the list, that many experiences do indeed check out, bingo!

LIFE TRANSITION ROUTINE

This book has been full of suggestions for intuitively developing many different areas of your life. But you may feel you need an extra development boost when you're going through a major life transition. This could include moments when you're experiencing an intense change or shift in jobs or careers, relationships, creative, spiritual or educational development, or at any time you find yourself involved in deep self-questioning.

For these periods, it would be wonderful if you could meditate (using the whole-focusing techniques in this book, or perhaps a meditation tape) at least five to thirty minutes a day (the longer, the better) to help break through any blocks you may be experiencing. To that end, pay special attention to your breathing. As well as spending a few moments a day doing deep breathing exercises, take deep breaths throughout the day whenever you think of it.

This, of course, is a form of mentally letting go, and anything physical you can do to give yourself a break would also help. Treat yourself to those yoga classes you've been meaning to take, step up your aerobics program, or try practicing the mind/body/spirit discipline of martial arts. Your body—and your life itself—will thank you.

For breaking stuck patterns, nothing beats getting away—for an hour, a day, a week . . . whatever you can manage. Consciously allow yourself to take in new sights, sounds, and experiences. The inspiration you need could hit you there—or when you come back, more refreshed and open.

Energy balancing (Exercise 17) could also be an especially important tool for you to use at these times. It really can help put you into a greater sense of alignment—both within yourself and with the changing world around you.

Keep tuning in to your white screen for a clearer picture of what's ahead, as well as for guidance through your present situation.

Pay special attention to the feelings and images that come to you at this time in your life—either through your white screen and other tuning-in exercises or just at any moment in your everyday life. So, too, make note of especially synchronistic events happening, or interesting coincidences. They could provide a vital clue to a new direction you should take or confirmation of a decision you've made or are in the process of making.

Keep noting these experiences in your intuition log and make sure to include any other interesting information you may be receiving, especially information from your dreams. Don't worry about all of it making sense. Your answers and direction will become clearer and clearer to you as you keep clearing your own path to inner wisdom.

You can also try tuning into your life path itself when going through a major life-change or at any time you want to get more clarity and guidance about your direction in life.

TUNING IN TO YOUR LIFE PATH

Focus on any topic of concern about your life. Close your eyes, take a deep breath, and send your breath and awareness to your white screen. Keep breathing as you visualize a road or path leading off to the horizon—your life path. Now see yourself on that path, traveling along it, and begin to tune into more details about where that path might lead you.

Where are you now? What do you see? feel? Do things get brighter as you go along the path? or darker? Is there an obstacle? Is the road bumpy or smooth? Is it going straight or does it twist and turn? Do you seem to make little progress down the path or move briskly and easily? Are you getting somewhere or have you reached a dead end?

What else do you sense/see/feel? Don't analyze. Let whatever pictures, feelings, symbols, words, and anything else emerge on this inner journey. For anything that's incomplete, silently ask your intuitive self to show or tell you more.

You can use this exercise to try to visualize different possibilities on your life path. The more you practice, the clearer your potential insight will be.

SETTING UP YOUR INTUITION LOG

I strongly encourage you to set up your own intuition log and to keep it handy when you try techniques and exercises. A good place to keep the log when it's not in use is on your night table, so you can jot down those dreams and flashes of inspiration in the morning before they flow back to the intuitive source.

You can use any of the following for your intuition log:

- black and white composition book

- a diary (with or without lock)

- looseleaf notebook

- accounting ledger with double columns

- steno pad

- spiral notebook of any size (the little ones with the spiral on top are good to carry around)

- index cards with a rubber band around them

- shoebox filled with slips of paper

- your personal computer and favorite word processing program

- a combination of any of the above, or whatever works for you!

If you like to dictate into a tape recorder, it's probably a good idea to keep a written log around because one of the great uses of an intuition log is to flip through it quickly to pick up patterns in symbols and images as you begin to work up your own intuition language. For most people, it's easier and quicker to review pages than it is to review audiotapes. Certainly continue taping your notes, but you might try to get into the habit of jotting down key images or insights in a small notebook—or even on the bottom line of your appointment book—as you record. Using the two methods together may even jog more insight.

WHAT AND WHEN TO WRITE IN YOUR INTUITION LOG

It doesn't matter how often you write in your log, as long as it feels right to you. Once a day, once a week, or once a month may be the perfect rhythm for you to collect your insights and spark more. Or you may find yourself writing feverishly every day for a few weeks or so and then not thinking about it for a few weeks. Writing in your log has its own special rhythm, just like developing your intuition. Sometimes the two intersect, and sometimes they don't.

It is a good idea, however, to date your entries. When you look back later, this will give you important information about how your insights developed in relationship with events in your life—which in turn will give you more insight about how to pinpoint the information your intuition has been giving you.

Use your log to jot down information about all your ongoing intuitive experiences. The discoveries you make with whole focusing, intuitive exercises alone or in a group, synchronicity, dreams, creativity, success, and even sessions with an intuitive counselor are all rich veins of intuitive experiences for you to record.

Start out by recording all of them, whenever you feel the need. Over time you may find you're especially interested in writing about your dreams or about the experiences you have with psychometry, finding the answers in the questions, or other intuitive experiences you've had helping others. Or you may find you have a lot to say about how your intuition comes through for you in your daily life. This is fine, too: Writing in your intuition log is all about fine-tuning your own unique intuitive talents and needs.

It's also a good idea to review your entries every once in a while to see what pops up for you and to write down your observations about patterns that come up, perhaps in a separate part of your log. (See the Patterns Checklist on page 218.)

YOUR CREATIVITY LOG

In Chapter 6 we discussed logging creative experiences. If you've already started a creativity log, you can combine your intuition log with your creativity log or run them separately. It's up to you. Some people find their intuitive experiences and creative ideas are so closely linked that each sparks the other. Others prefer the uncluttered feeling and enhanced focus that running two journals gives them. If you do opt to do them separately, try comparing them from time to time (maybe when you're doing your periodic review) to see what new creative ideas and personal insights are revealed.

PATTERNS CHECKLIST

- Key words or phrases in your entries

- Recurring images on your white screen

- Colors that keep coming up on your white screen, in your dreams, or during whole focusing (see Chapter 3 for interpretations, or use your own)

- Feelings or even physical sensations (chills, warmth, and so on) that come up during whole focusing or intuition exercises

- Signals that may be your personal forms of confirmation (literal physical sensations or a more general gut feeling, a sense of absolute conviction, examples of synchronicity. These can change from time to time.)

- Peak experiences in your intuition exercises (to pinpoint your special talents)

Even if you don't think you're going to find any patterns, check for them anyway. As you focus on reviewing your log, your right brain can suddenly tick out associations between experiences you'd forgotten or connections you've overlooked. If you don't find any patterns, don't be surprised if one so clear you can't believe it escaped your attention percolates up later in the day. When it does come up, don't forget to write it down. Finally, consider photocopying the Visual/Feeling Checklist (page 93) and the Patterns Checklist to staple inside the cover of your journal for quick reference. Or make up your own!

ABOUT
THE AUTHOR

Patricia Einstein is an internationally recognized intuitive counselor and teacher with an active practice that includes consultations, workshops, classes, and lectures for private and corporate clients. One of America's premier professional intuitives, she has been praised for her "uncanny accuracy and unique holistic approach."

Her popular Intuitive Path Workshops have proven to be highly effective for people from all walks of life—and at any level of development. A true intuition activist, Patricia is a co-founder of the innovative Inner Voyage conferences-at-sea—joining together an ever-increasingly interested general public with leading figures in the human consciousness field.

Patricia Einstein, who resides in New York City, has been hailed as one of the trendsetters of the '90s for her groundbreaking work in bringing intuition into the mainstream. She has been the subject of more than 200 radio and television interviews, as well as numerous magazine and newspaper articles featuring her practical techniques for easily applying intuition to everyday life.

FOR INFORMATION

about Patricia Einstein's
Workshops & Retreats,
Private Counseling Sessions,
Training Sessions, etc.
write to:
Patricia Einstein
561 Hudson Street
P.O. Box 27
New York, NY 10014

For news about The Inner Voyage conferences-at-sea
call the Inner Voyage information line
1-800-546-7871

Intuition: The Path to Inner Wisdom is the official manual of
Patricia Einstein's popular Intuitive Path workshops—which
helped launch the landmark Intuition Cruise and
Inner Voyage conferences-at-sea.